THE
RIGHT
DATA

by Edwin S. Rubenstein

D1279622

A NATIONAL REVIEW BOOK

TO BETH

for her patience, understanding, and love.

ISBN 0-9627841-3-3
Library of Congress Catalog Card Number 93-85579
Printed in the United States of America

ACKNOWLEDGMENTS

This work would not exist were it not for, naturally, its author, Ed Rubenstein. But the same can be said of Arthur Stetzner, the director of *National Review*'s annual fund appeal, who now also shares his many talents with National Review Books. Arthur was, well, just about everything to this project: from *The Right Data*'s editor to its production manager, in which capacity he oversaw the book's rise from a humble collection of photocopied articles and charts to the finished work you now hold in your hand.

Others played a role in this book's coming into being. Of course, *National Review* Publisher Ed Capano, who gave the project its green light and who provided much guidance along the way. Julie Crane, Karen Stevens, and Bob Tobin once again served National Review Books with distinction as proofreaders. Joe Vetter, in *NR*'s research library, assisted in fact-checking. *NR* Art Director Luba Kolomytseva designed the book's cover. And Terry Maloney and Galina Veygman, the front line of *NR*'s accounting department, were a source of endless inspiration.

Outside of *National Review*, Paul and Joan Zomberg of Shoreline Graphics in Rockland, Maine, typeset and designed the text and charts, often working magic that turned endless figures into beautiful graphs. To the Zombergs and to all who helped out, pitched in, and advised, our deepest gratitude.

—Jack Fowler
Assistant Publisher

CONTENTS

Contents

Contents

PART TWO • THE REAL REAGAN RECORD

Contents

FOREWORD

Will Bill Clinton's retroactive tax increases reduce the deficit and stimulate the economy? Or will they diminish incentives to work, save, and invest, resulting in a stagnant economy and little job creation?

Were the Reagan tax-rate reductions simply a giveaway to the rich? Or were they responsible for helping launch the greatest entrepreneurial explosion in American history, creating millions of new jobs along the way?

Were the 1980s a decade of greed? Or was it a decade of investment, jobs, and economic growth?

Read on. The answers to these and scores of other questions about America's economic past and future are vividly revealed in the pages of Ed Rubenstein's exciting, comprehensive, and informative new book, *The Right Data.*

President Reagan used to say that facts are stubborn things. In *The Right Data,* those are what Ed Rubenstein gives us—the facts. Myth after myth about the 1980s is shattered by Ed's compelling analysis. In the process, he makes an invaluable contribution toward overturning the revisionist history that has become the conventional wisdom—at least on the editorial pages of many of our major newspapers—about America's economic performance over the past 13 years.

Like other fans of Bill Buckley's *National Review,* I have been a devotee of Ed Rubenstein's columns since he began writing for *NR* in 1988. Ed's gift for cutting through the dense fog of numbers and statistics that obscures today's economic discourse has won him a loyal following among advocates of free-market economics. And you don't need a Ph.D. in economics to follow his analysis.

The publication of this book could not have been more timely. Today, the current Administration ridicules the 1980s as *a decade of greed.* The Left invokes its new mantra, "after 12 years of neglect," to justify every tax increase or social-spending scheme. And Reaganomics has been held responsible for causing everything from the S&L debacle to global warming.

The Right Data sets the record straight.

As Ed demonstrates, Reaganomics did precisely what its proponents said it would do and its opponents claimed was impossible, namely, combine rapid job creation with low inflation over an unusually long period of time. Remember the Phillips Curve, the Keynesian cul-de-sac that offered a bleak trade-off between high inflation and high unemployment, but denied that we could have both simultaneously? Well, we had *both* when Ronald Reagan took office and *neither* when he left.

From 1983 to 1989, the period corresponding with Ronald Reagan's economic policies, America experienced the longest uninterrupted economic expansion in our nation's history. Economic growth averaged 3.8 per cent—well above our nation's historical average. Inflation was cut from over 12 per cent in 1981 to under 4 per cent by the time Reagan left office. Small-business owners and entrepreneurs created more than 20 million new jobs and 4.5 million new businesses.

Entire industries, from computers to biotechnology, were born during this entrepreneurial boom. Microsoft started out as an idea in Bill Gates's head and within a decade had displaced IBM as America's technology leader. Wal-Mart revolutionized the retailing industry. And Silicon Valley, quite possibly the greatest center of entrepreneurial activity in our history, became a metaphor around the world for American creativity and innovation.

What policies produced this economic record, unmatched in American history? The core of the Reagan economic plan was based on three fundamental principles: a commitment to lowering tax rates by 30 per cent on all Americans; a commitment to limiting government spending; and a commitment to reducing government regulatory interference in the marketplace.

America's economy remained strong and growing as long as these three principles guided economic policy-making. But in the late 1980s and early 1990s, we began to move away from these principles. Federal spending began to climb as a percentage of gross domestic product (GDP). More and more federal regulations were imposed on American businesses. And finally, the 1990 Budget Agreement was passed, reversing the trend toward a flatter, fairer tax system designed to reward entrepreneurship, investment, and innovation.

Ed chronicles this tragic reversal and documents the resulting economic downturn which, many people believe, cost George Bush the Presidency.

Which brings us to the Clinton era. Bill Clinton likes to call himself a "new" Democrat. The truth is he is merely completing the fundamental reversal of the policies that created the economic boom of the 1980s. His recently enacted budget plan is simply the 1990 budget deal writ large. And the results will be the same: Higher taxes will not produce the expected revenues; the spending cuts will never materialize; and the economy will be faced with new and rising barriers to growth, job creation, and entrepreneurship.

All this in the name of deficit reduction. But while Bill Clinton blames Ronald Reagan for producing monster deficits, the fact is that the last Reagan deficit—$152 billion in 1989—is more than $60 billion less than the *best* deficit the Clinton Administration projects, even after his massive tax increases.

The outcome of the debate over America's economic past will help determine the course of our economic future. For years, Americans with an abiding faith in the power of entrepreneurial capitalism and free-market economics have found little aid and comfort in the academic research of the day. Until now.

The Right Data will quickly become the definitive reference guide on America's economic performance during the 1980s and early 1990s. Ed demonstrates which policies created growth, and which policies led to stagnation.

Bill Clinton can only dream of repeating the economic achievements of the President whose policies he, in his cavalier way, continually disparages. But there is no hope of his doing so until he understands the fundamental economic principles that encourage growth. To learn those, he'll have to read *The Right Data*.

Jack Kemp
October 1, 1993

INTRODUCTION

By now the spiel is familiar: Living standards for poor and middle-class Americans, after decades of progress, started deteriorating after the Republicans took the White House in 1981. To make matters worse, Ronald Reagan and his successor cut health spending and transfer payments. The federal tax burden shifted from wealthy Americans to the middle class.

However, none of these assertions is correct. Real income rose for *all* income classes, including the very poorest, from 1982 to 1989. Medicaid and Medicare have *always* been the biggest and fastest-growing programs in the budget. And IRS statistics show that the share of all taxes paid by the wealthiest 5 per cent of taxpayers *rose* substantially during the 1980s, while the poorest half paid less.

Providing statistics is an important part of what journalists do. Yet most of what passes for economic wisdom these days is based on politically inspired distortions of reality. *The Right Data* aims to expose the distortions and to provide the accurate statistics.

What we've done is to gather all of my "Right Data" columns from the pages of *National Review* (plus a few that were never published) and neatly assemble them under 14 timely categories. Someone interested in, say, capital-gains taxes will find five "Right Data" columns debunking (each in a slightly different way) the mythology that surrounds most discussions of this topic.

Part two of *The Right Data* contains "The Real Reagan Record," the special retrospective on the Eighties' economy published in *National Review* during the 1992 election campaign. The RRR contributors list reads like a *Who's Who* of conservative economists. It includes Paul Craig Roberts, Martin Anderson, and Alan Reynolds. Their insights (plus numerous charts and graphs) helped make it one of the most popular issues the magazine has ever published.

The final section, which we've dubbed "The Raw Data," contains just that: statistical tables and charts (along with explanatory text) covering more than a dozen topics. Here readers will find the vital background material missing from most media discussions of tax fairness, poverty, federal spending, health care, the deficit, and other issues.

All three sections are referenced in one comprehensive index.

A book like this has never been more timely. For while the Clinton Administration has put many of the "right questions" on the table—health care, deficits, trade, and technology policy, to name a few—its answers have been unfailingly wrong. *The Right Data* will, I hope, help Americans better understand the problems—and opportunities—facing the economy.

Edwin S. Rubenstein

PART ONE

THE RIGHT DATA COLUMNS

by Edwin S. Rubenstein

A. Clintonomics

Things to Come

September 6, 1993

When the President said the budget bill would "change the direction of the economy," he spoke the truth. For the economy *had been* showing signs of recovery. Car sales, fixed business investment, and new business formations are well above their year-ago levels. Nearly one million private-sector jobs were created in the six months prior to the bill's passage.

If history is any guide, this modest rebound is in jeopardy. Since 1960 each 1.0 percentage point rise in taxes as a percentage of GDP has been followed, after a one-year lag, by a 1.8 percentage point reduction in economic growth. This consistent trade-off is uncovered in an economic model developed by William C. Dunkelberg, dean of the School of Business and Management at Temple University. When applied to the Joint Tax Committee's projection of a 0.5 percentage point rise in the federal tax burden in 1994, the Dunkelberg model indicates a 0.9 percentage point drop in the rate of economic growth from the Clinton program.

So instead of growing at a rate of 3.0 per cent, we'll grow by 2.1 per cent. By 1998, according to the National Center for Policy Analysis, the new budget will destroy at least 1.34 million jobs that would have existed under current policies. A family of four will receive $4,000 less income that year because of this plan.

In analyzing this legislation, moreover, economists have focused exclusively on taxes. They have largely overlooked negatives on the spending side of the ledger.

Social-welfare programs will grab an unprecedented 14 per cent of GDP over the next five years. Some of this would have occurred no matter who was President, the result of an aging population reaching out for Social Security and Medicare. But the Democratic budget accelerates the growth of inflation-adjusted anti-poverty spending to 8.3 per cent per year from 1992 to 1998, up from 6.6 per cent in the previous decade. By 1998 we will spend $252 billion (con-

2

A. *Clintonomics*

Table 1-1. Composition of Federal Spending by Administration
Spending as a % of GDP

President (FYs)	Social Welfare	Net Interest	Defense	Other	Total
Nixon (1970–75)	9.4	1.4	6.7	2.6	20.1
Ford (1976–77)	11.9	1.6	5.2	3.0	21.7
Carter (1978–81)	11.6	1.9	5.0	3.3	21.8
Reagan (1982–85)	12.2	2.9	6.2	2.5	23.8
Reagan (1986–89)	11.2	3.2	6.2	2.0	22.6
Bush (1990–93)	12.6	3.4	5.1	2.3	23.4
Clinton (1994–97, est.)	14.0	3.4	3.8	1.6	22.8

Source: Congressional Research Service (calculations by author).

stant 1992 dollars) on these programs, or about two-thirds more than we do now.

Most recipients of AFDC, Food Stamps, housing subsidies, and Medicaid will lose benefits if they work full time. Of all means-tested programs only the Earned Income Tax Credit, a program for low-income workers with children, has effectively lifted people out of poverty without creating dependence. Yet EITC accounts for under 5 per cent of all anti-poverty spending.

Meanwhile, defense spending will decline to 3.8 per cent of GDP, a level not seen since before the Korean War. Other federal spending is also slated to fall, while interest payments, whose reduction was supposedly the goal of the entire exercise, will take the same share as during the Bush years. In a nutshell, Mr. Clinton's budget raises taxes on the most productive members of society to finance work disincentives for lower-income groups. Economic forecasts based only on the first part will seriously underestimate the eventual damage to the economy.

3

The New Math

August 23, 1993

In February President Clinton claimed his program would cut the deficit by $500 billion in four years. The number stuck. We now know, however, that the Clinton Administration was the first to use gross rather than net numbers in its budget presentation. The $500-billion figure did not subtract the $170 billion in new spending and tax cuts the President was simultaneously proposing. Eventually an additional year—1998—was tacked onto the plan to achieve the $500-billion net target.

In reality the entire concept of deficit "reduction" is suspect. The Administration's 1994 budget, for example, forecasts a modest decline in the deficit, from $322 billion this year to $250 billion in 1998. But most of this would have occurred anyway, the result of Social Security surpluses built into current law. When you net out Social Security, the deficit in 1998 becomes $341 billion, the same as last year's amount:

Table 1-2. The Clinton Plan
$ Billions

	Revenues	Outlays	Deficit	Deficit ex Social Security	National Debt
1992	$1,091	$1,381	$290	$341	$2,999
1993	1,146	1,468	322	367	3,304
1994	1,251	1,515	264	323	3,574
1995	1,328	1,574	247	312	3,827
1996	1,413	1,625	212	288	4,053
1997	1,476	1,690	214	297	4,294
1998	1,531	1,781	250	341	4,575

Source: Office of Management and Budget.

Under the Clinton plan federal spending would increase by an average of 3.9 per cent per year between 1993 and 1998, or twice the projected rate of inflation. The reconciliation bill is unlikely to alter this rate of growth. As a result, the "largest deficit reduction package

4

in history" will be accompanied by a whopping $1.0 trillion rise in federal debt over the next five years.

Another widely accepted claim is the 1-to-1 balance between spending cuts and tax increases. In Mr. Clinton's equation revenues from higher fees and excise taxes, stepped-up IRS enforcement efforts, and, most notably, the sharp increase in the tax on Social Security benefits are counted as "spending cuts." The Administration also pretends that defense cuts that have been in the pipeline for years are actually Mr. Clinton's, and that the projected reduction of debt service from lower interest rates is the result of presidential action. When the smoke and mirrors are cleared away, tax hikes outweigh spending cuts by a margin of 15 to 1, according to the Heritage Foundation.

On the tax side, the broad-based energy tax, for example, is scored as a $72-billion revenue increase over the next five years. This figure ignores the tax's projected economic impact: 500,000 jobs lost, and a 1 per cent reduction in GNP. The resulting loss in payroll, personal-income, and corporate taxes will reduce net energy-tax revenue to a mere $5 billion per year, according to the Institute for Research on the Economics of Taxation.

Equally questionable is the more than $100 billion in revenues attributed to raising the top personal-income-tax rate. Taxpayers are skilled at turning taxable income into non-taxed perks, deferring compensation, or simply working less. Martin Feldstein has shown that even a 5 per cent reduction in taxable income will mean a net reduction in taxes paid.

Fanciful tax estimates are not new. In its euphoria following the 1990 budget agreement, the CBO predicted that the deficit would plunge to a mere $29 billion by 1995. Since then the CBO has repeatedly lowered its revenue projections by amounts that now total more than $100 billion per year.

The Static Model Lives

June 21, 1993

One of the most important promises President Clinton made in his State of the Union address was to increase the accuracy of federal revenue estimates. The current budget bill, however, represents a big step backward.

We are told, for example, that higher tax rates on income, payrolls, and corporate profits, along with an entirely new tax on the BTU-generating capacity of different fuels, will raise an additional $250 billion over the next five years. While Mr. Clinton's tax package has been hotly debated, the revenue estimates are rarely questioned.

In fact, the higher tax rates may not produce a cent of new revenue. The Administration's revenue estimates are based on the CBO's static model of the economy, in which an X per cent rise in tax rates invariably produces an X per cent rise in revenues. This mindset enables the CBO to assume blithely that the proposed increase in the top personal-income-tax rate from 31 per cent to 39.6 per cent will bring in an additional $115 billion from affluent Americans over the next five years.

History shows that wealthy taxpayers will either shift to tax-exempt forms of income, increase their use of existing tax deductions, or—worst of all—cut back on their work and investment effort to avoid paying taxes at higher rates. Even a small change in taxpayer behavior can send revenues south in a hurry. Martin Feldstein points out that if a couple with $180,000 of taxable income were to reduce their income by just 10 per cent, they would pay $3,700 less in tax under Mr. Clinton's tax rates than they do under current rates.

Similarly, luxury taxes imposed in 1990 ended up costing the government money when thousands of middle-class workers in the yacht and aircraft industries were thrown out of work. The sharp drop in asset sales after capital-gains taxes were raised in 1987 resulted in an equally sharp drop in federal capital-gains revenues. The elimination of passive-loss deductions in 1987, touted as a big revenue raiser, contributed to the collapse of the commercial real-estate market.

A. Clintonomics

Anyone seriously interested in cutting the deficit should propose: No new taxes. In the absence of new taxes, revenues will be $305 billion higher in 1998 than in 1993. Cap spending, and the deficit battle is won.

Debunking Clinton

March 1993

Had it been a commercial, President Clinton's deficit speech would have been yanked off the air for deceptive advertising. Among his more egregious misstatements were these:

1. *A Balanced Program.* He claimed his plan would cut the deficit by $494 billion over four years (1994–97), with spending cuts and tax hikes accounting for equal shares. To achieve this "balance," however, he counted the $21 billion raised by hiking the tax on Social Security benefits as a reduction in Social Security benefits. Similarly, higher Medicare premiums, user fees, and other tax hikes were labeled "spending cuts." When these sleights of hand are corrected for, and the spending hikes in infrastructure, education, and health care are added in, the net deficit reduction drops to $339 billion, with taxes accounting for nearly three-fourths of the total.

Most important, defense and interest are the only areas to suffer net reductions. The Clinton plan calls for a $10 billion rise in domestic spending over the next four years—that is, $10 billion more than the $245 billion increase already in President Bush's last budget.

2. *Shared Sacrifice.* Clinton insists he reneged on the middle-class tax cut only after learning that the deficit was higher than the Bush Administration told him it was. Not so. A widely disseminated OMB report released last July warned that the 1994 deficit would be more than $60 billion larger than the amount forecast in February.

In reality, Mr. Clinton is taxing the middle class for the same reason that Willie Sutton robbed banks: That's where the money is (see Table 1-3). Middle-class households—those with incomes between $30,000 and $200,000—accounted for 32.7 per cent of all tax returns and 64.2 per cent of total gross income in 1990. Although individuals earning $200,000 and above pay far more tax per capita and as a per cent of income, there simply aren't enough of them to yield the revenues that Clinton wants. He had to tax the middle class.

3. *The Deficit and Investment.* The notion that government borrowing "crowds out" private sector investment makes sense only if you assume that the amount available for investment is fixed. It isn't, however. When Ronald Reagan cut the top income-tax rate from 70

8

Table 1-3. The Distribution of Income and Taxes, 1990

Gross Income Bracket	No. of Returns	Adjusted Gross Income	Income Tax	Average Tax per Return	Tax as % of AGI
($1,000s)	(Mils.)	——— ($ Billions) ———			
$0–$30	75.7	$ 912.2	$ 65.9	$ 871	7.2%
30–50	20.7	821.1	90.2	4,357	11.0
50–75	10.9	657.2	87.2	8,000	13.3
75–100	3.3	279.5	44.4	13,455	15.9
100–200	2.3	305.6	57.8	25,134	18.9
200–1 Mil.	0.8	275.1	64.3	83,506	23.4
1 Mil. +	0.06	154.7	37.3	616,495	24.1
Total	113.7	$3,405.4	$447.1	$ 3,932	13.1%

Source: Internal Revenue Service (calculations by author).

per cent to 50 per cent in 1981, upper-income individuals earned more, saved more, and switched funds from tax shelters to economically productive, taxable investments. Between 1982 and 1984 U.S. capital outflows dropped from $121 billion to $22 billion, as U.S. firms took advantage of lower U.S. corporate income taxes. In addition, foreign investment poured into the country at unprecedented rates.

The net result was that business investment increased from 10.57 per cent of GNP during the 1975–79 period to 11.51 per cent during 1980 to 1984.

4. *Public Investment Panacea?* Over the past four years, while state, local, and federal "investment" spending rose by 37 percent, or $30 billion, total employment actually declined. Public works projects can create jobs—but at a cost ranging from $136,000 to almost $400,000 per job, according to a 1979 OMB survey. Since the typical job created by the private sector costs only $40,000, it follows that whenever a public works program costs more, the number of jobs created by the economy will actually fall.

Clintonomics Exposed

October 19, 1992

Bill Clinton's plan to spend our way out of economic malaise has drawn generally favorable reviews from the media. A detailed analysis prepared for Representative Dick Armey of the Joint Economic Committee (JEC) shows, however, that far more jobs would be destroyed than created:

Defense Cuts. Mr. Clinton would cut defense outlays by $58.5 billion more than the reductions already requested by President Bush for 1993–96. The result: 240,685 more jobs lost in 1993 than under the Administration's proposal.

Health Care. By requiring employers either to provide health-care coverage for employees (play), or contribute 7 per cent of payroll to finance a government-operated program (pay), the Clinton health-care plan would increase employment costs by $42 billion, and force employers to lay off 710,000 workers in the first year. Forty-three per cent of the job loss would occur in businesses that employ fewer than 20 workers.

Minimum Wage. Mr. Clinton has endorsed the notion of indexing the minimum wage to inflation. Had such an adjustment been made in 1991, the minimum wage would have increased by 4.2 per cent, displacing 42,021 low-wage workers.

Family and Medical Leave. Mr. Clinton has promised to sign the bill, twice vetoed by President Bush, requiring employers to provide three months of unpaid leave with health benefits to new mothers and to those taking care of a sick relative. This mandate would raise labor costs by more than $3.3 billion, translating into 60,000 lost jobs.

Environment. A carbon tax designed to cap CO_2 emissions at 1990 levels could reduce GNP by up to 2 per cent by the year 2000, and put 195,000 workers out of work as early as 1993. The Democratic ticket has also pledged to raise the average automobile fuel economy standard from the present 27.5 mpg to 45 mpg. Assuming a four-year, 3-4-5-5 mpg phase-in, the first-year employment loss would be 75,840 jobs.

Tax Hikes. A new higher tax bracket for the top roughly 2 per cent of taxpayers, a 10 per cent surtax on millionaires, and higher taxes on corporations that invest abroad will reduce private-sector investment in this country. The JEC estimates that 437,000 jobs would be lost.

Job Training Tax. The "Lifetime Learning" initiative would require employers to spend at least 1.5 per cent of their payrolls on worker education and training programs, thereby adding $21 billion to the $16 billion that employers already spend on such programs. The new payroll tax would force the dismissal of 265,000 workers in its first year.

Government Downsizing. The Putting People First plan promises to reduce federal administrative expenses by $15 billion annually. This will require eliminating 100,000 government jobs. (Though that one's hard to oppose.)

And the job gains? The Clinton people claim that spending an additional $23 billion annually on highways, high-speed rail, and other public infrastructure will create 275,000 jobs directly, and many times more indirectly, as the economy responds to the spending stimulus. Unfortunately, there is no evidence that public spending exerts the kind of "multiplier" effect Keynesians claim for it. Indeed, if such a relationship existed, our present problems would have vanished long ago.

As a practical matter, an acceleration in public-works spending may be difficult to achieve. Only 60 per cent of the funds authorized under the current highway bill, for example, have been spent by the states. New funding would either remain unspent or be wasted on pork-barrel projects.

The bottom line for Clintonomics? A new loss of over 1.8 million jobs, and an unemployment rate 1.5 points above what it would otherwise be.

B. Health Care

Spending More for Less

June 7, 1993

While details are not yet known, Hillary Clinton's plan will significantly increase government's role in health-care finance. The trend
has been under way for almost thirty years:

Table 1-4. Health Care Expenditures
$ Billions

	Total ($ bils.)	Percent of GDP	Percent Financed by:		
			Government	Private Insurance	Out of Pocket
1950	$ 12.1	4.6%	25.3%	15.8%	58.9%
1960	27.1	5.3	24.3	26.7	49.0
1965	41.9	5.9	26.2	28.1	45.7
1970	74.4	7.3	37.0	28.6	34.4
1980	250.1	9.2	42.2	34.1	23.7
1990	666.2	12.2	42.4	37.2	20.4

Source: Health Care Financing Administration (HCFA).

Until the mid-Sixties the government paid for about 25 per cent
of all health care, limiting its involvement to prevention and medical
research. With the advent of Medicare and Medicaid the government's share rose rapidly, as did that of private health insurance,
much of it subsidized by federal tax deductions. As a result, the share
of total health costs paid out of pocket by consumers plummeted,
and the percentage of GDP consumed by health care soared.

What do consumers get for all of this? As it happens, the link
between spending and the amount of care actually received has
grown increasingly tenuous. Hospital costs per person, for example,
rose from $71 (1982 dollars) in 1965 to $545 in 1989, and yet the
number of beds per 1,000 population *declined* by almost 50 per cent.
Most of the rise in hospital spending was absorbed by the salaries of

doctors, nurses, and technicians: personnel per occupied bed doubled between 1946 and 1965; it more than tripled after Medicare started.

The decline in hospital beds, of course, could be a "healthy" sign: a healthier population needing less hospitalization, and technological advances that reduce the average length of hospital stays. But in a recent paper Milton Friedman found no evidence that advances in the quality of hospital care have accelerated since 1965.

The apparent anomaly of higher expenditures and lower output is, in fact, typical of highly socialized industries—c.f. the U.S. public-school system. Medical-care prices have increased more than 50 per cent faster than consumer prices over the past 25 years. In the private economy such price hikes would induce lower demand and higher supply, thereby mitigating the upward pressure on prices. In the medical marketplace, however, third-party payers eliminate the need for consumers to restrain their demand. Government inhibits the supply side by licensing medical personnel, regulating the introduction of new treatments, and capping the fees paid by Medicare and Medicaid.

Liberals contend that government intervention is needed to make medical care accessible to all. Yet price controls have hurt the poor. Pregnant women on Medicaid, for example, are denied access to most OB/GYN physicians because the program pays doctors less than half their normal fees.

In fact, the OMB estimates that only 21 per cent of total health-care expenditures paid for by federal tax money goes to poor people. Medicare, the largest health entitlement, is not means-tested. Medicaid, although ostensibly aimed at families on welfare, channels about half of its annual $80 billion to middle-class people who have hidden their assets. Nearly all of the tax subsidy allowed for employer-provided health insurance accrues to people who are not poor.

If history is any guide, another expansion of the Federal Government's role will widen the disparity between the medical haves and have-nots.

Mr. Clinton's Prescription

March 29, 1993

"The pharmaceutical industry is spending $1 billion more each year on advertising and lobbying than it does on developing new and better drugs. Meanwhile, its profits are rising at four times the rate of the average Fortune 500 company."

The President's statistical indictment of the drug industry ignores crucial evidence to the contrary. *Most* industries spend far more on marketing their products than on developing them. The drug industry spends about equal amounts on each—a ratio more than justified by the number of new products that require detailed explanation.

Since 1982, drug-industry profits have averaged about 13.5 per cent of sales, according to the Department of Commerce. That's slightly above the profit rate for the soap, food, and soda industries. And with only one out of every four thousand drugs screened making it to the market, the industry probably doesn't offer investors a rate of return commensurate with the risks involved.

Nevertheless, Mr. Clinton's remarks suggest that drug companies will bear the brunt of his near-term efforts at cost control. Senator Pryor (D., Ark.) has already introduced legislation to curtail tax benefits of drug companies that raise prices faster than the CPI. In the proposed vaccination program for children, drug makers will probably be required to provide vaccines at whatever price the government deems reasonable.

The political rationale is obvious: Unlike doctor or hospital bills, drug expenses are usually paid out of the patient's pocket. Medicare, for example, doesn't cover prescriptions.

In purely economic terms, however, the drug industry is an odd first target. Since 1965 drug prices have risen only two-thirds as fast as the prices for all medical care; pharmaceutical costs have declined from 8.9 per cent of overall health-care spending in 1965 to 4.8 per cent in 1991. Americans spend a smaller fraction of GDP on prescriptions than Germans, Frenchmen, or Japanese. Even Canada, where the government controls drug prices, could do no better than match the U.S., at 1 per cent of GDP.

14

Furthermore, much of the rise in prescription prices is unrelated to actions taken by drug companies. Almost the entire rise in the price of whooping-cough vaccine (up 6,000 per cent since 1970) has been attributed to the courts. Drug companies have been forced to buy hefty liability insurance, even though the vaccine was found to be safe.

Seven conditions—osteoporosis, diabetes, depression, arthritis, Alzheimer's disease, cardiovascular diseases, and cancer—account for more than half of total health-care costs in the United States. There are 262 drugs currently being developed for these seven conditions. New drugs have already eliminated the need for most ulcer surgery and have reduced the costs of treating schizophrenia.

Bashing the pharmaceutical industry may kill the only truly painless way to control health-care costs.

Canada's Health Plan: A Second Opinion

May 1991

Fact: During the 1960s both Canada and the U.S. spent about 6 per-cent of GNP on health care. Fact: Canada adopted a universal gov-ernment-run health-care system in 1971, while the U.S. still relies on the private sector to provide medical care for its non-poor, non-elderly population. Fact: The U.S. now spends about 12 per cent of GNP on health care, while Canada has held health costs to 8.5 per cent of GNP since 1978.

A superficial analysis of the "facts" suggests that the Canadian system, in which the government controls all medical fees, is better at cost control.

Unfortunately, the true cost of "free" medical care is not reflected in national economic statistics. Canadians must endure long, potentially dangerous, waiting periods for surgical procedures that are readily available in the U.S. A survey recently published by the Fraser Institute in Vancouver, Canada, found that patients in British Columbia wait an average of 23.7 weeks for coronary bypass surgery, 16.3 weeks for a hysterectomy, and 14.1 weeks for disc sur-gery. Of course, patients of doctors who have seniority rights or who have political pull wait less than others.

Diagnostic procedures are rudimentary compared to American standards. Until recently there was only one functioning CAT-scanner in Newfoundland (population 570,000), resulting in a two-month wait and the requirement that a specialist order the proce-dure. The safest diagnostic device yet invented is the magnetic reso-nance imaging (MRI) machine, of which there are more in the state of Michigan than in all of Canada.

Such rationing might be acceptable if it resulted in a more efficient use of medical resources. But political considerations, not efficiency, drive the rationing procedure. Routine doctor visits are available without wait to all Canadians for the simple reason that they affect the largest number of people. Serious illness affects a rela-tive few. To maximize their political appeal, national health insu-rance plans invariably allocate a disproportionate share of resources to routine maladies at the expense of critical illnesses.

B. Health Care

Even the much vaunted savings achieved in Canada appear questionable. For example, the share of GNP devoted to medical care grew more slowly in Canada because economic growth was higher: from 1967 to 1987 real GNP per capita grew 74 per cent in Canada versus only 38 per cent in the U.S. Real per capita health spending grew at about the same rate in both nations over this period, with Canada spending about 25 per cent less per capita both before and after the introduction of universal government funding.

The remaining difference can be explained by other factors. Canada is a younger nation (11 per cent of the population over age 65 versus 12.2 per cent in the U.S.), and does not have the large inner-city populations that drive up medical costs in this country. The age difference alone accounts for one-fifth of the spending difference between the two nations, according to a recent study.

Malpractice insurance accounts for a far larger fraction of doctors' fees in this country, and U.S. doctors are far more likely to practice "defensive medicine," prescribing many tests and procedures not out of medical necessity but in order to say in court that everything that could be done for the patient was done. This, of course, is a problem of tort law reform, not medical finance.

Despite these negatives, in many respects U.S. health costs are below Canada's. A recent study compared per capita costs in Canada with those of the largest American health management organizations (HMOs), which are private plans giving the same universal health coverage available in Canada. The HMOs had per enrolee costs $300 to $500 below the Canadian average, without the accessibility problems seen in Canada.

The Health of Nations

September 1, 1989

Every day this year, Americans will spend $200 million more on health care than they did last year, the total coming to $620 billion, or 12 per cent of GNP. By comparison, Japan and the UK devote only 6 per cent of their economies to health care, but enjoy higher life expectancies and lower infant-mortality rates. Data published in 1987 by the Organization for Economic Cooperation and Development (OECD) hint at possible explanations:

Table 1-5. Health Costs and Consequences

	U.S.	UK	Japan
Physicians per 1,000 persons	1.9	1.3	1.4
Hospital admission rate (% of pop.)	17.0	12.7	6.7
Hospital beds per 1,000 pop.	5.9	8.1	12.1
Average hospital stay (days)	9.9	18.6	55.1
Hospital expenditure per day	$360	$140	$60
Caesareans per 100 deliveries	18	9	8
Infant mortality rate (males)	12.8	12.2	6.6
Life expectancy (males)	70.9	71.3	74.8

Source: Organization for Economic Cooperation and Development (OECD).

Contrary to the prevailing wisdom, the U.S. does not have excessive hospital capacity. Our bed-per-thousand-population figure—5.9—is less than half Japan's and 27 per cent below the UK's. Nevertheless, our hospital admission rate—total admissions as a percentage of population—is nearly three times Japan's and one-third higher than the UK's.

Clearly something has to give. We compensate by keeping the average hospital stay considerably shorter (9.9 days), albeit more expensive, $360 per day in 1982, the latest year for which comparable figures for all three countries are available. Although many factors, including different mixes of medical cases, might account for these differences, the prevailing medical practice in this country

18

seems to favor shorter, more technologically intensive hospital stays, as opposed to the longer, more deliberate therapies practiced in Europe and Japan.

Many widely used medical procedures in this country are now being called into question. Glaucoma, for example, has for years been treated first with drugs and then, if the drugs fail, with laser therapy or surgery. Yet in a recent review of the medical literature, Dr. David Eddy of Duke University found that three of the four clinical trials in which these treatments were compared with doing nothing at all indicated that the disease was more likely to progress in the treated patients.

Caesarean sections are performed far more frequently in this country than in the rest of the developed world, even though they are much more dangerous for the mother: death rates are two to four times greater than with vaginal delivery, and complication rates are higher. The U.S. ranks 17th in infant mortality among the 24 OECD nations.

From one-fourth to one-third of the 200,000 coronary-artery bypass operations done annually are now regarded as unnecessary. Our hysterectomy rate is six times that of Sweden, the nation with the best health indices in the world. Carotid endarectomy—surgery to clear the carotid artery—is done on fifty thousand patients without symptoms each year at a cost of about $250 million, although the procedure confers no certain benefit to these patients and carries a risk of death or stroke that is several times that associated with the untreated condition. Just being in a hospital can be dangerous to your health: the Centers for Disease Control attribute $2.5 billion in medical costs and twenty thousand deaths to infections acquired in hospitals.

C. Capital Gains

Gunning for Gains

July 19, 1993

There they go again. The Senate Finance Committee wants to raise capital-gains tax rates to 30.8 per cent from the current 28 per cent. The move is supposed to increase revenues and, more important, shift the burden of taxation toward the wealthy. Of course, we heard the same arguments in 1986, and look what happened then:

Table 1-6. Capital Gains Realizations

Income Bracket	Total ($ Bil.) 1985	1991	Average per Return 1985	1991	Change
Under $50K	$ 31.2	$13.1	$ 6,670	$ 3,422	–49%
$50K to $100K	26.2	16.4	15,450	7,656	–50
$100K to $200K	22.6	15.9	50,089	17,514	–65
$200K to $500K	23.9	15.9	150,052	48,418	–68
$500K to $1 Mil.	14.2	9.4	427,840	132,329	–69
$1 Million +	36.0	27.5	2,488,938	800,093	–68
Total	$154.1	$98.2	$21,916	$13,430	–39

Source: Internal Revenue Service.

Capital-gains realizations in 1991 came to more than $55 billion below the level of 1985, the year before tax "reform" raised capital-gains tax rates. On a per-return basis the decline was far more precipitous, approaching 70 per cent in the upper brackets. There were plenty of gains to be realized that year: the NYSE composite stock average rose 27.1 per cent, reaching a record high on December 31, 1991. Taxpayers simply opted to hold onto their gains rather than sell and give 28 per cent to the Federal Government.

The decline in realizations is the mirror image of what occurred when tax rates were cut. The top capital gains rate was reduced from 48 per cent to 28 per cent in 1978, and to 20 per cent in 1982. By

C. Capital Gains

1982 realizations were double the level of 1977, especially remarkable considering that the recession of that year was the deepest of the postwar period. Taxes paid on capital gains, after sinking to as low as $4 billion a year in the mid-1970s, soared to a record $53 billion in 1986. Upper-bracket taxpayers paid most of this.

The "fairness" issue goes beyond the distribution of the tax burden, however. The failure to adjust capital gains for inflation means that investors are taxed on the purely inflationary part of capital gains as well as the real part. Thus an asset bought for $1,000 in 1975 and sold for $2,000 in 1993 will generate a $280 tax bill for its owner even though, after inflation, he has lost more than $700 on the deal. Wheeler-dealers get in and out too quickly to care about inflation, but small businessmen, farm families, and long-term investors get clobbered.

The economic stimulus from indexation has been extensively studied. An analysis by former Treasury economists Gary and Aldona Robbins finds that indexation would raise real growth by 1 per cent and create nearly 2,500,000 jobs by the end of the century. The Robbinses also find that, contrary to what nearly everyone "knows," most of the benefits of indexation go to wage earners. More capital per worker makes workers more productive, enabling employers to pay higher real wages without a reduction in profits.

President Clinton favors targeting capital-gains tax relief to taxpayers who buy stock in start-up companies. This would do nothing to unlock the accumulated capital gains that taxpayers are already sitting on. The numbers are staggering: $8 trillion of unrealized gains, according to Polyconomics, of which $1 trillion are real. A better alternative is the one sponsored by Representative Charles B. Rangel (D., N.Y.) and Senator Malcolm Wallop (R., Wyo.): terminate the provision that "steps up" the basis for capital gains at death, but index all capital gains. The Treasury will ultimately collect an additional $280 billion as investors reinvest their old gains in situations likely to produce new gains.

Who Has Capital Gains?

April 16, 1990

Only 296,000 taxpayers had Adjusted Gross Income (AGI) of $200,000 or more in 1985, according to the IRS. But this small group, only 0.3 per cent of all taxpayers, accounted for 5.8 per cent of total income and 45.3 per cent of all capital-gains income that year. Taken at face value this shows an overwhelming concentration of capital gains at the upper incomes. But how much of the apparent high income of capital-gains recipients is due to the gains themselves, and therefore not likely to be repeated in subsequent years? A sizable proportion, judging from data provided by the Joint Tax Committee:

Table 1-7. Percentage of Capital Gains Going to Various Income Groups, 1985

Income Group	AGI	AGI Less Capital Gains
Less than $10,000	6.27	15.08
$10,000 to $30,00	6.66	11.40
$30,000 to $50,000	10.38	11.94
$50,000 to $75,000	10.72	13.26
$75,000 to $100,000	6.09	9.13
$100,000 to $200,000	14.62	13.81
$200,000 and over	45.26	25.38

Source: Joint Committee on Taxation.

When income is defined so as to exclude capital gains, the percentage of capital gains going to individuals making $200,000 and over falls from 45.3 per cent to 25.4 per cent, while the percentage going to people earning $30,000 or less rises to 26.5 per cent from 12.9 per cent. If income is defined as wages and salaries, individuals earning $200,000 and above received only 13.0 per cent of all capital gains in 1985.

There is good reason to exclude capital gains in measuring wealth. A businessman who retires and sells his business for a

$500,000 gain will be counted among the nation's very wealthiest individuals in the year he retires, though his normal income may be very modest. The same thing happens, albeit to a lesser degree, to people who sell stock or bonds to pay for their children's college tuition or a wedding. To the extent that gains are one-time or sporadic events, annual income including the gain will overstate the "permanent" income of the taxpayer, and overstate the concentration of gains among the wealthy.

Such examples appear to be the norm rather than the exception. An analysis of IRS data for the years 1979 through 1983 found that only 16 per cent of taxpayers with capital gains reported gains every year; 44 per cent reported them only once. In 1984, 43 per cent of taxpayers reporting capital gains of $100,000 or more had ordinary, predictable income of $50,000 a year or less.

The tax code recognizes this problem in the case of the sale of a home, where taxpayers age 55 and over are allowed a lifetime capital-gains exclusion of $125,000. But capital-gains taxes still overburden the elderly, who have had time to accumulate assets: taxpayers over age 65 pay about 11 per cent of the nation's total income tax but more than 26 per cent of the capital-gains tax.

Inflation exacerbates the problem of measuring the "wealth" of capital-gains recipients. Consider a farmer who bought his farm for $50,000 in 1949. If the price of his farm kept pace with inflation, he would be able to sell it for $260,000 at his retirement in 1989. Although in real terms he is no wealthier now than he was forty years ago, for tax purposes he is considered five times as wealthy, and must pay nearly $59,000 in capital-gains tax.

Until 1987 these problems were mitigated by excluding 40 per cent of gains from taxable income. Now, with capital gains taxed as ordinary income, the tax code does not distinguish between those who are king for a day and those who live like royalty their entire lives.

Quid Pro Stupidity

June 1989

Jim Wright may be gone, but his bad ideas still flourish. Three years ago the former House Speaker suggested that a federal excise tax be imposed on securities sales as a means of cutting the deficit. The Democrats have resurrected this idea as part of a deal to cut capital-gains tax rates.

A 0.5 per cent tax on stock sales would produce distressing results for many investors. Obviously, people selling stocks at a loss would incur still greater losses because of the tax. For those selling stock at a gain the tax would act like a capital-gains surtax imposed, perversely, at a lower rate the higher the gain.

For example, suppose a person buys $1,000 of common stock and sells it two years later for $1,100. Under current law the investor pays $28 in capital-gains taxes. Under Bush's capital-gains tax cut proposal, 10 per cent of the capital gain on assets held for one to two years would be excluded from tax. The investor would thus pay $25.20 in capital-gains taxes, or $2.80 less than currently. However, the excise tax liability on this transaction would come to $5.50 (0.5 per cent of $1,100), bringing total taxes to $30.70. This investor's capital-gains tax rate would effectively rise from 28 per cent to 30.7 per cent because of the stock transfer tax.

Had the investor been lucky and sold the stock for $2,000 instead of $1,100, the effective tax rate on the gain would be less. Under Bush's proposal his capital-gains tax payment would be $252. His transfer tax liability would come to $10, bringing the total tax bill to $262, or less than the $280 paid now. In general, the higher the rate of return, the lower the average tax rate on the capital gain—exactly the opposite of what one would expect from a tax designed to remove the "pro rich" bias from the capital-gains tax cut.

In fact, the wealthy do not care much about capital-gains or stock-transfer taxes. They can avoid paying either tax by simply bequeathing stock to their heirs or investing in municipal bonds. The biggest losers are people who don't have wealth but aspire to it. The stock-transfer tax would fall particularly hard on pension funds, most of which are exempt from capital-gains taxes.

C. Capital Gains

Of course revenues, not redistribution, may be the determining factor. Based on current trading volume, a 0.5 per cent stock transfer tax would bring in $8.0 billion per year. But with brokerage commissions averaging 0.42 per cent of the value of traded shares, this tax would more than double the cost of selling stock. Stock market volume would fall by 12.7 per cent, and prices would decline by as much as 14.6 per cent in response to such a tax, according to a 1987 Congressional Research Service study.

Foreign competition will exacerbate these losses. Americans can easily shift their trading to tax-free Canadian stock exchanges, where 180 NYSE stocks are listed. Four European countries—the UK, Germany, the Netherlands, and Ireland—plan to eliminate stock transfer taxes by late 1991. While many Americans might be reluctant to do business abroad directly, they might happily invest in overseas mutual funds targeted at Americans wanting to trade American securities. Attempts to control the flight of American capital to tax-free havens abroad, primarily tax and currency restrictions, would result in our financial markets resembling those found in many third world countries.

A Rich Man's Tax?

April 21, 1989

Citizens for Tax Justice calls it an "outrageous giveaway to the wealthy." The *New York Times* asks "Why Stroke the Rich?" And even the *Wall Street Journal* reports that "New Tax Proposals Would Benefit Corporations, Wealthy . . ." The notion that capital gains are the province of the super-rich is the driving force behind the opposition to the Administration's proposal to cut the rate at which capital gains are taxed. Yet recently published IRS data show most taxpayers with capital-gains income to be of fairly modest means:

Table 1-8. Distribution of Capital Gains, 1987

Gross Income	Number of Returns (Millions)	Capital-Gains Income (Billions)	Capital Gains per Return (Average)
$0–10,000	1.4	$ 2.2	$ 1,571
10–25,000	2.2	5.1	2,318
25–50,000	3.4	11.9	3,500
50–100,000	2.5	21.6	8,640
100,000 +	0.8	39.3	49,125
Total/Average	10.3	$80.2	$ 7,786

Source: Internal Revenue Service.

Nearly 70 per cent of the 10.3 million tax returns reporting capital-gains income in 1987 were filed by taxpayers with gross incomes below $50,000; more than one-third had incomes below $25,000. Not surprisingly, the dollar amounts are weighted heavily toward the upper incomes, with 49 per cent of all capital-gains income accruing to the 8 per cent of capital-gains taxpayers with incomes in the $100,000-plus bracket.

The specifics of the President's proposal point toward a still more egalitarian disposition of tax benefits. In general, 45 per cent of capital-gains income would be excluded from the tax base, thereby cutting the maximum effective capital-gains tax rate from 28 per cent to 15 per cent. But individuals earning less than $20,000 will be granted a 100 per cent exclusion, virtually absolving them from the tax. Gains arising from the sale of "collectibles"—old masters, antique furniture, etc.—will not qualify for the lower rates. Ditto for gains arising from the sale of entire buildings or the capital gains of corporations; and starting in 1995 all assets will have to be held for at least three full years before qualifying for the 15 per cent rate, effectively excluding all but the most passive investors from direct tax-cut benefits.

It's fair to say, however, that the indirect benefits of lower capital-gains taxes redound to all stockholders, not just those who sell stock in a given year. A New York Stock Exchange survey conducted in mid-1985 put the median household income of the 47 million shareholders in public corporations at $36,800, with a median portfolio of only $6,200. The Exchange also estimated that as of year-end 1980—the latest figures available—an additional 133 million individuals owned stock indirectly, via pension plans, life-insurance policies, mutual savings bank accounts, etc.

There may be legitimate reasons to oppose the Administration's capital-gains tax proposal. A pro-rich bias, however, is not one of them.

The Twenty-Year Bear Market

May 27, 1988

Wall Street is not quite sure whether the current backing and filling is a short-term bull market within a long-term bear market, or vice versa. For perspective on long-term market trends:

Table 1-9. Average Daily Close of S&P 500 Stock Index
1941–43 = 10

Period	Actual	Adjusted for Inflation	Average Capital Gains Tax Rate
1948–52	19.20	12.32	25.0%
1953–57	37.18	21.83	25.0
1958–62	57.62	31.30	25.0
1963–67	83.32	42.07	25.0
1968–72	97.45	40.80	34.2
1973–77	95.33	29.30	46.9
1978–82	113.11	22.32	29.6
1983–87	206.18	30.78	21.6

Source: The Economic Report of the President (calculations by author).

Adjusted for inflation, the stock market peaked in the mid Sixties. The recent stock-market boom actually reflects lesser heights than those of the 1963–67 period (the highest individual year was 1968, when the index reached 45.62). Steady erosion had pushed the index down to a post-1968 low in 1982 (19.94), and even five years of the late, great bull market produced only a 40.59 average (in 1987). The index finished the year at 34.96 after bottoming out at 31.82 on October 19.

Historically the market moves south when capital-gains-tax rates move north. The 1948–67 rise in equity prices coincided with a 25 per cent tax rate on capital gains, moderate compared to the 90 per cent rate on ordinary income during much of that period. Starting with the Tax Reform Act of 1969 and culminating with the Tax Reform Act of 1976, Congress progressively raised the maximum tax rate on capital gains from 25 per cent to 49.1 per cent. In 1978 rates were cut to 28 per cent, and then to 20 per cent via the 1981 Reagan tax cut.

The 40 per cent increase in the top capital-gains tax rate that took effect January 1, 1987, ended nearly a decade of rate reductions and what was mistakenly regarded as one of the greatest bull markets in history. For many investors, these rates more than doubled: a married couple with taxable income of $40,000 had a capital-gains tax rate of 13.2 per cent under the old law, but now faces a rate of 28 per cent.

In a perverse way the initial impact of these tax changes was positive, because many investors liquidated their positions in late 1986 in anticipation of the rate increase, and those who didn't were reluctant to sell at the higher tax rates. These factors held down the supply of stock for sale in the first part of 1987, propping up prices.

Also, foreign investors were induced to buy U.S. equities when the dollar declined, but gradually became unnerved when it appeared that the dollar's fall would be longer and deeper than anticipated.

Taxes are only one of many factors influencing equity prices, but there can be little doubt that the 1986 changes were a setback to the stability of the stock market and to long-term investing.

D. Tax Fairness

Mr. Clinton's Corporate Tax

July 5, 1993

The proposed hike in corporate income-tax rates—from 34 to 35 per cent—has attracted little attention compared to other elements of the Clinton tax package. Supporters point to a long-term decline in corporate taxes relative to other federal taxes:

Table 1-10. Measuring the Corporate Tax Burden
$ Billions

	Corporate Income Taxes	Total Federal Revenues	Corporate income taxes as % of:	
			Federal Revenues	Corporate Profits
1950	$17.0	$ 50.4	33.7%	39.6%
1960	20.6	96.9	21.2	40.6
1970	27.1	195.4	13.8	34.9
1980	58.6	553.0	10.6	32.9
1982	33.8	635.4	5.3	22.3
1986	66.0	827.2	8.0	24.3
1987	85.4	913.8	9.3	26.7
1990	88.5	1,107.4	8.0	24.5
1991	81.7	1,122.2	7.3	23.5

Source: Office of Management and Budget; U.S. Department of Commerce.

In 1950 corporate income taxes accounted for about one-third of all federal revenues. Despite continued revenue growth the tax share plummeted steadily, to a low of 5.3 per cent in 1982. Liberals blame the decline on tax loopholes or deductions available to corporations.

In reality the decline reflects the failure of pre-tax profits to grow as fast as other forms of income taxed by the government. In 1950 corporate profits accounted for 18 per cent of GDP. Throughout the 1970s they hovered at around 11 per cent. They plunged to 4.9 per cent in 1982, and are currently between 6 and 7 per cent.

D. Tax Policy

Take a look at the recent history of corporate tax law. The Tax Reform Act of 1969 repealed the investment tax credit then available and imposed a minimum tax on depreciation allowances. Significant corporate tax reduction in 1981 was canceled by the Tax Equity and Fiscal Responsibility Act (TEFRA) in 1982, followed by smaller tax hikes in 1984, 1987, and 1988.

None did more damage than the monumental Tax Reform Act of 1986. While cutting the top corporate rate from 46 to 34 per cent, this law abolished the investment tax credit, which had saved companies billions of dollars a year. Perhaps the most damaging feature of the 1986 law was an Alternative Minimum Tax imposed on corporations that earn little or no profit but have large depreciation write-offs. The cumulative effect of this law—and one of its main selling points—was to shift $120 billion in tax payments from individuals to corporations in the first five years.

Corporations currently pay nearly 25 per cent of their pre-tax profits to the Federal Government. And state and local corporate income-tax collections—$25 billion in 1992—have grown faster than the federal tax in recent years. Social Security taxes represent a still larger tax liability for business. All in all, the effective tax rate on profits exceeds 80 per cent, according to the Tax Foundation.

Treasury officials fear that if the top personal income-tax rate rises to 36 per cent while the corporate rate remains at 34 per cent, there would be a surge of phony incorporations. Perhaps. But the corporate tax already creates a notorious double taxation of profits—when earned by the corporation, and when distributed to shareholders as dividends. Norman Ture of the Institute for Research on the Economics of Taxation estimates that taxes paid on corporate profits are 40 per cent greater than the amount shareholders would have paid if earnings flowed directly to them and were taxed at personal income-tax rates.

Corporate taxes are ultimately paid by individuals, in the form of lower wages for employees, higher prices for consumers, and lower returns to stockholders. An ideal tax system would have no corporate tax whatsoever.

31

Finally, Fairness

November 2, 1992

The rich get richer, and pay less tax. The poor get poorer, and pay more.

Variations on this theme have haunted Republicans since the early days of the Reagan Administration. There is, however, a slight revisionist trend at work. In October the most liberal of *New York Times* economics writers, Sylvia Nasar, retreated from her earlier line about Reagan-Bush tax unfairness. Drawing on new CBO research, Mrs. Nasar reported that while the overall federal tax burden remained about the same, the income-tax changes legislated during the Eighties benefited *all* American families.

She omitted the details:

Table 1-11. Personal Income-Tax Rates by Income Group
Tax as Percentage of Income

Income Quintile	Top Income in Bracket	1980	1992	Percentage Reduction, 1980–92
Poorest 20%	$20,300	−0.5	−3.2	540.0
Second 20%	36,800	4.5	2.8	38.7
Third 20%	54,500	7.9	6.2	21.5
Fourth 20%	82,400	11.0	8.7	20.1
Richest 20%	—	17.2	15.5	9.9
All Taxpayers		12.3	10.9	11.4
Richest 1%	$324,100+	23.9	22.0	7.9

Source: Congressional Budget Office.

The 1981 tax act slashed the top marginal tax rate—the rate paid on the last dollar of income—from 70 per cent to 50 per cent, and lowered other rates by nearly one-quarter. In 1986 the top rate was cut again, to 28 per cent. That year's tax reform also expanded the alternative minimum tax, which ensures that wealthy taxpayers cannot escape paying tax altogether, and increased the standard deduction, thereby removing millions of low-income taxpayers from the tax rolls. Tax policy took an unfortunate turn at the 1990 budget summit, when the top marginal tax rate was increased to 31 per cent.

These reforms increased the progressivity of the personal income tax. As seen in the table, the richest 1 per cent (1992 income of at least $324,100) saw their tax rates decline by only 7.9 per cent between 1980 and 1992. Middle- and lower-income groups received significantly larger percentage cuts over this period. In fact, the poorest fifth of taxpayers now receive a tax refund equal to 3.2 per cent of their pre-tax income. In 1980, their average refund equaled only 0.5 per cent.

Unfortunately, what income-tax reform giveth, less visible tax changes take away. Corporate taxes increased dramatically with the passage of the Tax Equity and Fiscal Responsibility Act (TEFRA) in 1982. Five "Deficit Reduction Acts" produced additional revenues, *but no deficit reduction*, throughout the 1980s. Most of the added tax burden was in the form of Social Security taxes. As a result of legislation passed during the Carter Administration (1977), payroll-tax rates rose from 12.26 per cent in 1980 to 15.3 per cent in 1990. This, along with more modest changes enacted in response to the Greenspan Commission's recommendations in 1983, generated an extra $300 billion in Social Security taxes—most of it from middle-class taxpayers. None of this was the result of Reagan tax reform, which focused on income taxes.

Tax Myths

February 1992

A number of durable misperceptions have resurfaced in the wake of President Bush's State of the Union speech:

1. *We Are Actually Undertaxed.* When the U.S. is compared to other developed nations, this argument seems to have merit. In 1989 federal, state, and local taxes (including Social Security taxes) appropriated 30.1 per cent of GDP in the U.S., versus 43.8 per cent in France, 38.1 per cent in Germany, 36.5 per cent in the UK, and 30.6 per cent in Japan. Of the 24 nations in the Organization for Economic Cooperation and Development, only Turkey taxes away a smaller share of GNP—29.0 per cent. The cost of tax-financed national health insurance plans explains a good part of the difference, and this, of course, is not something we should emulate. More important, while average tax rates—taxes as a percent of GDP—are lower in the U.S., marginal tax rates—taxes on the next dollar of income—are not. Our 33 per cent top marginal capital gains tax rate, for example, is highest except for Australia's, and we are the only OECD member to tax dividends twice. Since marginal tax rates influence economic incentives, we are hardly undertaxed.

2. *Tax Cuts Will Inevitably Increase Employment.* Not necessarily. The demand for workers is ultimately derived from the demand for things that workers make, e.g., the demand for auto workers goes up when people buy more cars. If consumers use their tax cuts to pay off debts rather than buy more goods, there obviously will not be a major increase in the derived demand for labor. The Social Security payroll tax (FICA), on the other hand, influences the cost of labor directly, and would stimulate employment if reduced. Even marginal changes would be welcome. The elimination of FICA taxes on restaurant tips earned above the minimum wage, for example, would create 39,000 jobs in the restaurant industry, according to a recent study by Ohio University economist Richard Vedder.

3. *A Capital Gains Cut Favors the Wealthy.* The hoariest myth of all. Yes, although capital gains are received by every income group, the wealthy predominate: in 1989 the 0.7 per cent of taxpayers with income above $200,000 received 59.0 per cent of total capital-gains

34

income. The distributional story doesn't stop here, however. Lower CG tax rates will stimulate investment, increase the ratio of capital-to-labor, and, because labor productivity is inextricably linked to this ratio, increase real wage rates. A recent study by the National Center for Policy Analysis concluded that more than 90 per cent of the rise in after-tax income stemming from lower taxes on capital will flow to wage earners, not investors. While workers may not own capital, they benefit disproportionately from its increase.

4. *Only Congress Can Cut Taxes.* The Administration can unilaterally change the timing of revenues and expenditures to move fiscal stimulus from 1993 to 1992. Some departments have already been ordered to speed up the spending of funds already appropriated—a traditional election year tactic. More problematic is the President's decision to cut withholding rates without cutting the basic tax rates. Next spring the resulting increase in income tax payments and refunds decrease may be a severe blow to the economy. Most of the really substantive tax changes do require Congressional approval. Paul Craig Roberts recently alerted his readers to a conspicuous exception: capital gains indexation. According to Roberts, the definition of "cost" in computing taxable capital gains is set by regulation, not by statute. The President can unilaterally change that definition to mean the inflation-adjusted, rather than the nominal, value of the asset. By subjecting only the real gains to tax, this will cut tax rates significantly.

5. *The March 20th Deadline Is Unrealistic.* The smart money says it will be June or July before we have a growth package. But history shows that Congress can pass complex legislation quickly: The Emergency Banking Relief Act was enacted in one day (March 9, 1933), and last year Congress authorized aid to the Kurdish rebels in 19 days. Prolonged wrangling can have chilling economic effects, as investors and consumers postpone decisions. In 1990 tax negotiations started in May, when Mr. Bush disowned his "Read my lips, no new taxes" pledge, and ended with the signing of the budget agreement on October 26th. The economy worsened significantly during that period; the recession started in July.

Reaganomics Revisited

February 3, 1992

The longest peacetime economic expansion in U.S. history took place between November 1982 and July 1990. During those 92 months—a period three times longer than the average economic recovery since 1919—real GNP rose 32 per cent, or 4.2 per cent per year. There were 19.3 million more Americans working at the end of the cycle than in 1982, and median family income, which had declined from $34,156 (1990 dollars) in 1978 to $32,037 in 1982, hit a record $36,062 in 1990. The poverty population, which grew by 7 million during the Carter years, shrank by 4 million during the Reagan boom.

It has become fashionable, however, to denigrate the Reagan achievement, often via the use of selective or misleading statistics. A case in point: the recent nine-part series in the *Philadelphia Inquirer*, entitled "America: What Went Wrong?" Authors Donald L. Barlett and James B. Steele of the *Inquirer* staff cite tax-return data to demonstrate the (alleged) enormous disparity between rich and middle-class income growth during the Reagan years: "Between 1980 and 1989 the combined salaries of people in the $20,000–$50,000 income group increased 44 per cent," but "During the same period, the combined salaries of people earning $1 million or more a year increased 2,184 per cent."

They never say whether these are real (inflation-adjusted) or nominal growth rates, or whether they reflect growth in the aggregate income or in the per-capita income of each bracket—a crucial point in determining whether the rich really got richer, or whether there were simply more of them.

More important, because the tax laws change so frequently, IRS statistics are virtually useless for measuring the true distribution of income. The 1986 tax-reform act, for example, disallowed passive real-estate tax shelters, forcing many high-income individuals to include previously sheltered income in their adjusted gross income (AGI). Barlett and Steele interpret the resulting rise in AGI as evidence of "the rich getting richer," when it really signals that the rich are being taxed on a larger fraction of their true income.

36

D. Tax Policy

At the other extreme, the 1986 law removed millions of the working poor from the tax rolls. The resulting decline in the AGI of poor taxpayers is interpreted by Barlett and Steele as a decline in their economic fortunes rather than a progressive tilt to the tax code.

Of course, the rich *did* get richer during the Eighties, but not without making others richer also. Department of Commerce statistics show the average real income of the wealthiest 20 per cent of American households increased 22 per cent between 1980 and 1989, while that of the middle three quintiles rose by a range of 8 to 19 per cent. Unlike IRS statistics, these data are consistent over time and include transfer payments.

Perhaps the most blatant distortion involves allegations of a pro-rich bias in the 1986 tax law. The authors note—correctly—that the number of wealthy taxpayers paying the Alternative Minimum Tax (AMT), which was designed to ensure that nobody escapes paying at least some tax, fell by 75 per cent between 1986 and 1989, and that the average AMT payment fell by 90 per cent. But this trend actually reflects a more progressive income tax, not the "illusory" tax hike on the rich claimed by the authors.

In fact, AMT payments rise or fall with the number of loopholes or "tax preferences" available to wealthy taxpayers. (The minimum tax is levied on the amounts of such exemptions.) The 1986 tax reform eliminated many loopholes available to wealthy taxpayers— e.g., the passive real-estate tax shelters mentioned above. Thus while AMT payments fell after 1986, the total amount of income taxes collected from individuals earning $100,000 and above rose by more than $50 billion between 1986 and 1989, and their share of all income-tax payments went from 29.0 per cent to 35.9 per cent.

Middle-Class Malaise

December 2, 1991

According to official economic statistics, the recession started in July 1990. For the typical middle-class family, however, federal taxes have been producing a "recession" in living standards ever since 1987:

Table 1-12. Income and Taxes of the Median Two-Earner Family
1991 Dollars

	Gross Income	Income Tax	Federal Taxes Social Security	Other	After-Tax Income
1981	$47,998	$6,532	$3,192	$3,842	$34,432
1987	53,086	6,306	3,795	3,943	39,042
1989	53,606	6,576	4,026	4,165	38,839
1990	53,883	6,762	4,122	4,290	38,709
1991E	53,265	6,493	4,075	4,350	38,347

Source: Tax Foundation.

From 1981 to 1987 the typical American household—two earners employed full time, with two dependent children—enjoyed an 11 per cent rise in gross income, from $47,998 to $53,086 in 1991 dollars. After paying federal taxes this family was left with $39,042 in 1987, a healthy 13 per cent more purchasing power than it had at the start of the Reagan Administration.

That was the peak of the boom for them. Although income continued rising, it was outpaced by federal taxes. In 1991, according to Tax Foundation estimates, this family will have $695 less after-tax income than four years earlier.

Interestingly enough, in real dollars, the family pays less income tax now than it did in 1981. But the Social Security tax rate has been increased six times since 1980, from 6.13 per cent to 7.65 per cent, and the level of earnings to which this tax is applied has rocketed from $25,900 to $53,400. Combined income and Social Security taxes absorb 19.8 per cent of the family's income in 1991, down only slightly from the 1981 peak of 20.3 per cent.

D. Tax Policy

The "other" category reflects taxes that are passed on to consumers by business. The 1990 budget agreement increased many of these indirect taxes, including excises on gasoline, cigarettes, beer, and wine. In 1991 these taxes are expected to absorb a record 8.2 per cent of the family earnings.

In reality, the middle-class squeeze may be far more serious than shown here. After borrowing heavily during the Eighties, the average American family now devotes 10 per cent of total spending to interest payments, up from 7 per cent in 1980. (Homeowners typically spend over 40 per cent of gross income on mortgage payments.) Day-care expenses are, on average, equal to 20 to 30 per cent of the wife's earnings. State and local taxes have risen even faster than federal revenues, and will take an additional $5,273 from the two-earner family in 1991.

Out of each dollar of income, this family pays an average of 37.9 cents in combined federal, state, and local taxes, and spends 16.7 cents on housing, 11.4 cents on food, 9.1 cents on health care, and 7.5 cents on transportation. This leaves only 17.4 cents of each dollar for clothing, recreation, and other discretionary spending.

At that, the two-earner family is doing comparatively well. Its income—$53,883 in 1990—was 50 per cent higher than that of the average American family, and three times larger than the income of a typical female-headed family. Most families are hunkering down—cutting consumption and paying off their debts—in this recession. But government is oblivious: on the heels of last year's federal hike, 26 states have increased taxes this year.

An Unaffordable Tax

May 1991

The attempt to "soak the rich" with a luxury tax has already thrown thousands of middle-class workers out of work and will cost the government far more than it raises, according to a recent study prepared for Representative Olympia Snowe (R., Me.) and Senator Connie Mack (R., Fla.). The ten per cent tax on high-priced automobiles, airplanes, pleasure boats, jewelry, and furs was supposed to yield $25 million this year and $1.5 billion over the next five years.

Unfortunately, these figures are based on a static analysis, ignoring the rise in unemployment attributable to the tax. In 1991, for example, 19,000 production workers in the boat-building industry will lose their jobs, according to the National Marine Industry Association. While nearly two-thirds of them would have become unemployed anyway—the victims of the recession—7,600 of the 19,000 will lose their jobs solely because of the deleterious impact of the tax on new boat sales, according to the report.

Even if these workers had been paying income taxes at the low 15 per cent tax rate, and find new jobs after only four months of unemployment—unreasonably conservative assumptions—the government will still lose $16.1 million in reduced income and Social Security tax receipts, plus $2.1 million in higher unemployment insurance outlays. The total cost to the government—$18.1 million—exceeds the luxury tax revenue expected from boat sales by a six-to-one margin.

Perhaps the most dramatic evidence of tax-inflicted damage occurs in the aircraft industry: domestic aircraft shipments fell 13.3 per cent in the first quarter of 1991, while the number of exported aircraft, which are not subject to the luxury tax, rose 5.6 per cent. The tax is responsible for all of the estimated 1,470 jobs lost in fixed-wing aircraft manufacturing in 1991, according to the Snowe/Mack report. Offsetting revenues are minuscule: preliminary IRS data show only six returns with aircraft luxury-tax payments during the first quarter of 1991, bringing in only $120,000.

Luxury tax proponents argue that these are temporary setbacks, the result of people accelerating luxury item purchases late last year to beat the January 1st imposition date. But economic theory, as well as common sense, indicates that putting a tax on items that have non-taxed substitutes will depress demand for the taxed items for as long as the tax is in place. Indeed, the depressing effect of the tax may grow worse over time as, for example, people learn to use charter services, and commercial airlines, and to extend the life of used airplanes.

The time, paperwork, and confusion involved in complying with the tax represent another overlooked cost. The automobile luxury tax, for example, applies to cars valued at more than $30,000. But customers can easily buy a car with a base price of $28,000 at one dealership, purchase $10,000 worth of options at another, and avoid the tax entirely.

The jewelry tax, which applies to purchases in excess of $10,000, is loaded with regulatory nonsense. If a granddaughter inherits a ring valued at $20,000 and has it reset at a cost of $1,000, the tax law requires that tax be paid on the full $21,000 piece of jewelry. She would thus face a $1,100 luxury tax liability on a new purchase valued at only $1,000.

Wealthy taxpayers seem to be avoiding the luxury tax in droves, perhaps because art, antiques, and luxury real estate are among the many luxuries not subject to tax. Unfortunately, workers who have lost their jobs because of the tax usually do not have as many options.

The Family Tax

May 27, 1991

The tax-fairness debate invariably focuses on whether the rich pay sufficiently more than those of more modest incomes. Yet family size rarely enters the discussion, even though most would agree that a "rich" five-person family with income of, say, $100,000, is no better off than a single person earning half as much.

In earlier years the tax code fully recognized the importance of the family by granting substantial personal exemptions for dependents, most of whom are children. But exemptions for dependents have dramatically failed to keep pace with inflation.

Table 1-13. The Dwindling Personal Exemption			
	In Nominal Dollars	In 1989 Dollars	As % of Median Family Income
1950	600	3,087	18.1
1960	600	2,513	10.7
1970	625	1,997	6.3
1980	1,000	1,505	4.8
1985	1,040	1,152	3.6
1989	2,000	2,000	5.8

Source: Office of Senator Dan Coats (R., Ind.).

Figures prepared by the office of Senator Dan Coats (R., Ind.) show that in constant dollars the personal exemption was worth $1,087 more in 1950 than in 1989. Forty years ago the $600 exemption represented 18.1 per cent of a median family's income; today's exemption ($2,050 in 1990) shields less than 6 per cent of this family's income from taxation.

Singles needn't worry: they've gained far more from higher standard deductions over the past thirty years than they've lost from smaller real personal exemptions. Similarly, upper-middle-class and truly wealthy families pay a smaller fraction of income to the government now than they did in earlier years because of the sharp reductions in the top marginal tax rate. Poor families are also not harmed because, thanks to the 1986 tax reforms, they pay no income tax.

D. Tax Policy

But for lower-middle-class families the withering of personal exemptions has brought a substantial decline in after-tax income: in 1960 a four-person family earning the equivalent of $22,100 paid no taxes; today that family has a tax liability of more than $2,000.

Mr. Coats would double the personal exemption for all taxpayers, at a cost of some $30 billion to $50 billion in foregone income-tax revenues, according to some estimates. A tax-relief bill sponsored by Congressman Frank Wolf (R., Va.) would target families, raising the exemption to $3,500 for each child under age 18. This would hold costs down to the $8- to $12-billion range.

And other tax-code changes could easily recoup these losses. We might, for example, include the value of employer-provided medical insurance in employees' taxable income, thereby raising as much as $30 billion while putting a socially desirable brake on medical costs. The deduction for state and local taxes subsidizes high-tax states and cities; eliminating it would raise $15 billion. That most sacred of all loopholes, the mortgage-interest deduction, could be capped at $20,000, bringing in another $2 billion annually. A higher personal exemption would make the child-care tax credit redundant; its elimination would save $4 billion and also undo the tax code's bias against mothers who stay at home to care for their children. Surely it is fairer to distribute tax relief on the basis of mouths to feed rather than home ownership, child-care arrangements, or fringe benefits.

In fact, the cost of doubling the personal exemption may be vastly overstated. Millions of working-class families would be dropped from the 31 per cent tax bracket to the 15 per cent tax bracket, or be removed from the tax rolls entirely. The supply-side boost to the economy would keep costs far below the static estimates.

Taxing the Elderly

October 13, 1989

Most Americans face lower tax rates now than at the start of this decade, the top marginal tax rate having been slashed from 70 per cent to 28 per cent. But according to a study published by the Dallas-based National Center for Policy Analysis (NCPA), two tax changes enacted during the past few years are preventing elderly, middle-class workers from deriving any benefit whatever from the Reagan-era tax cuts.

First, there is the taxation of Social Security benefits. Since 1983, for each additional (taxable) dollar earned by certain Social Security recipients (couples with non-Social Security income over $32,000; singles with non-Social Security income above $25,000), 50 cents of their benefits from Social Security become taxable as well. Thus while non-elderly workers face tax rates of from 15 per cent to 28 per cent, elderly workers are facing tax rates that are, effectively, one and a half times as high, ranging from 22.5 per cent to 42 per cent.

On top of this there is the Medicare surtax imposed this year to cover the cost of catastrophic-illness insurance. Calculated as $22.50 per every $150 of federal income tax, the surtax raises effective tax rates by another 15 per cent, to as high as 48.3 per cent. Although the Administration is having second thoughts about it, as things currently stand the surtax rate will rise to 28 per cent in 1993, meaning that elderly taxpayers will be paying the IRS 53.8 cents for each dollar of additional earnings.

When you factor in the impact of the "earnings test," which causes workers to lose $1 in Social Security benefits for every $2 in earnings (in effect a 50 per cent tax on earnings), many elderly workers are actually better off earning less than trying to earn more. The NCPA study found, for example, that an elderly widow earning twice the minimum wage would see her total income fall by $27 if she were to get a $1,000 raise. A married man earning $8,800 would experience an $18 decline in after-tax income if he were foolish enough to accept a $1,000 raise. These absurd marginal rates do not apply to the richest elderly, who already pay the maximum amount of surtax and benefits tax, but to those with non-Social Security income between $20,000 and $45,000 per year.

The assumption would be that at least the rest of us gain from these inequities imposed on older Americans—but not so. Today 83 per cent of all men and 92 per cent of all women over the age of 65 are completely retired. Considering only the healthy individuals in this group, the United States has lost about 17.5 million workers— some 14 per cent of the total civilian labor force. If one-third of the retired men aged sixty and over re-entered the labor market, even if they earned as little as $5 per hour, national income would rise by $58 billion, generating an addition $12 billion in income and Social Security taxes.

So far, the entry of married women into the labor force has more than made up for the withdrawal of the elderly, but this bonanza will not last forever. By the year 2030, according to the Social Security Administration, there will be only two workers for every retiree—compared to 17 in 1950.

Jesse Jackson's 38.5 Per Cent Solution

May 13, 1988

Jesse Jackson says that if elected President he will raise the top tax rate back up to 38.5 per cent for individuals earning more than $192,000 a year, a move that he claims will raise an addition $20 billion.

That's good money if you can get it, but according to Harvard economics professor Lawrence Lindsey, there isn't enough taxable income above $192,000 to generate that kind of revenue:

Table 1-14. Taxable Income and Taxes at Each Marginal Tax Rate, 1988			
Tax Bracket for 4-Person Family	Marginal Tax Rate (Per Cent)	Taxable Income ($ Billions)	Income Tax Generated ($ Billions)
$0–$29,750	15%	$1,354	$203
$29,750–$71,900	28	361	101
$71,900–$192,930	33	113	37
$192,930 +	28	120	34
		$1,948	$375

Source: National Bureau of Economic Research.

Only 6 per cent of taxable income currently falls into the highest bracket, generating $34 billion of taxes. Raise the rate on that income to 38.5 per cent, and at best you would get an additional $12 billion.

In reality, the government would be lucky to get any additional revenue, considering the likely response of high-income taxpayers. Because of tax shelters, many taxpayers in this bracket qualify to pay the Alternative Minimum Tax (AMT) at a 21-per-cent marginal rate. Raising the rate on the top bracket to 38.5 per cent would increase the spread between ordinary and AMT rates from 7 per cent to 17.5 per cent, making tax shelters that much more attractive.

Consider what happened after 1981. The top marginal rate on earnings, which had effectively been 70 per cent despite the statutory maximum of 50 per cent, was lowered to 50 per cent. From 1982 to 1985, according to Lindsey's calculation, high-income taxpayers (those with taxable incomes above $200,000) reported $86.8 billion more taxable income than they would have at the pre-cut rate. This wasn't a case of the rich getting richer—in fact, dividend and interest income was below expectations. But the income of entrepreneurs, lawyers, and doctors—people who have enormous discretion as to how much and when they pay themselves—was nearly three times what we would have expected.

Over the past decade, while marginal tax rates on the highest incomes were being cut by 60 per cent, the share of taxes paid by the wealthiest 1 per cent of families rose 22.1 per cent, and that of the poorer half fell 7.8 per cent. Mr. Jackson's tax plan would reverse this trend.

Truth in Taxation

February 19, 1988

The 1986 Tax Reform Act was billed as a $25-billion shift of tax burden from individuals to corporations. Understandably, in selling the package to the American people, both Treasury and the Joint Tax Committee focused almost exclusively on the personal-income-tax side of things. Charts were prepared showing all income brackets paying less under the new law, with reductions in 1988 ranging from 2.4 per cent for taxpayers with incomes above $200,000, to 65.1 per cent for those with incomes below $10,000. The average taxpayer, we were told, would pay $194 less in 1988 because of this legislation.

But corporate taxes are paid by people also, not directly, but indirectly—first in the form of lower dividends and capital-gains income, and then, in cases where corporations are able to pass the tax on to their customers, in the form of higher prices for goods and services.

Recent research has worked through the net impact of the total tax package, including the corporate tax increase, on the tax liabilities of individuals, and has discovered that, when corporate taxes are factored in, all income brackets above $50,000 pay more in taxes under the new tax law. Considerably more.

Individuals earning $200,000 and above will see their combined personal- and corporate-tax liabilities rise by $18,770 in 1988, a 12.9 per cent increase over what they would have been paying under the old tax law. Taxpayers with incomes between $100,000 and $200,000 will pay, on average, $3,335 more; between $75,000 and $100,000, $1,113 more; and between $50,000 and $75,000, $243 more, according to the National Bureau of Economic Research.

Taxes are reduced for those earning less than $50,000, but not by nearly as much as had been promised: individuals earning less than $10,000 will pay 17.6 per cent less; they had been promised a cut nearly four times as large. Taxpayers in the $40,000 to $50,000 group will pay 4.4 per cent less—not the 9.5 per cent reduction originally advertised.

Taxpayers over age 65 will pay more under the new law no matter what bracket they are in, reflecting the importance of capital-

48

gains income among older retired or partially retired individuals in all income classes. The combined tax increase ranges from 17 per cent for elderly taxpayers in the $10,000 to $20,000 income group, to 8 per cent for those in the highest income group.

E. Federal Spending and the Deficit

Behind the Deficit

February 15, 1993

When confronted with the last deficit projection for 1993, and the forecasts of still larger imbalances in future years, Dick Darman said, "I thought we'd have more time." Based on the budget director's performance, we're glad he didn't:

Table 1-15. Federal Spending, Revenues, and Deficit
$ Billions

	1989	1993	% Change
National Defense	$303.6	$289.3	−4.7
Social Security	232.5	304.7	31.1
Medicare	85.0	132.8	56.2
Health Programs	48.4	105.0	116.9
Transfer Payments	136.0	207.4	52.5
Infrastructure	51.9	72.8	40.3
Net Interest	169.3	202.8	19.8
Other	116.5	160.1	37.4
Total Spending	$1,143.2	$1,474.9	29.0
Total Revenues	989.7	1,147.6	16.0
Deficit	$153.5	$327.3	113.2

Source: Office of Management and Budget (calculations by author).

The Federal Government will spend $332 billion, or 29 per cent, more this year than it did the year George Bush was inaugurated. By comparison, consumer prices rose 16 per cent, and economic growth was a mere 6.6 per cent over the same period. Revenues kept pace with inflation, but they were no match for spending. The deficit more than doubled.

Although Social Security is the largest federal program, and accounted for one-quarter of the budget growth since 1989, it is not responsible for the current deficit. Indeed, the Social Security trust fund will record a surplus of more than $100 billion this year, reflecting the excess of payroll-tax receipts over benefits paid to retirees. The surplus is spent on other government programs, a practice that has been widely criticized.

The real culprits are federal health programs. Medicaid spending, for example, after being held to a 14 per cent average annual growth rate under President Carter, and 9.5 per cent under Ronald Reagan, exploded at a 25 per cent annual rate in the Bush/Darman régime. Medicare and other federal health programs will account for 16.1 per cent of the budget this year, versus 11.7 per cent in 1989.

Apologists insist that this trend was inevitable, given the recession and the enormous inflation in health costs. But Medicaid eligibility was expanded in recent years, along with the number of covered services. Significant liberalization also occurred in the Head Start program, child nutrition, unemployment insurance, prenatal care. The nation's largest welfare program—Aid to Families with Dependent Children—saw its enrollment increase by 25 per cent since January 1989, far faster than the rise in the poverty population.

Public-policy experts estimate that the recession, the aging U.S. population, and inflation together explain 60 per cent of the increase in domestic spending. The remaining 40 per cent reflects program changes proposed by the Bush Administration, or congressional initiatives approved by it.

Social Security, Medicare, and Medicaid are well protected politically. Interest payments must be made. President Clinton might in theory cut the deficit in half by attacking the waste, fraud, and mismanagement that the General Accounting Office says costs the taxpayers $180 billion each year. But only the most exuberant optimist could imagine a government free of waste, fraud, and mismanagement.

There was a glimmer of hope last year. The deficit forecast for fiscal 1992 was reduced from $400 billion at the start of the year to $325 billion by mid-year. The actual deficit was only $290 billion. Good news? Not exactly. Most of the decline was due to Congress's failure to enact additional funding for the S&L bailout, a delay that many believe will eventually increase the total cost of the cleanup. When it comes to the deficit, even good news is bad news.

The Deficit's Damage

July 1992

The federal budget hasn't been in surplus since 1969, yet the economy still hasn't collapsed. Americans may be excused for thinking that deficits simply do not matter.

But economists agree that investment is the key to long-run economic growth, and deficits, by enabling government to take more resources from the private sector, reduce the income available for productive investment. During the 1960s the budget deficit absorbed approximately 2 per cent of net private savings; in 1990, 58 per cent of these savings was needed to finance the federal deficit. This year's deficit, currently estimated at $400 billion, could easily absorb the entire net amount saved by the rest of the economy.

A recent GAO study compared the long-term economic consequences of different deficit trends:

Table 1-16. Deficits and the 2020 Economy			
	1992 Actual	——— In 2020 (1992 dollars per capita) ———		
		No Action	Muddling Through	Budget Balance
Real GNP	$23,500	$23,875	$30,374	$32,353
Federal Debt	12,067	45,816	16,702	4,665
Foreign Debt	1,765	19,243	8,460	3,748
Source: General Accounting Office (GAO).			

According to GAO's model, if we take "No Action" and simply continue current spending and tax policies, total federal outlays will equal 42.4 per cent of GNP in 2020 (versus 22.9 per cent in 1990), and the deficit will explode to 20.6 per cent GNP, or more than three times its current share. The composition of expenditures will change drastically, with defense falling to just 8.2 per cent of total spending (versus 24.6 per cent in 1990), and interest payments becoming the largest single expenditure item, comprising 31.5 per cent of the budget. Nearly 40 per cent of the 2020 budget is Social Security, Medicare, and other mandatory health spending.

E. Federal Spending & the Deficit

As seen in Table 1-16, a "No Action" policy brings economic growth to a halt. Real per-capita GNP in 2020 is about equal to today's figure, and per-capita federal debt is nearly four times larger.

The "Muddling Through" scenario assumes that deficits are held to 3 per cent of GNP, or at about the levels CBO projects for the mid 1990s. This only postpones the date of confrontation with the underlying problem. When baby-boomers start to retire (after 2005), massive spending cuts are required to keep the deficit at 3 per cent. Although economic growth resumes, "Muddling Through" implies higher per capita federal debt and an endless stream of trade deficits and foreign borrowing.

Under the "Budget Balance" scenario sharp spending cuts are enacted in the mid- to late 1990s, producing a balanced budget in 2001 that is maintained. People are initially worse off and forced to consume less under this scenario than under "Muddling Through." The sacrifices pay off after 2001, however, when the higher national savings rate brought about by deficit reduction increases GNP and consumption, and lowers foreign indebtedness.

The GAO model probably understates the benefits of a balanced budget. It assumes, for example, that productivity continues growing at a steady one per cent per annum rate despite the collapse of investment under a "No Action" policy. GAO also assumes that interest rates are unaffected by higher deficits, and that foreign investors will buy unlimited amounts of U.S. government bonds despite a deteriorating U.S. economy.

The "No Action" scenario may be the least likely of all, since an economic crisis of the magnitude forecast by GAO would make fundamental spending reforms politically possible.

Who's Entitled?

April 13, 1992

George Bush claims that he agreed to raise taxes in 1990 in return for "serious controls on spending." The second part of that deal never materialized: led by entitlements, domestic federal spending (excluding the S&L bailout) will increase more during Bush's first four years than during Ronald Reagan's eight:

Table 1-17. Domestic Federal Spending
Billions of 1992 dollars

	Mandatory Enrollments		Discretionary Spending		
	$	% of Budget	$	% of Budget	$ Total
1970	226.0	31.1	143.6	19.8	369.6
1980	442.4	43.7	220.8	21.9	663.2
1988	563.6	45.2	185.4	14.9	749.0
1991	617.2	45.3	201.4	14.8	818.6
1992E	675.5	45.7	216.2	14.7	891.7

Source: Congressional Budget Office (CBO).

The 1990 Budget Act "controlled" entitlements by requiring new spending to "pay for itself" via offsetting tax hikes or reductions in other entitlements. Congress easily circumvented this rule by putting automatic spending increases into existing legislation. Indeed, by their very nature, entitlements are difficult to control. Social Security and Medicare—which together account for 60 per cent of all entitlement spending—are available to anyone over age 65, whether needy or not. Congress has steadfastly refused to impose a means test for Social Security, or to modify its annual cost-of-living adjustment. Unemployment benefits are paid to wealthy executives and poor laborers alike.

Since the start of the Great Society in 1966 entitlement spending has increased more than tenfold, after adjusting for inflation, dwarfing the 81 per cent rise in real GNP. The rise has been continual, even during the Reagan years: real entitlement spending in 1989 was 17 per cent higher than in 1981, although the poverty population increased less than 1 per cent over that period.

Even during a recession the potential for cutting entitlements seems enormous, especially considering that only one-fourth of all so-called anti-poverty spending actually trickles down as cash to the poor. In New York State, for example, people with incomes as high as $1,565 per month *after* the subtraction of medical expenses, and with assets totaling as much as $62,580 after these expenses, are eligible for Medicaid—the health program for the poor. Similarly, half of the $2 billion spent nationally on school lunch and breakfast programs goes to families with incomes of over $25,000 per year, or 185 per cent of the poverty level. Agricultural subsidies are available to farmers with non-farm incomes of more than $125,000, and middle-income families are eligible for student loans and grants that are desperately needed by the neediest college students.

The Bush budget acknowledges the entitlement problem. But its proposed remedy—a "cap" on mandatory spending growth set equal to growth in population plus CPI plus 4.1 per cent—seems little better than the current situation. Indeed, despite the economic recovery forecast by OMB for 1992 to 1997, the budget foresees higher real entitlement spending over this period.

A Decade of Debt

August 12, 1991

The doomsayers are sure that the high levels of debt accumulated during the 1980s will limit economic recovery in the Nineties. There were excesses, of course, but today debtors appear to be mending their ways—all but the Federal Government.

Table 1-18. Government vs. Private Debt
Year End, $ Billions

| | Government Debt | | Private- | |
	Federal	State/ Local	Sector Debt	Total Debt
1980	743	287	2868	3898
1989	2,269	634	6902	9,805
1990	2,568	649	7,342	10,560
Average Annual Percentage Change				
1980–89	13.2	9.2	10.2	10.8
1990	13.2	2.3	6.4	7.7
As Percentage of GNP				
1980	27.2	10.5	105.5	143.2
1990	47.0	11.8	134.3	193.2

Source: Federal Reserve.

From 1980 to 1989 non-financial debt more than doubled, to $9.8 trillion. Persistent deficits pushed federal debt up at a 13.2 per cent average annual rate during this time, faster than the overall debt rise. And in 1990, while the recession and the credit crunch forced other governments and the private sector to ease up on credit demands, federal debt rose at the same breakneck pace as in the Eighties.

More recent data show an even greater divergence between federal and private-sector debt trends. From May 1990 through May 1991, commercial bank loans rose only 3.6 per cent, the slowest pace since August 1975. Business debt outstanding actually fell in the last three months of 1990. Meanwhile, the 1991 deficit is expected to reach $318 billion, so that federal debt will grow at a faster rate this year than it did during the Eighties.

E. Federal Spending & the Deficit

Of course, the economy also grew in the Eighties. But the ratio of debt to GNP, after holding remarkably steady at 140 per cent (debt 1.4 times as large as GNP) during the 1950s, 1960s, and 1970s, shot up to 190 per cent during the 1980s. Federal debt, which had declined relative to GNP from 1945 to 1980, rose from 27 per cent of GNP in 1980 to 47 per cent in 1990.

Those who believe a tax increase will be needed to reverse this trend err on two counts. First, much debt is used to finance roads, bridges, defense installations, schools, and other capital projects that will increase future GNP and thus pay for themselves in higher tax revenues. A recent study of government balance sheets by economist Robert Eisner found that the value of assets owned by the Federal Government was only slightly less than that of outstanding federal debt. When state and local government assets are included (much of which the Federal Government helped finance), total government assets exceed government debt by well over $1 trillion. Unfortunately, Eisner also found that the "net worth" of government, i.e., the amount by which public assets exceed public debt, has been shrinking since 1983, as federal debt is increasingly used to finance items other than tangible, productive assets.

More important, federal taxes already consume 19.4 per cent of GNP, higher than the 19.2 per cent average tax burden of the Carter years, and sharply higher than the 18.1 per cent Reagan level of 1983 and 1984. Budget "summits" were convened in 1982, 1984, 1987, 1989, and 1990, to deal with the deficit. Taxes were raised each time, and in every case the deficit rose the next year as new spending outstripped the new revenues.

Expenditure control, perhaps aided by a balanced-budget amendment or the requirement that new taxes be approved by a 60 per cent supermajority of Congress, seems the only way out.

The Deficit (Non-)Problem

October 15, 1990

A recent Congressional Budget Office study highlights the role of the S&L bailout in pushing up the deficit:

Table 1-19. The Deficit and the S&Ls					
	Cost in Billions			**As % of GNP**	
Fiscal Year	**Base Deficit, Ex S&L Costs**	**S&L Costs**	**Total Deficit**	**Base Deficit**	**S&L Costs**
1989	$143	$ 9	$152	2.8	0.1
1990 (June est.)	159	36	195	2.9	0.7
1990 (Sept. est.)	159	55	214	2.9	1.0
1991 (Sept. est.)	164	70	234	2.8	1.2
1992 (Sept. est.)	158	60	218	2.5	1.0
			Source: Congressional Budget Office.		

In June, the CBO estimated that the deficit for fiscal 1990, which ended on September 30, would be $195 billion, including $36 billion spent for the S&L bailout. But that has now been swollen by $19 billion in additional bailout costs, pushing the deficit above $200 billion for the first time since 1986. (For what it's worth, the Gramm-Rudman target was $100 billion.)

Next year looks even bleaker, with the estimated costs of closing insolvent thrifts and paying depositors ranging from $70 to $100 billion. Higher oil prices, by helping the economies of the oil-producing states, where many failed S&Ls are located, could lower costs.

The cost of American operations in the Gulf—$2.5 billion in fiscal 1990 and $1 billion per month thereafter—seems puny by comparison. In fact, when the bailout costs are excluded, the base deficit figure—not counting any steps Congress may take to cut it—is expected to decline as a percentage of GNP. In a meaningful economic sense, not in the sense of Gramm-Rudman, the federal budget is now in balance.

Does the enormous upsurge in costs associated with the S&L bailout warrant a tax increase? Many economists think not. Unlike federal borrowing to pay for transfer payments or salaries or military hardware, the deficit incurred to cover deposit insurance does not reduce the funds available to private-sector borrowers. Nearly all the money the government raises for this purpose is pumped right back into the financial system, as recipients deposit the funds in new accounts.

Economist Robert Eisner likens the bailout to replacing $180 billion of currency that got washed down a sewer or lost in a fire. In replacing the lost funds the government is not adding to the wealth of depositors. Raising taxes to reimburse those who lost money would only compound the problem: their wealth would be restored at the expense of the rest of us. It would be far better to borrow the funds, and authorize the printing of additional money to pay off the debt. But, according to Eisner, failing to replace the lost money is no solution: it would be deflationary, and would probably trigger at best a financial crisis and at worst a sharp depression.

This is not to say that the S&L debacle hasn't hurt the economy. But the economic impact occurred in the past, when the bad loans and fraud diverted the savings of depositors from more productive uses. Borrowing to close the remaining insolvent S&Ls doesn't add to those problems, it forestalls additional ones.

Time Bombs

February 19, 1990

Continued economic growth and falling interest rates have brought a sort of fiscal nirvana to Washington, with talk of a "peace dividend" heard on both sides of the aisle. Yet the potential for unpleasant surprises, *à la* the S&L fiasco, is greater now than ever before:

1. *The Pension Benefit Guarantee Corporation* (potential federal liability: $2.0 trillion). This shadowy government corporation insures the private pension benefits of 66 million Americans, taking over if employers cannot meet their pension obligations. In theory such pension plans are required to police themselves by undergoing periodic outside audits, but in November the General Accounting Office reported that nearly half of the plans it surveyed had never been audited, and that 43 per cent of the pension-plan assets involved were officially unaccounted for. The corporation's potential exposure is greater than that of the Social Security Trust Fund and the savings and loan industry combined.

2. *Federal Mortgage Insurance* (potential federal liability: $0.9 trillion). During the Eighties the share of mortgages directly held by federal agencies rose from 17 per cent to 29 per cent. (This is over and above the 49 per cent of all mortgages currently held by S&Ls and commercial banks where deposits are federally insured.) Unfortunately, while the government acted to shore up the private thrift industry, its own mortgage agencies were allowed to deteriorate. Technically they are insolvent. Mortgage defaults, which in the case of the Federal Housing Administration (FHA) went from $2.6 billion in 1986 to an estimated $6.7 billion in 1989, have long since overwhelmed their cash reserves. And a bill sponsored by Senators D'Amato and Cranston would aggravate the situation by lowering the required down payment on FHA-insured mortgages to 1 per cent from the already far too low 3 to 5 per cent, while simultaneously increasing the loan limit from $101,250 to as much as $190,000 in some sections of the country.

3. *Federal Pensions* (potential federal liability: $0.8 trillion). Imagine the condition of the Social Security Trust Fund a few decades hence if it hadn't accumulated a surplus to help pay for future

benefits. That is exactly what awaits the Civil Service and Military Retirement systems, where benefits will exceed income by a combined $775 billion (in 1988 dollars) over the next forty years. Of course, many believe that there is no real need to fund these liabilities now. After all, the Federal Government—unlike a private company, where such underfunding would be illegal—is never going to go out of business. Six years ago the Grace Commission warned that to amortize the unfunded liability of the Civil Service Pension system would require setting aside an amount equal to 85 per cent of the federal payroll for each of the next forty years, compared to the 30 per cent of payroll spent on pensions now.

4. *Federal Deposit Insurance Corporation* (FDIC) (potential federal liability: $1.7 trillion). In 1988 the FDIC registered its first loss—$4.2 billion—which reduced its reserves to $14.1 billion, the lowest level it has ever been at relative to insured deposits. Meanwhile, the commercial banks the FDIC insures have devoted increasing shares of their loans to real-estate and corporate-takeover ("junk bond") ventures. Ironically, therefore, the S&L bailout exacerbates the problem faced by commercial banks, since much of the property owned by insolvent thrifts will be auctioned off over the next few years, keeping real-estate prices depressed.

Dividends of Peace

December 31, 1989

The proposed defense cutbacks are seen by many as the first significant reduction in military spending since the end of the Vietnam War. In fact they simply reinforce a trend under way for the past four years:

Table 1-20. The Rise and Fall of Defense Spending

Fiscal Year	Defense Authorizations*		Defense Outlays	
	Total	Weapons Procurement	As % of Budget	As % of GNP
1980	$210.1	$ 51.5	22.7%	5.0%
1985	320.0	105.1	26.7	6.4
1986	307.5	98.4	27.6	6.5
1987	304.4	84.9	28.1	6.4
1988	303.4	83.2	27.3	6.1
1989	298.8	79.2	26.2	5.8

* In billions of 1989 dollars.

Source: Office of Management and Budget.

Defense spending started falling in fiscal 1986. That year Congress slashed the Administration's budget request by 10 per cent, and, for the first time since the end of the Vietnam War, authorized defense spending dropped in nominal terms. By 1989 real defense-spending authority was nearly 7 per cent below its 1985 peak; weapons-procurement authority, which had doubled in real terms between 1980 and 1985, was 25 per cent lower. Defense outlays, which lag behind authorizations, started to fall relative to GNP in 1986, and as a share of the budget in 1987.

Even absent further cuts, the Reagan/Bush Administrations have already presided over both the largest defense buildup, and the largest decline, in the nation's peacetime history.

From a broader perspective, defense spending has been declining for more than a quarter of a century. During the late Fifties and early Sixties defense accounted for about 52 per cent of the federal budget, and about 10 per cent of GNP. Real defense spending fell in the years immediately following the 1962 Cuban missile crisis, and by 1970, despite the Vietnam War, defense's share of the budget fell to 42 per cent. At its post-Vietnam low, in 1978, defense accounted for only 22.8 per cent of federal spending and 4.8 per cent of GNP.

Although this earlier "peace dividend" dwarfed anything now contemplated by Defense Secretary Dick Cheney, it did not prevent the onset of higher inflation and chronically poor economic performance. The problem, of course, was that federal spending continued rising as a percentage of GNP throughout this period, as social programs more than filled the void left by defense. A $300-billion defense budget supports, directly or indirectly, between 7 and 8.5 million jobs, or roughly 6 per cent of the nation's total employment. Five states—California, Virginia, Texas, New York, and Massachusetts—account for nearly half of the value of DOD procurement contracts, and a similar share of defense-related civilian employment. Sixteen states—California, New York, Massachusetts, Virginia, Washington, Utah, New Mexico, Missouri, Mississippi, Georgia, South Carolina, Maryland, Connecticut, New Hampshire, Alaska, and Hawaii—receive more in military spending than they contribute to the defense budget in taxes.

The economic impact of defense spending is most pervasive in the research-and-development area, where approximately one-third of the nation's scientists and engineers work on DOD-sponsored projects. While many critics argue that defense R&D crowds out private-sector R&D, in fact the big surge in defense and space research during the 1950s and early 1960s, and the defense-related expansion in the 1980s, were both accompanied by strong growth in non-federal, civilian R&D. During the 1970s, when defense-related R&D was cut in real terms, civilian R&D grew more slowly.

Defense-related research is credited with the creation of entirely new civilian industries, such as computers, semiconductors, jet aircraft, nuclear power, and satellite communications. A sharp cutback would have ominous economic implications.

The Privatization Potential

November 10, 1989

Governments around the world have privatized $160 billion worth of assets over the past five years, according to *Privatization 1989*, published by the Reason Foundation. The U.S., described as "virtually alone in having no serious national commitment to privatization," accounted for only $7.2 billion of the total—$1.6 billion from the 1987 sale of Conrail, the rest from the sale of agricultural, veteran, and student loans.

The potential in this country is great, however. While we don't have the national monopolies in steel, airplanes, and communications that have fueled privatization in Europe and Japan, we do have land. More than one-third of the nation's land area is owned by the Federal Government. Much of it is leased for commercial use at rates far below the cost of managing the land. Privatizing the 375 million acres of timberland and grazing land managed by the U.S. Forest Service and the Bureau of Land Management could yield $160 billion over a ten-year period, according to Reason's calculations. The Bush budget highlights some less well-known privatization possibilities, including:

Naval Petroleum Reserves: Established by Woodrow Wilson to help the Navy make the transition from coal to oil, they have long since lost their strategic importance. Selling the government's oil fields at Elk Hills, California, and Teapot Dome, Wyoming, could raise $1 billion in up-front cash plus in-kind payments of oil (50,000 barrels per day) for the Strategic Petroleum Reserve.

Spectrum License Fees: The Federal Government has awarded licenses for use of radio frequencies since 1927. Although most frequencies were assigned years ago, the FCC regularly makes new assignments as technological advances make more of the spectrum useable. Auctioning off the rights to six megahertz of unused cellular-radio frequencies would raise $3.4 billion over two years.

Helium Processing: The Federal Government began processing helium in 1929 and was the sole supplier until 1961. Today the private helium industry can satisfy both the government and private-sector demand for this substance. Sale of the federal production facility and its hundred-year supply of helium would raise $60 million.

Alaska Power Administration: The Federal Government produces 6 per cent of the nation's electricity, mainly from hydro power. With few exceptions its energy pricing policies are the same as those that prevailed when the federal dams were built in the 1930s. As a result the government sells power worth $4 billion for $2.5 billion. Negotiations are under way to sell the dams and transmission lines that provide power to Anchorage and Juneau to a consortium of utilities and the State of Alaska. Probable revenue: $85 million.

These initiatives, while modest in scope, may face tough sledding. Congress has passed 37 laws explicitly blocking privatizing, including some that prevent agencies from even studying the possibility of saving money through privatization. Some laws prevent federal unions from participating in privatization negotiations, making agreement virtually impossible to achieve. A little *perestroika* seems in order here.

A Nation of Savers?

October 27, 1989

The notion that the deficit is sopping up an ever-larger share of our personal savings, seemingly valid for most of the Seventies and Eighties, is seriously threatened by the savings surge of the past few years:

Table 1-21. The Deficit and Personal Savings
$ Billions

Calendar Year	Federal Deficit	Personal Savings	Deficit as % of Savings
1973	5.6	89.0	6.3
1980	61.3	136.9	44.8
1986	206.9	124.9	165.7
1987	161.4	101.8	158.5
1988	145.8	144.7	100.8
1989	146.5 *	201.5 *	72.7

* Annualized rate based on first six months.

Source: Office of Management and Budget; U.S. Department of Commerce.

In 1973 the deficit absorbed only 6.3 per cent of personal savings, leaving more than $80 billion to finance private-sector investment. The savings rate (savings as a percentage of disposable personal income) took a dive after 1973, falling from 9.4 per cent that year to 3.2 per cent in 1987, and the deficit/savings ratio deteriorated to the point that in 1983, for the first time since 1945, the federal deficit exceeded total personal savings. By 1986 the deficit was $80 billion larger than personal savings, creating what many, but by no means all, see as a dangerous reliance on foreign capital to finance the deficit.

Things have improved over the past two years, however. The savings rate increased one full percentage point in 1988, to 4.2 per cent, making for the largest year-to-year increase since 1973, and during the first six months of 1989 Americans saved a robust 5.6 per cent of disposable income, a rate which if continued for the rest of the year will generate a record $202 billion of personal savings.

Why the resurgence? The reduction in the top personal-income-tax rate to 28 per cent undoubtedly played a part, as does our aging population. A Bureau of Labor Statistics survey found that households headed by individuals under 25 years of age had negative savings rates, spending nearly 20 per cent more than they earned, but those headed by people between 35 and 44 (the largest baby-boomer contingent) saved, on average, 5.0 per cent of their income. Those with incomes $40,000 and over saved an enviable 20.1 per cent of income.

The reduction in international tensions may also have contributed to our improved savings performance. University of Michigan economist Joel Slemrod finds a strong negative relationship between the perceived likelihood of nuclear war and a country's rate of private saving: an increase of 10 per cent in the fraction of the population that believes a world war likely is associated with a 4.1-percentage-point drop in the savings rate. In a Gallup Poll released in January 1987, 49 per cent of the respondents in the U.S. indicated they thought there was at least a 50–50 chance of a world war occurring within the next ten years. In Japan, where personal savings rates are consistently in the 16 to 18 per cent range, only 15 per cent expressed a high fear of world war.

A higher savings rate is not an unmitigated economic blessing. But in economics, as in sex, gratification is often greater for being delayed.

Fiscal Legerdemain

July 14, 1989

The official national debt—debt sold by the Treasury to finance the deficit—now exceeds $2 trillion, nearly triple what it was in 1980. This figure does not include the more than $1 trillion of federal obligations kept off the official ledger, specifically, the debt of government-sponsored enterprises (GSEs) and guaranteed federal loans:

Table 1-22. Federal Debt Obligations
$ Billions

	Treasury Debt	GSE Debt	Guaranteed Federal Loans	Total
1980	709.3	126.1	298.5	1133.9
1985	1509.9	351.6	410.4	2271.9
1988	2050.2	663.2	550.0	3263.4
Average Annual Percentage Increase				
1980–85	16.3	22.8	6.6	14.9
1985–88	10.7	23.6	10.3	12.8

Source: Federal Reserve.

The success of Gramm-Rudman in throttling the growth of Treasury debt since 1985 has, at the same time, spurred the use of federal loan guarantees, which do not result in budget outlays unless they go into default, and in GSEs, which are off budget and therefore immune from that law's limits.

Technically, GSEs are private corporations chartered by the U.S. Government to perform certain "public" functions, which originally meant providing credit to certain sectors of the economy. There were legitimate economic reasons for the early GSEs: the Farm Credit System helped redress the imbalances between the supply and demand for farm credit caused by restrictions on interstate banking. Fannie Mae did the same for mortgage lending. The traditional GSE is profitable and doesn't cost the taxpayer a dime.

Not so the new ones. Instead of helping private-sector business and individuals, their sole mission has been to channel public funds to failed government agencies or other GSEs, circumventing Gramm-Rudman. The S&L bailout, for example, will be transacted via a GSE created specifically for that purpose. The Resolution Financing Corporation (Refcorp) will be authorized to raise $50 billion by means of thirty-year bonds, none of which, if the Bush Administration gets its way, will be recorded in the budget although taxpayers will pay interest amounting to about $5 billion per year, or $150 billion over the life of the bonds.

The sleight of hand does not end here, for Refcorp will be obliged to turn over the bond proceeds to the government, where they will be logged in an "offsetting receipt," a type of revenue that has the effect of reducing budget outlays. Ergo, the 1990 budget can show spending on deposit insurance as *declining* by $14 billion from the current year.

If accounting principles were the only issue, these shenanigans would be of little interest. After all, a dollar spent off budget does not hurt us any more than one spent on budget. But by going off budget the government puts itself in the position of having to pay interest rates at least 75 basis points higher than it would on straight Treasury debt, increasing the cost to taxpayers anywhere from $2 billion to $8 billion over the life of the bonds. In addition, the phony deficit reduction gives the Administration leeway to propose new spending initiatives without offsetting spending cuts in the 1990 budget.

The Common Defense

June 30, 1989

The disproportionate defense burden shouldered by the United States is quantified in a report of the Secretary of Defense released in April:

Table 1-23. Defense Spending and Manpower, 1987			
	Spending as % of GDP	Per-Capita Spending	Military Personnel as % of Population
	Spending ($ Bils.)			
U.S.	$288.1	6.5	$1,181	1.4
France	34.8	4.0	626	1.3
W. Germany	34.1	3.1	558	1.1
UK	31.6	4.7	555	0.9
Japan	24.4	1.0	200	0.2
Non-U.S. NATO	157.3	3.3	391	1.1

Source: U.S. Department of Defense.

According to the Pentagon, approximately 60 per cent of total U.S. defense outlays are directly related to NATO, which implies that we spend 10 per cent more defending Western Europe than the 14 other NATO countries combined. The share of our population engaged in defense-related activity (1.4 per cent) is also above the NATO average, and seven times as high as Japan's. Only Greece (2.3 per cent) and Turkey (1.8 per cent) devote a larger share of population to defense, arguably arrayed against each other as much as against the Warsaw Pact forces.

The burden-sharing problem is compounded by the considerable, albeit indirect, contributions to Soviet defense spending made by Western European and Japanese banks. Gross Soviet indebtedness to Western commercial banks reached $36.8 billion at the end of 1988, more than doubling in the past four years (it stood at $16.6 billion at the end of 1984). In a spate of highly publicized deal-making, the Soviet Union secured an additional $9 billion in credit lines from Western banks in October of last year. West German banks led the way with a $1.8-billion package, followed by banks in Italy ($775 million), Britain ($1.8 billion), and France ($2 billion). Japanese and Canadian banks accounted for another $3 billion; U.S. banks, which account for less than 0.5 per cent of total Western private-sector loans to the Soviet Union, did not participate in the latest deals.

The unusual publicity surrounding the October credit-market blitz has convinced some financial observers that it was intended to reassure the Soviet military establishment, a few weeks before the December troop-cut announcement, that an inflow of Western resources can partially offset the military cuts.

On paper it's hard to see why the Soviet Union needs to borrow at all. Countries with trade surpluses tend to be net international lenders, not borrowers, and the Soviet Union's hard-currency trade surplus with the non-socialist world reportedly rose from $1.5 billion in 1985 to $8.4 billion in 1987, before falling oil prices in 1988 pushed the surplus down to about $1 billion. It turns out, according to PlanEcon, a Washington-based economic consulting firm, that while Soviet statistics show a large trade surplus vis-a-vis Third World countries, the bulk of it is on paper only, reflecting the fact that Soviet "sales" of arms and capital goods to Libya, Nicaragua, and other client states are basically giveaways, consummated with long-term export credits rather than hard cash. Western banks have provided the bridge loans needed to finance these transactions.

Moscow has avoided overplaying its Western-credit card. There has been nothing resembling a debt crisis involving the Soviet Union: indeed, in 1986 Gorbachev went so far as to pay off on defaulted 1917 Czarist bonds still held by the Bank of England. The Soviets have kept their debt-service ratio down to a manageable 20 to 25 per cent of exports, for which they have been rewarded with extremely favorable interest rates by Western banks.

Raise Money, Not Taxes

April 7, 1989

Here, in no particular order, are a few ways the Federal Government can raise revenues without raising taxes:

1. *Crack Down on Loan Deadbeats.* As of September 30, 1987, the Federal Government was owed $339 billion, of which $32.1 billion was delinquent agricultural, housing, and assorted other loans. This represents a 24 per cent increase in current receivables and a 108 per cent increase in delinquencies since the end of fiscal 1982. As a "lender of last resort," the government is often obliged to make loans that would never have been approved by private financial institutions (indeed, the inability to secure private financing is often a prerequisite for federal-loan approval). Even so, the Grace Commission estimates that more aggressive debt collection by federal lending agencies could cut delinquencies by 25 per cent within three years, bringing in an additional $8 billion.

2. *Sell Amtrak.* Despite fare increases and a successful cost-cutting effort since 1981, passenger fares cover only two-thirds of Amtrak's costs; on some long-distance lines, the per-passenger subsidy exceeds the cost of a plane ticket. Selling the economically profitable portions of the rail system (primarily the Northeast-corridor routes) could reportedly fetch $1 billion, while phasing out the remainder of the system would relieve taxpayers of an ongoing subsidy ($597 million in 1987). A successful privatization would also increase federal tax revenues: in the six months ended June 30, 1988, Conrail (sold last year to a private railroad for $1.6 billion) paid $87 million in corporate taxes. A possible Amtrak buyer: its management and employees.

3. *Privatize the Postal Service.* Since 1970 the cost of a first-class stamp has outpaced the Consumer Price Index by 30 per cent, yet the Postal Service has needed more than $28 billion in federal subsidies to break even. Employee wages and fringes account for 85 cents of every dollar spent by the Postal Service, leaving little for capital improvements. Nevertheless, the Postal Service *could* become profitable if it were allowed to enter new lines of business (electronic mail, for example) and if private companies were allowed to offer

alternative first-class mail service, thereby forcing the federal service to operate under the discipline of competition rather than as a protected monopoly. Largely because of its extensive real-estate holdings, the net worth of this enterprise is about $13 billion, according to a Reason Foundation study. A public stock offering *à la* British Telecom or Nippon Telegraph would allow millions of Americans to own a part of what would then be one of America's largest corporations (annual sales of $30 billion).

We Are Rich Enough to Be Strong

March 10, 1989

In revoking the 2 per cent rise in national defense budget authority proposed in Reagan's last budget, the Bush budget ensures the largest real decline in defense spending since the early 1970s:

Table 1-24. National Defense Spending, 1985–91
Billions of 1982 Dollars

	Budget Authority	Outlays	Outlays as Percentage of GNP
1985	$264.6	$230.0	6.4
1988	241.2	252.9	6.1
1989E	237.1	250.0	5.8
1990E			
Reagan	241.1	244.6	5.5
Bush	236.2	242.4	5.5
1991E			
Reagan	244.6	245.6	5.4
Bush	237.1	241.1	5.3

Source: Office of Management and Budget.

Although budget authority has declined each year since 1985, national defense outlays managed to increase in real terms until this year, reflecting the momentum of the earlier defense build-up. Conversely, even if the Bush defense cuts are undone immediately, military outlays will continue to fall well into the 1990s because of long lead time between authorizations and outlays.

It's unfortunate that the public debate over defense spending is carried out in the context of the federal budget, where defense historically represents 25 per cent to 50 per cent of total expenditures, rather than in the context of the overall economy, where defense now accounts for less than 6 per cent of GNP. Last year Americans spent $3.2 trillion (66 per cent of GNP) on clothes, food, housing, and all other kinds of personal consumption. A 1 per cent reduction—roughly a decline from $13,000 to $12,870 in per capita consumption—would free up enough resources to finance a $32-billion rise in defense spending. This realignment of national priorities need not require higher taxes, but could be achieved by fairly modest reductions in federal transfer programs, which currently underwrite 15 per cent of all private consumption.

In fact, higher defense outlays may themselves generate sufficient economic growth to permit even higher levels of personal consumption than before. During the 1950s and 1960s defense spending accounted for 8 to 14 per cent of GNP, but was more affordable than it is now because the economy was stronger, industrial productivity grew at a steady 3 per cent per year, and the nation ran large trade surpluses in virtually every manufacturing sector relevant to the military. The big surge in defense and space research during this period, as well as the expansion in defense in the early 1980s, was accompanied by strong growth in non-federal, commercially oriented R&D. During the 1970s, when defense and space research was cut back, non-federal R&D also grew more slowly, and productivity growth slowed to 1 per cent annually.

No Apology Needed

February 10, 1989

In his farewell speech the President could have cited, but did not, a number of mitigating factors behind the Administration's deficit performance:

1. The sharp recession of 1980–82 was responsible for approximately $640 billion, or 38 per cent, of the total growth in national debt since 1980, according to the Office of Management and Budget.

2. The 1988 deficit—$155.1 billion—was equal to 3.2 per cent of GNP, the lowest ratio since 1981.

3. According to figures released in December by the Organization for Economic Cooperation and Development (OECD), the budget surpluses run by state and local governments will cut the United States' overall deficit/GNP ratio to 1.7 per cent, or considerably below the 2.9 per cent average for the European countries in 1988.

4. Federal spending this decade is expected to grow at the slowest rate since the 1920s:

Table 1-25. Percentage Increase in Real Federal Spending, by Decade	
1920s	−30.7
1930s	212.4
1940s	165.0
1950s	54.4
1960s	49.6
1970s	37.2
1980s (est.)	26.0
Source: Heritage Foundation.	

5. Federal outlays accounted for 22.3 per cent of GNP in 1988, slightly more than the 22.1 per cent share in 1980. By 1990 we will have experienced the first decline over a full decade since the 1920s (see Table 1-26).

6. Federal purchases of goods and services accounted for only 36 per cent of total spending, or 8 per cent of GNP last year. In 1980, 9 per cent of GNP was purchased by the Federal Government, and in the 1960s, more than 10 per cent.

Table 1-26. Federal Spending as a Percentage of GNP

1920	6.9
1930	4.2
1940	9.9
1950	16.2
1960	18.0
1970	19.8
1980	22.1
1990 (est.)	21.0

Source: Heritage Foundation.

7. The "deficit problem" is to a large degree a transfer-payment problem: in 1988, transfer payments, in the form of payments to individuals, grants to state and local governments, and interest on the federal debt (which may be thought of as a transfer from taxpayers to bond-holders), accounted for about two-thirds of all spending.

8. Although cumulative defense spending over the last eight fiscal years (1981 through 1988) was 36 per cent higher, in real terms, than over the preceding eight years, the share of GNP currently devoted to defense—6.1 per cent—is still smaller than at any time during the 1950s and 1960s.

9. Despite the tax cuts, federal revenues have averaged 18.9 per cent of GNP since 1981, up slightly from the 18.3 per cent share in the 1970s.

Is a Tax Increase Unavoidable?

September 16, 1988

Notwithstanding both candidates' studious disavowal of any future tax increase, higher taxes are widely regarded as increasingly probable.

Conventional Wisdom (hereafter CW) has it that the U.S. is so far in debt that a tax increase is required in order to avoid a collapse of investment.

Right Data disagrees: The deficit is manageable, given the size of the economy. It stands at 3.1 per cent of GNP this year, down from 6.3 per cent in 1983. State- and local-government surpluses bring the total deficit in the governmental sector down to $103 billion, only 2.3 per cent of GNP. Since 1983, real private fixed investment has increased at a 6.6 per cent average annual rate, exceeding the growth in every other major industrial country. But during the two years prior to the 1981 tax cut, private-sector investment fell, as many U.S. companies invested heavily abroad to avoid high taxes and inflation at home.

CW: A tax increase will lower the deficit and reduce interest rates.

RD: History demonstrates that a substantial part of any tax increase will be diverted to new spending rather than used to reduce the deficit. The $29-billion tax hike enacted following the October market crash was expected to lower the deficit by no more than $21 billion, with the remainder destined for spending.

Interest rates would fall if individuals saved more following a tax increase, but the Treasury Department finds that, at least for the first few years, people defray a tax increase by drawing down their savings. On balance, the recent tax hike increased government spending more than it reduced private spending, thus forcing a rise in interest rates.

CW: Tax cuts are responsible for the deficit.

RD: What tax cuts? From 1973 to 1980, federal revenues averaged 18.5 per cent of GNP. Since Ronald Reagan has been in office, revenues have averaged 18.9 per cent of GNP. Total revenues were $140 billion higher under Reagan than they would have been if pre-Reagan tax rates had prevailed.

CW: Government spending must go up in order to meet America's needs.

RD: Federal spending has increased 70 per cent since 1980, soaking up 22.8 per cent of GNP last year, versus 22.1 per cent in 1980. All the major safety-net programs grew in real terms between 1980 and 1987: Social Security up 2.9 per cent per annum; Medicare, 6.9 per cent; AFDC, 1.2 per cent; housing subsidies, 6.7 per cent. The major exception: unemployment compensation, off an average 4.7 per cent per year, reflecting the record increase in employment.

The $48,000 K Car

July 8, 1988

The 380 per cent Korean tariff on Chrysler K cars was widely publicized by Congressman Gephardt and others as the archetypal unfairness to American goods in foreign trade. It later turned out that this example was more metaphor than reality: K cars were never marketed in Korea; if they had been, they would have sold for "only" $29,000 (as opposed to about $10,000 in this country).

Despite the bad PR, no more than 15 per cent of the trade deficit can reasonably be attributed to tariffs and other unilateral restraints imposed by our trading partners. Instead, a major and seemingly intractable factor is the spending propensity of the American consumer vis-à-vis his foreign counterparts:

Table 1-27. Consumption and Savings as a Percentage of GNP				
	Private Consumption		**Gross Domestic Savings**	
	1965	**1985**	**1965**	**1985**
Singapore	79	45	10	42
Japan	58	58	33	32
Korea	84	59	7	31
Germany	56	57	29	24
Canada	60	57	25	23
U.S.	62	65	21	16
				Source: World Bank.

Since the mid-1960s, Korea has cut private consumption 30 per cent relative to GNP, increased its savings rate more than fourfold, and transformed a trade deficit, which ran as high as 12 per cent of GNP, into a robust surplus. The U.S., meanwhile, muddles along, consuming an ever larger fraction of national income, while saving proportionately less. A heavy reliance on income taxes is part of our problem (see Table 1-28). Income taxes are anti-saving in the sense that when a dollar is saved, the interest or investment income from

Table 1-28. Taxes on Income and Consumption as a Percentage of Government Revenue, 1985

	Income Taxes	Consumption Taxes	Ratio of Consumption Taxes to Income Taxes
Korea	25.3	57.4	2.3
Germany	17.0	21.6	1.3
Singapore	30.1	18.6	0.6
Canada	48.5	24.8	0.5
Japan	68.8	18.7	0.3
U.S.	50.0	6.1	0.1

Source: Organization for Economic Cooperation and Development (OECD).

that saving is taxed, while a dollar spent on consumption gives rise to no additional income-tax liability.

We ought at least to consider substituting a federal tax on consumption for part of the federal income tax. A 5 per cent Value Added Tax (VAT) levied on all U.S. personal consumption, for example, would raise about $150 billion. If medical care, food, and clothing were declared exempt from tax, the VAT would still raise $115 billion, or enough to permit a 30 per cent reduction in personal income taxes or total elimination of the corporate income tax.

Besides lowering the overall consumption rate, a VAT could directly aid the foreign-trade account by being applied to imports while being rebated on exports. Income taxes, on the other hand, are unalterably embedded in the price of domestically produced goods, whether exported or not.

Undertaxed or Overspent?

June 10, 1988

During the 192 years before Inauguration Day, 1981, the Federal Government accumulated $914 billion in debt. The national debt is now more than $2.6 trillion, and is still rising by over $125 billion each year. Many see this as prima facie evidence of the failure of Reaganomics, which had claimed, among other things, that we could cut tax rates without increasing the deficit.

Was it all pure voodoo? A historical perspective is helpful:

Table 1-29. Federal Taxes, Spending, and Deficits as a Percentage of GNP		
		Surplus or
	Revenues	Outlays	(Deficit)
1960	18.3%	18.2%	0.1%
1970	19.5	19.8	(0.3)
1980	19.4	22.1	(2.7)
1987	19.4	22.8	(3.4)

Source: Office of Management and Budget (OMB).

Increased outlays account for the entire rise in the deficit since 1980. Despite the sharp cut in tax rates (the top marginal rate went from 70 per cent in 1980 to 38.5 per cent in 1987), total revenues as a percentage of GNP remained exactly the same in both years. Tax receipts averaged 18.2 per cent of GNP during the 1960s (when the top income tax rate was as high as 90 per cent), 18.3 per cent during the 1970s, and 18.8 per cent since 1980.

To blame tax reductions for the rise in national debt is tantamount to blaming them for increased spending relative to GNP. We might want to assign full blame for this to Congress, but that also would be wrong. Relatively uncontrollable factors such as interest rates and the business cycle play a large role and, in fact, are responsible for 80 per cent of the 1987 deficit according to a Treasury study released last October. Less than 20 per cent (only $29.4 billion) of the deficit is due to imbalances in fiscal policy.

Of course, the economic impact of persistently large deficits may be the same no matter what their source. Nobel laureate James Buchanan argues that every dollar of debt incurred to finance consumption represents a net reduction in the nation's future wealth.

But not all federal spending is for consumption: outlays for dams, highways, hospitals, weapons procurement, and other physical assets came to over $102 billion in 1987, according to the Office of Management and Budget. An additional $24 billion of federal funds was transferred to states and localities to support their capital projects, and federal loans to the private sector accounted for another $30 billion. In toto these capital investments represented 15.5 per cent of all federal outlays last year.

The benefits from these investments will redound to future generations of Americans. Debt finance insures that future generations will also bear some of the costs.

Cut Defense Spending Gracefully

April 15, 1988

Cutting federal spending has become a code phrase for cutting the defense budget. The latest budget recommends that the Defense Department's spending authority for 1989 be cut by $33 billion below the level deemed prudent just one year ago. Meanwhile, spending on transfer payments is projected to be at least $140 billion more over the next five years.

The six-hundred-ship Navy is now on indefinite leave. More than a dozen weapons projects have ended. SDI spending is cut 25 per cent below last year's level. The army must make do with two thousand fewer helicopters, the armed forces with 36,000 fewer men, at a time when our conventional-force vulnerabilities are exacerbated by the INF treaty.

An additional $170 billion in defense cuts will have to be made by 1993 to keep us on course for the zero-real-growth target set by the new Defense Secretary, and the newly appointed National Economic Commission is rumored to have the Pentagon's budget in its sights for still further hits.

Instead of this sort of indiscriminate budget-slashing, Peter Grace has already shown how defense spending can be cut without impairing our ability to defend ourselves. His commission found, for example, that military pensions are six times greater than typical private-sector plans. Putting the military on an equivalent retirement basis could save us $28 billion over three years. There are four thousand military installations in the United States, but only 326 of them are considered essential to national defense by the Department of Defense. Closing the obsolete bases would save $2 billion annually.

On another front, more than $28 billion could be saved by giving a businessman's touch to the way weapons are procured— managerial changes like writing multi-year contracts and purchasing spare parts from a source other than the manufacturer of the original equipment. (These manufacturers tend to low-ball the original contract, figuring they can make up the difference on the spare parts.) Do these things and the $90 screw is history.

Defense Spending in Historical Perspective

March 4, 1988

In his bestseller *The Rise and Fall of the Great Powers*, Paul Kennedy finds economic overextension, specifically the tendency of mounting military expenditures to overwhelm the economy's productive capacity, to be behind the demise of every great power since the Habsburgs.

Will defense spending be our economic Trojan Horse?

In 1961, when President Eisenhower first warned us about the military-industrial complex, total national defense spending amounted to only $48 billion. By fiscal 1987 it had reached $282 billion, a 26 per cent rise after adjusting for inflation.

But economic burden is best measured not by dollars but by the share of the total economy devoted to government spending:

Table 1-30. Federal Spending as a Percentage of GNP				
	National Defense	Transfer Payments	Interest	All Categories
1960	9.5	4.8	1.4	18.2
1970	8.3	6.5	1.5	19.8
1980	5.0	10.4	2.0	22.1
1987	6.4	9.2	3.1	23.0

Source: Office of Management and Budget.

On the heels of the largest defense buildup in peacetime history, national defense appropriates roughly 33 per cent less of the total economy today than in 1960. Meanwhile, transfer payments are nearly twice, and interest on the national debt more than twice, as burdensome relative to the size of the economy now.

If Professor Kennedy's historical dialectic is valid, then surely the Soviet Union, which devotes approximately 17 per cent of its GNP to defense (up from 12 per cent in the early 1970s), is the more likely candidate for political oblivion.

If it should be us, however, our army of social engineers will be at least as much to blame as the military—if not more.

F. Trade Policy

MYTHTA

October 1993

Despite years of debate, the Mexican trade pact remains an unknown quantity to many. A self-serving mythology has been created—by opponents as well as by those favoring the agreement:

1. *Thousands of Jobs Will Vanish.* NAFTA will produce a modest gain in U.S. employment, according to most independent research. The study most often cited, by Gary Hufbauer at the Institute for International Economics in Washington, forecasts the creation of 325,000 new jobs. This dwarfs the 150,000 unskilled factory jobs he reckons will be lost to Mexico.

For perspective: the current round of defense cuts will displace ten times as many workers as NAFTA. Moreover, the pact contains safeguards—a 15-year phase-in period for tariff reductions on the most heavily protected American manufactures, for example—to minimize the chance of long-term unemployment.

2. *We Will Be Inundated with Cheap Mexican Goods.* The door is already open: U.S. tariff rates on Mexican imports average a mere 3 per cent. Mexican tariffs, although sharply lower than they were a few years ago, still hover in the 10 per cent range. Still, the liberalization of the past few years has produced a trade windfall for the U.S.:

Table 1-31. Warming Up for NAFTA

Billions of Dollars

	U.S. Exports to Mexico	U.S. Imports from Mexico	U.S. / Mexico Trade Balance
1988	$19.8	$22.6	$-2.8
1989	24.1	26.5	-2.4
1990	27.5	29.5	-2.0
1991	32.2	30.4	1.8
1992	39.6	33.9	5.7

Source: U.S. International Trade Commission.

F. Trade Policy

Since Mexican tariffs are still a multiple of our own, further liberalization will undoubtedly increase our trade surplus with Mexico.

3. *Our Wage Level Will Sink toward Mexico's.* Most economists who have analyzed NAFTA conclude that the average wage of U.S. workers will increase as a result of the agreement. The biggest gainers will be workers in export-related jobs, where wages are already well above the national average. Unskilled workers in protected industries will inevitably lose ground, although this might be offset somewhat by a reduction in illegal immigration if NAFTA improves Mexico's ability to create jobs.

U.S. workers may take heart from the experience of Japan. That country has been shifting its labor-intensive operations to Malaysia and other low-wage Pacific-rim countries for more than a decade, with no discernible impact on the pay of its unskilled workers.

4. *U.S. Investment Will Be "Sucked" South.* If anything, the reverse is true. For example, the Mexican government currently requires U.S. automakers to produce domestically rather than sell cars imported from the U.S. Under NAFTA this captive investment would return to the U.S., and U.S. auto exports to Mexico should increase.

People forget that the Mexican economy is one-twentieth the size of our own. Even if the entire flow of additional Mexican investment—about $15 billion per year—were financed solely from U.S. sources, it would amount to only 1 to 2 per cent of our annual savings. And nearly everyone agrees that, absent NAFTA, much of America's new Mexican investment would have gone to Hong Kong, Malaysia, and other low-wage countries.

5. *States Will Relinquish Their Sovereignty.* Opponents raise the specter of international tribunals preventing states from easing up on their environmental regulations or labor laws. While the side agreements do establish tri-national commissions, they make it nearly impossible for them to impose fines or sanctions. In any case, the U.S. is always free to reject the panel findings and refuse to pay. The offended country can, at that point, impose its own sanctions, but it can do that now.

In other words, even in the worst-case scenario, no country will be worse off under NAFTA than it is now.

The BeGATTs

April 27, 1992

After six years of negotiations, the U.S., Germany, and Japan seem close to a Uruguay Round trade agreement. Seven earlier rounds of talks under the General Agreement on Tariffs and Trade (GATT) have lowered average tariff rates from 40 per cent in 1947 to (roughly) 5 per cent today; world trade volume increased by a factor of 20 during that time.

Since 1960, U.S. foreign trade (exports plus imports of goods and services) has grown by 495 per cent, or more than three times as fast as total GDP. From 1988 to 1991, U.S. GDP rose $129.8 billion in constant dollars. Merchandise exports accounted for 70 per cent of that growth. Had exports not grown in 1991, the economy would have shrunk by 1.4 per cent, or twice the actual 0.7 per cent decline.

Table 1-32. The Globalization of the U.S. Economy
Billions of 1987 Dollars

	GDP	Exports	Imports	Foreign Trade as % of GDP
1960	$1,973.2	$88.4	$96.1	9.4
1980	3,776.3	320.5	289.9	16.2
1990	4.884.9	505.7	557.0	21.8
1991	4849.9	538.9	558.8	22.6

Source: U.S. Department of Commerce.

The Council of Economic Advisors estimates that a successful Uruguay Round would add $1.1 trillion (constant 1989 dollars) to U.S. GDP over the next ten years—an additional $1,600 per year for the average U.S. family of four. The world as a whole would gain more than $5 trillion in additional purchasing power.

Why, then, did the Uruguay Round talks flounder for so long? For one thing, protectionist policies today are far more sophisticated and less obvious than the import tariffs that occupied earlier GATT rounds. Domestic agricultural subsidies, for example, enable Europe's small, inefficient farmers to export a wide range of products to Third World nations. The subsidies offer protection equivalent to that of a 60 per cent import tariff.

Japan's protectionist policies include a discriminatory internal distribution system, regulations that limit the size of retail outlets, and fiscal policies that keep the cost of business capital low. These are not addressed by GATT, although they have been the subject of bilateral talks between the U.S. and Japan.

The U.S. cloaks its protectionism under the guise of unfair-practice laws, permitted under a GATT loophole. Since 1980 Washington has investigated more than 750 charges of dumping and unfair subsidization. These cases triggered major policy decisions, including "voluntary" steel import quotas, import restraints on Canadian lumber, and the U.S.–Japan semiconductor accord. Americans pay $75 billion more a year for goods because of these restraints, a sum equal to 13 per cent of total imports.

The most dangerous obstacles to the GATT trading system are the regional trading blocs coalescing in North America, Europe, and the Pacific rim. Regional free-trade agreements invariably discriminate against products produced outside the region. In 1960, for example, more than 60 per cent of the foreign trade of the 12 EC nations was conducted with nations outside the EC. Today 60 per cent of the EC's foreign trade stays within the EC. EC-92 and the possible inclusion of the former Communist bloc nations will undoubtedly accelerate the trend.

Fast Track, Sí!

June 24, 1991

American labor leaders insist that a Free Trade Agreement (FTA) with Mexico—which seems nearly inevitable now that President Bush has "fast track" negotiating authority—will increase corporate profits and reduce U.S. employment. They are only half right.

An FTA would be the latest in a series of trade moves that have increased employment on both sides of the Rio Grande. Since 1985 Mexico has lowered its tariffs from an average of 30 per cent to 10 per cent. As a result, U.S. exports to Mexico nearly tripled, rising from $11.9 billion in 1986 to $28.4 billion in 1990. (In 1988 Mexico replaced West Germany as our third largest trading partner, behind Canada and Japan.) Every $1 billion of exports creates an additional 22,800 jobs, so the expansion in trade with Mexico over the past few years created 376,000 jobs that would not exist otherwise.

Even at 10 per cent, Mexican tariffs are still considerably higher than the U.S. average of 4 per cent. Major areas of trade, including electronic equipment, steel, and textiles, are still subject to restrictive quotas. The mutual elimination of these barriers under an FTA would enable the U.S. to increase its non-oil trade surplus with Mexico, creating still more jobs in this country.

Perhaps the best way to gauge an FTA's likely impact is to look at areas where free trade between the two nations already exists. Under the border plant or *maquiladora* program, introduced in 1965, U.S.-made components are shipped duty free to U.S.-owned subsidiaries in Mexico, where they are assembled and re-exported, also duty free, back to the United States. Since 1986 the number of Mexicans employed in the plants has doubled to 460,000. The *maquiladoras* now provide about one-fifth of all manufacturing jobs in Mexico.

The big draw for U.S. companies is cheap labor: a $12-an-hour job in the U.S., burdened with Social Security taxes and health benefits, can be done for between $1.50 and $2 an hour in Mexico. Some low-skilled U.S. workers have undoubtedly been displaced by Mexican labor. But by allowing American businesses to cut costs, the southern migration has saved a hundred thousand jobs in directly export-related industries, and created perhaps twice as many jobs in industries such as warehousing, real estate, and transportation. While most of the jobs are in Arizona, California, New Mexico, and Texas, even in non-border states such as Michigan and Illinois workers manufacture components for assembly in Mexico.

Labor leaders assert that an FTA will induce U.S. firms to expand the scope of their Mexican operations beyond the benign *maquiladoras*. They forget that the current restrictions on U.S. investment in Mexico simply divert U.S. investment to more distant Third World countries, with far more deleterious effects for U.S. labor. A recent analysis by the International Trade Commission notes that when U.S. companies transfer operations to Mexico most of their work force remains in the U.S., particularly high-paying jobs in administration, sales, management, and component manufacturing. A move to Asia or Europe, on the other hand, results in a loss of high-paying production jobs as well as low-skilled assembly work.

An FTA would also ameliorate another labor bogeyman: illegal immigration. More than 1.05 million Mexicans cross the border every year in search of employment. Increased job opportunities such as would occur in the aftermath of an FTA may be the only way to stem the illegal influx of Mexicans.

G. International Comparisons

Are We Undertaxed?

August 30, 1993

"It leaves the tax burden in the United States far less onerous than those in most other Western nations. If the electorate is serious . . . about eliminating the deficit and cutting the national debt, it will eventually have to accept far more than this modest effort to increase revenues."

New York Times correspondent R. W. Apple is only half right. U.S. taxpayers will indeed face the lowest average tax rates in the industrialized world, even after the Clinton tax hike. But there is no discernible link between tax rates and deficit reduction.

Table 1-33. Tax and Consequences

	— Tax Revenues — 1982	1992 as % of GDP	Surplus/ Deficit, 1992	GDP per Capita, 1991	Employment Growth, 1982–92
U.S.	30.5%	30.7%	–4.7%	$22,204	15.9%
Japan	29.4	34.0	+1.8	19,107	14.4
UK	42.1	37.4	–6.7	15,720	4.4
Canada	38.8	43.3	–6.4	19,178	11.0
Italy	36.2	43.7	–9.5	16,896	4.3
Germany	45.7	46.6	–2.8	19,500	6.6
France	47.6	48.1	–3.9	18,227	3.2

Source: Organization for Economic Cooperation and Development; International Monetary Fund.

Tax revenue as a per cent of GDP rose significantly in most European countries during the past decade, despite—or perhaps because of—widespread cuts in the top personal income-tax rate and corporate tax rates. Yet deficits remained high. The additional revenues went mainly to support social insurance and national health programs, leaving deficits (as a per cent of GDP) generally larger than our own.

It is, of course, difficult to isolate the effect of tax policy on a nation's fiscal condition since other factors, including spending decisions, play a key role. But the futility of raising taxes to reduce budget imbalances seems universal: A study of 19 industrial countries by the Organization of Economic Cooperation and Development found that countries that raised revenue most were just as likely to have large budget deficits as countries with much smaller changes in revenue.

The "undertaxed" U.S. enjoys the highest living standard in the world, as measured by real GDP per capita. While our lead narrowed during the 1970s, no OECD country enjoyed a better combination of income, employment, and productivity growth during the 1982 to 1992 period. And notwithstanding our sub-par recovery, the U.S. economy will grow faster than that of Japan, Germany, and France this year.

We rank a distant last in one vital area, however. Over the past two decades Americans saved an average of 6.8 per cent of disposable income. Japan had a personal savings rate for this period of 17.3 per cent; West Germany's was 12.7 per cent; Canada's was 12.5 per cent.

Our tax system may be to blame. Although our overall tax rate is lower than that of other industrialized countries, the U.S. relies more heavily on income taxes and offers fewer and less generous saving incentives. For example, our capital-gains-tax rate on long-term gains—28 per cent—exceeds that of all other OECD countries except Australia and the UK, and even they index asset prices to inflation. Germany gives shareholders a credit against personal income taxes to offset taxes paid at the corporate level, and imposes no taxes whatever on capital gains. Britain, France, Italy, Canada, and Japan give corporations and individuals a partial credit or deduction for dividends. Only in the U.S. is corporate income taxed twice, when earned by corporations and when distributed to shareholders.

93

If It Ain't Broke . . .

December 28, 1992

The election was about "change," especially change designed to create jobs and improve living standards. But change can be counter-productive, if the wrong kinds of change are visited on an economy that already out-performs the rest of the developed world.

Our economic lead is now documented in a comprehensive new study of worker productivity by McKinsey and Co. In 1990 a full-time American worker produced $49,600 worth of goods and services. In terms of equivalent purchasing power, French workers produced $47,000, German workers, $44,200, and Japanese workers just $38,200.

The findings were a surprise, "and not only because they contradict the widely held view that the U.S. has fallen behind." Most economists had expected that by now—nearly fifty years after the end of World War II, with technology and capital flowing freely among nations, and with foreign workers at least as well educated and skilled as our own—full economic convergence would have occurred.

In fact, the productivity gap is much narrower in manufacturing, where many elite Japanese and German firms dominate international markets. But 63 per cent of U.S. workers, and nearly 60 per cent of Japanese and German workers, are employed in the service sector, where our productivity lead is enormous.

The U.S. telecommunications industry, for example, handles 2.5 times more calls per employee than Japan's, and nearly 4 times more than Germany's. In retailing—the largest service-sector employer in the advanced economies—the typical U.S. worker generates $25,003 in value added, compared to $20,595 and $11,039 for his counterparts in the UK and Japan, respectively. As a result, workers in many U.S. service industries are paid better than manufacturing workers.

Traditional explanations such as capital per worker, firm size, managerial skills, and relative prices cannot explain the international productivity gap. The most powerful explanation, according to the study, is the high degree of competition found in the U.S. economy, and Washington's relative reluctance to regulate business.

Japanese law prevents large domestic or foreign firms from opening stores unless small shop owners approve the new competition. The policy, justified as a means of preserving social harmony, has deprived that country's consumers of the one-stop shopping efficiencies enjoyed here. And while the deregulated U.S. airline and telecommunications industries have undergone painful restructurings, state-owned operations in Europe are explicitly not allowed to reduce costs by laying off workers.

Does higher productivity mean fewer jobs? The record speaks for itself:

Table 1-34. The American Job Machine

	Civilian Jobs Created, 1973–90		Unemployment Rate, 1990	% Unemployed for More Than 6 months, 1989
	Number	*Increase*		
U.S.	32.9 mil.	37%	5.4%	10
Japan	9.9	19	2.1	37
Germany	1.5	6	5.1	67
UK	2.3	9	6.9	57
France	0.9	4	9.0	64

Source: McKinsey & Co.

Our more productive labor force has created more new jobs than Japan, Germany, France, and the UK combined. Rapid job creation enabled the U.S. to move from having the lowest percentage of working-age population employed among the advanced economies in 1973 to having the highest percentage (71) in 1989.

The moral of the story? The best jobs program is no jobs program.

The Lazy American?

February 17, 1992

Yoshio Sakurauchi said that the problem with the U.S. economy is that "U.S. workers are too lazy. They want high pay without working." Although many Americans undoubtedly agree with this statement, a recent survey by the Department of Labor found that U.S. workers were significantly more productive than their foreign counterparts:

| Table 1-35. Annual Output per Worker |||||
| *1990 U.S. Dollars* |||||
	U.S.	**Japan**	**Germany**	**UK**	**Korea**
1960	$31,842	$7,676	$15,748	$17,414	NA
1970	38,526	18,242	23,841	22,573	$6,737
1980	40,600	26,038	30,684	27,179	10,773
1990	45,165	34,711	35,736	32,161	19,550

Source: U.S. Department of Labor.

The Japanese produced an average of $34,711 worth of goods and services per worker in 1990, 23 per cent less than the $45,165 produced by American workers, and 3 per cent less than Germany's $35,736 figure. (In converting local currencies to U.S. dollars the Labor Department used the actual purchasing power of each currency rather than official exchange rates.)

Japan has steadily narrowed the productivity gap, however. Between 1960 and 1990 output per worker grew by 41.8 per cent in the U.S.; Japanese output grew by 352 per cent. This does not mean that American workers are growing increasingly "lazy." Worker productivity rises or falls with the amount and quality of tools workers have to do their jobs. Japanese firms, facing much lower tax rates on new investment than U.S. firms, increased their capital per worker at an 8 per cent annual rate during most of this period. In the U.S. the increase was less than 2 per cent per year.

If "laziness" is measured by the number of hours spent on the job rather than the amount produced, then indeed Mr. Sakurauchi has a point. Japanese office workers are notorious workaholics, putting in 500 more hours per year than their German counterparts, and 225 more hours than their American ones.

Indeed, the Japanese are working themselves to death. The *Japan Times* reported that in 1989 more than 1,300 claims were filed against companies in which widows asserted that their spouses were victims of *karoshi,* or death from overwork. Some *karoshi* victims worked fifty days straight and logged more than one hundred hours of overtime each month. One man commuted daily between Tokyo and Osaka (a distance of 220 miles) and was putting in 135 hours of overtime monthly. Although the Japanese government has reluctantly acknowledged the *karoshi* problem, it is unlikely to be able to reverse it. A rapidly aging population, a shortage of skilled workers, and the corporate obsession with productivity have pushed overtime statistics to all-time highs.

Not all "work," however, takes place in the workplace. Painting the house, making beds, cleaning the carpet—all are examples of the productive household activity that never gets counted in GNP. A survey by University of Michigan economist F. Thomas Juster found that American men spend an average of 14 hours per week doing household chores, compared to just 3.5 hours for Japanese men. When you add this time to the time spent at the office, American men work an average of 57.8 hours per week, versus 55.5 hours for Japanese men.

American children, on the other hand, do qualify as world-class lazy. Juster found that Japanese schoolchildren spend 42 hours a week in class, compared with the Americans' 26 hours. More important, Japanese students put in an additional 19 hours each week studying outside the classroom, versus just 4 hours for the Americans.

An Economic Pearl Harbor?

December 30, 1991

The December 7 anniversary, coming amidst signs of economic weakness in the U.S., has renewed fears of Japan's "unstoppable economic expansion" at the expense of an America that, in the words of a recent *New York Times* op-ed piece, "cannot cope with Japanese power or fathom Japanese intentions." The author, Karel van Wolferen, warns that "believers in the wonders of 'natural' free-market forces must understand the 'unnaturalness' of the arrangements in the Japanese political economy . . ."

Mr. van Wolferen is not alone. Many erstwhile free-traders believe that efforts to lower Japan's formal import barriers are pointless: Japan's governmental-industrial complex will prevent even the most efficient foreign firm from penetrating the domestic market. The only agreements that will work under such conditions are those that manage trade—granting American manufacturers a specific share of the Japanese market, while limiting Japanese exports to this country.

But the facts don't support this view. While Japanese cars, VCRs, and camcorders are ubiquitous, in fact Japanese bought more U.S. products last year—$395 per person—than Americans bought Japanese products—$359 per person. In 1990 Japan imported $49 billion of U.S. goods—second only to Canada's $84 billion, and far ahead of our next largest market, Mexico, at $28 billion. More important, Japan devotes a larger share of its GNP to the purchase of imports from the U.S. (1.7 per cent) than we devote of our GNP to the purchase of imports from Japan (1.6 per cent).

Since peaking in 1987, Japan's trade surplus with the U.S. has fallen by $15.3 billion, or 27 per cent. U.S. exports to Japan grew 33.4 per cent in 1988, 18.2 per cent in 1989, and another 9.2 per cent in 1990—faster than the growth of exports to the rest of the world. Nor is it a case of Japanese buying our raw materials and selling us the finished products. Nearly two-thirds of U.S. exports to Japan are manufactured goods—chemicals, aluminum, aircraft, scientific instruments, computers, and many other products. About half of these—30 per cent of all U.S. exports to Japan—are considered "high tech" by the Commerce Department.

G. International Comparisons

By many criteria the economic interdependence has benefited the U.S. more than Japan. Some 350,000 Americans currently work for Japanese-owned companies. Some of them—Firestone and Columbia Pictures come to mind—were in serious financial trouble before the Japanese invested in them. Japanese auto companies now produce more than 1.7 million cars and trucks in the U.S. each year, many of which are exported to Japan. And the Japanese technology and management skills acquired via joint ventures with Japanese steel companies virtually rescued the U.S. industry in the early 1980s, when one-fifth of America's steel-producing capacity was in Chapter 11. Although smaller than it once was, the American steel industry is again internationally competitive.

Attempts to keep Japanese products out of the U.S. have hurt us more than they've helped. Since 1984, for example, steel-import restrictions have saved an estimated 17,000 jobs in the steel industry. But industries that use steel, such as producers of farm and construction equipment, have lost 54,200 jobs as a result of the higher cost of steel, according to a study by the St. Louis-based Center for the Study of American Business. More recently, a 63 per cent tariff on Japanese computer screens forced the American-based computer manufacturers that use the component either to cease production or, in one case, to move operations to Japan.

If standard of living is the criterion by which an economic régime is judged, furthermore, Japan Inc. has not done well at all. Although Japan's per-capita GNP is slightly above our own, prices of most goods are far higher in Japan. In terms of real purchasing power, the Japanese consumer is only 60 per cent as well off as his American counterpart.

Another Road to Serfdom?

January 1991

To give or not to give? Since February the IMF and World Bank have committed nearly $10 billion to the nations of Eastern and Central Europe. A $25-billion Eastern European Development Bank, modeled after the World Bank, is being capitalized by Western European Governments. Senator Bill Bradley (D., N.J.) wants Congress to set aside an amount equal to 1 per cent of the defense budget for Eastern Bloc reconstruction, and financial guru Henry Kaufman thinks a new Marshall Plan is needed because " . . . meeting Eastern Europe's financing needs is a political priority and not a matter that can be left to a standard market determination of risk and reward."

But suddenly the World Bank is having second thoughts. In its year-end report on the Soviet economy, Bank economists suggest that large-scale foreign aid is best postponed until economic reforms, including a free-market price system, the clarification of private property rights, and the privatization of the larger state enterprises, are in place. This caught many by surprise: for decades the Bank has zealously financed state-run enterprises in Eastern Europe identical to those it now finds counterproductive in the USSR.

Yugoslavia, for example, has been the institution's favorite Eastern European client, receiving more than $5 billion since 1945. On paper these loans were to foster "structural adjustment," the funds targeted to the most efficient and profitable sectors of the economy. However, the "commercial" banks entrusted with allocating World Bank funds were founded and often were managed by workers of state-run enterprises whose sole agenda, quite naturally, was the perpetuation of the parent. Incessant lending to insolvent state-run businesses necessitated a bailout by the Yugoslav Central Bank, which produced, in turn, a 2,800 per cent inflation rate in 1989. Bank losses in Yugoslavia, Hungary, and Poland now average 30 per cent of gross domestic product, according to World Bank reports.

Although Bank officials are fully aware that rigged banking systems frustrate true private enterprise in Eastern and Central Europe, they routinely approve additional loans to prop up failed banks: In April 1990 a $400-million loan went to Yugoslavia to "strengthen the country's financial sector." By insulating banks from financial risks the Bank has created conditions similar to those that produced the S&L debacle in the U.S.

More than $2 billion in World Bank agricultural loans enabled Rumanian dictator Nicolae Ceausescu to set up centralized state "villages" to which peasants were forcibly relocated throughout the 1970s and 1980s. While Rumania's economy was being destroyed by Ceausescu, World Bank bureaucrats were dutifully parroting the official version of things. In a recent *Forbes* interview Sir Alan Walters, former chief economic advisor to Margaret Thatcher, quotes from a 1979 World Bank country study, "Rumania—The Industrialization of an Agrarian Economy under Socialist Planning": "Between 1950 and 1975 the economy grew rapidly within the framework of comprehensive economic planning made possible by the state's control of the major productive resources and its monopoly over foreign trade. . . . According to official statistics, Social Product and National Income grew at 9.8 percent per annum for 25 years."

As Walters notes, this analysis is not worth the paper it's printed on. In 1975 Rumania's per capita income was between $700 and $800. If the country had grown at 10 per cent per year over the previous 25 years as claimed, Rumanians would have died from starvation in 1950.

Feeding Russia

January 1991

A 25 per cent drop in agricultural output, Gorbachev's persistent entreaties, and the approach of winter have convinced even the most skeptical that the Soviet Union needs our food to avoid starvation. The U.S. Department of Agriculture is not so sure, however.

Despite its problems, the Soviet Union remains the world's largest producer of wheat, and one of the largest producers of grain, potatoes, and sugar beets, according to a recent USDA report. Indeed, the food crisis has developed despite a massive increase in U.S. food exports to the USSR during the Gorbachev era:

Table 1-36. Supplying Food to the Soviets
$ Millions

| | U.S. Exports to USSR | | | USSR |
	Total	Agri-cultural	% Agri-cultural	Crop Output (Mil. Tons)
1986	$1,257	$ 658	52%	210.1
1987	1,492	938	63	211.4
1988	2,849	2,246	79	195.0
1989	4,412	3,597	82	211.0
1990	3,092	2,262	73	233.8

Source: U.S. Department of Agriculture; Planecon.

Supply is not the problem. The 1990 harvest, for example, was the second largest ever. But instead of alleviating the shortage, the bumper crop created a monumental transportation crisis that actually worsened the food shortage in Moscow and other major cities. Limited storage capacity means that crops are often left to rot in the fields: only 14 million metric tons (mmt) of the 36 mmt of grain threshed in the Russian Republic by August 1990 was delivered to state storehouses. Even imported food purchased with Western credits has remained unloaded or in storage in the West for lack of adequate domestic storage facilities.

The demand side of the equation is at least as much to blame for the chronic food crisis. Between 1985 and 1990 average wages increased 42 per cent, or six times faster than the productivity of the average Soviet worker. In the West this imbalance would create inflation, eventually bringing supply and demand into balance. But for political reasons the Soviet Union tried keeping prices fixed, especially for foodstuffs, thus keeping demand greater than supply.

As the ruble becomes increasingly worthless, goods—including food—have become the main store of wealth. As a result, farmers increasingly barter their crops for scarce fuel, equipment, and fertilizer, rather than sell them to the government distribution apparatus for rubles. And consumers hoard whatever they can get their hands on. According to one Soviet economist, more than 80 per cent of the Soviet population has accumulated food stocks two to four times larger than their needs.

Gorbachev has gamely tried to reform the system. Back in 1987 he announced a plan to let farmers sell food produced in excess of state quotas at free market prices. In 1989 individual entrepreneurs were allowed to farm state-owned land under long-term lease agreements. Another decree that year authorized the government to purchase certain crops with "convertible rubles," or currency that could be used to purchase foreign farm equipment or foreign consumer goods.

None of these initiatives got off the ground. There are, you see, three million people in the Soviet Union who earn a living administering agricultural prices, quotas, and contracts. (By comparison, there are two million *farmers* in the United States.) Fearing for their jobs, the bureaucrats have in many cases withheld information essential for implementing the proposed reforms.

On the other hand, many Soviet farmers are reluctant to give up the guaranteed income of a collective farm for the risks associated with private plots. According to one USDA official, farm workers feel they've been manipulated by the government so many times in the past that they distrust the system. Whether the official demise of communism has changed all this remains to be seen.

The More the Merrier

December 17, 1990

A population time bomb hangs over the world, threatening humanity with overcrowding, starvation, and conflict. So argued the World Bank and most other international development agencies—until recently. But the stellar economic success of many "overcrowded" countries has led some economists to revise their thinking on the role of population:

Table 1-37. Population Matters

	Population per Square Mile	GNP per Capita	
		Dollars, 1988	Average Annual Percentage Growth, 1965–88
Singapore	11,910	9,070	7.2
Hong Kong	9,744	9,220	6.3
South Korea	1,189	3,600	6.8
Japan	844	21,020	4.3
India	658	340	1.8
China	288	330	5.4
Argentina	30	2,520	0.0

Source: World Almanac; World Bank.

The population of capitalist Hong Kong grew from 700,000 in 1945 to 5.6 million in 1987, yet earnings rose at unprecedented rates. Singapore also flourished, and is now forced to import labor to alleviate a labor shortage. Of course these are small city-states, but does anyone think that a large hinterland attached to them would be as poor as Mainland China?

At the other extreme, sparsely populated, statist Argentina has stagnated for at least 25 years.

In the short run Malthus is right: another baby or another immigrant invariably lowers living standards for those around him. Over periods measured in decades, however, economists (including Nobel laureate Simon Kuznets, perhaps the greatest economic historian of modern times) have found no evidence that population growth decreases economic growth. Since World War II, per-person income in less-developed countries has grown faster than that of developed countries despite far faster population growth in the developing world.

How does population growth spur economic growth? In *Population Matters* (1990), Julian Simon notes that American fathers work the equivalent of two to five weeks a year extra for each additional child, more than offsetting the mother's withdrawal from the workforce. Population growth increases the demand for investment and reduces the risk of overbuilding in housing and other highly cyclical industries. Other things being equal, countries with large populations enjoy higher and more rapidly growing output per worker.

Largely unnoticed amidst the current economic gloom, the U.S. seems to be pulling out of a long demographic slump. The nation's fertility rate climbed to an estimated 2.1 lifetime births per woman in the first half of 1990, the highest figure since 1971. Based on the earlier rates, the Census Bureau had forecast a declining U.S. population by the year 2038.

Further, the new immigration law provides for a 30 per cent annual increase in slots, from 540,000 to 700,000, with the number of those admitted because of specific skills increasing proportionately more. But we are in no danger of becoming a nation of immigrants: there were 800,000 immigrants in 1980, and at the turn of the century immigration topped one million for six consecutive years. Only 6 per cent of the U.S. population today is foreign born— less than in Britain, France, and Germany; far less than in Canada and Australia.

Still Number One

July 23, 1990

The fear that the U.S. is slipping and may already have lost its economic lead has energized the movement for an interventionist industrial policy. In fact, the latest data show we are comfortably ahead of other nations in terms of worker productivity.

Table 1-38. GNP per Employed Person
1989 Dollars

| | U.S. | As Percentage of the U.S. | | | |
		Japan	Germany	UK	Canada
1950	$24,972	15.2	34.5	53.8	76.0
1973	39,198	50.8	64.9	61.8	85.4
1980	39,011	62.7	77.5	66.5	91.5
1989	43,673	72.7	82.0	71.5	94.0
	Average Annual Percentage Change				
1950–73	2.0	5.3	2.8	0.6	1.3
1973–80	(0.1)	3.1	2.6	1.1	1.0
1980–89	1.3	1.7	0.6	0.8	0.3

Source: U.S. Department of Commerce.

The typical Japanese worker produced 72.7 per cent as much as his American counterpart in 1989, up from only 15.2 per cent in 1950. Economists who study these trends claim that it is only natural for once-poor countries to draw closer to the leader. They can leap forward by replacing obsolete equipment with state-of-the-art technology produced elsewhere, whereas the leader must often wait for new technology to evolve before making new advances. However, once a degree of affluence is reached the situation changes. The nearly universal decline in the rate at which these countries are converging on the U.S. is evidence of this.

Economic convergence is beneficial for both the leader and the laggards. (Would we be better off if we were the only developed country?) The slowdown in our productivity growth is troubling, but even here there may be less to worry about than meets the eye. In

G. International Comparisons

Productivity and American Leadership (MIT Press, 1989), Princeton economist William Baumol assembles data showing that our manufacturing productivity rebounded spectacularly in the 1980s, "bringing rates of growth higher than any previously experienced in postwar American history." He finds no sign of "deindustrialization": the U.S. share of world industrial output grew from 36 per cent in 1973 to 39 per cent in 1986. During the past quarter-century both the U.S. and Japan increased their share of world industrial employment, while Britain, West Germany, and France saw their share shrink.

Paradoxically, the very success of U.S. manufacturers may have contributed to the overall productivity slowdown. As industry learns to produce more with fewer workers, more of the labor force is absorbed into service jobs. Unlike manufacturing, productivity gains in service jobs are difficult to achieve. As Baumol points out, it takes as much labor to play a Scarlatti sonata on the harpsichord today as it did in the eighteenth century.

Service employment has therefore grown rapidly, while industrial workers account for an ever-smaller share of the U.S. labor force. But this has not occurred because other countries are taking away our high-wage manufacturing jobs and leaving us with McDonald's. Each of the 19 countries Baumol analyzed has experienced the same shift. If anything, labor is moving into services less rapidly in the U.S. than in our trading partners. While the U.S. service/industry ratio grew 10 per cent between 1965 and 1980, West Germany's grew 19 per cent and Japan's, 31 per cent.

Perestroika Stumbles

July 9, 1990

The Soviet economy is in an "unstable state" where inflation and shortages have "made daily life miserable for all but the most privileged segments of society," according to a recent CIA study. Prospects for even a modest recovery appear remote, and a number of events—strikes in fuel and transportation sectors, ethnic unrest in economically vital regions such as the Ukraine, consumer panic that brings hyperinflation and greater reliance on barter trade—could reduce output by as much as 20 per cent over a year or two.

In this chaos the traditional measure of overall economic performance—GNP—is less informative than in the past:

Table 1-39. The Rise and Fall of the Soviet Economy
Average Annual Percentage Change

	GNP	Component of GNP		
		Agriculture	Industry	Transportation
1970–80	2.4	–1.1	4.0	5.1
1980–85	1.6	1.1	2.0	2.2
1985–88	2.5	2.0	2.8	2.2
1989	1.4	3.4	0.0	–0.1

Source: Central Intelligence Agency.

Total output grew 1.4 per cent last year. That hardly seems catastrophic, although it's considerably below the 2.5 per cent rate of Gorbachev's first few years. But the other figures show where the problems are. Most of last year's rise occurred in agriculture, attributable to good weather. Industrial production was stagnant as declines in defense production canceled increases in consumer goods. And chaotic transportation conditions (reflected in that sector's decline) meant that consumer goods and agricultural output increasingly ended up in freight cars or warehouses instead of store shelves. A survey of state stores found that only two hundred of the 1,200 standard consumer goods were available last August; by year end that figure had plunged to fifty.

None of the consumer-oriented policies appears to be working well. Gorbachev's plan to convert defense factories to consumer-goods production has foundered because of shortages in the necessary retooling equipment. Imports rose a hefty 23 per cent last year, but oil exports dwindled and the USSR's hard-currency trade balance slipped from surplus to deficit. Debt incurred to finance imports has doubled since 1985, impelling Western bankers to tighten credit and charge higher interest rates. The recent trade agreement is unlikely to change things in the short-run, both because of the USSR's limited export potential under current conditions and because similar agreements with Japan and the European Community already grant USSR products Most Favored Nation (MFN) treatment. This accord is of little importance to the success or failure of *perestroika*, for oil, gas, and gold—items not affected by MFN treatment—comprise four-fifths of current Soviet exports.

Even reforms aimed at economic decentralization have proven counterproductive so far. Since 1987 many state enterprises have been allowed to set output so as to maximize profits. But without market prices for a guide, profitable items are not necessarily what consumers want or need. To make matters worse, newly autonomous enterprises used their growing "profits" to increase wages, thereby exacerbating the imbalance between consumer demand and supply.

A prominent casualty of the economic turmoil has been Gorbachev's anti-alcoholism campaign. Apparently vodka is one consumer good the USSR *can* still produce in quantity. Presently its value as a work incentive is regarded as outweighing the risks of increased alcoholism.

The Other Path

April 30, 1990

A social-security system lurching from crisis to crisis as unprecedented inflation pushes benefits up while high unemployment holds payroll taxes down: sound familiar? Both the U.S. and Chile confronted these problems in the early 1980s. The U.S. responded by increasing the role of the government, while Chile became the first nation in the world to dismantle a social-security system through sweeping privatization.

In the U.S. the Greenspan Commission proposed, and Congress approved, still further increases in payroll taxes. Tax rates went from 6.65 per cent in 1983 to 7.65 per cent in 1990, while the maximum annual payment escalated from $2,393 to $3,924. The 1983 "reforms" also subjected up to half of the benefits received by certain high-income retirees to income taxation, and increased the age of eligibility for full benefits from the current 65 to 66 by 2009 and 67 by 2027. As a result, the Social Security Trust Fund is expected to accumulate a surplus of nearly $3 trillion (1989 dollars) by the year 2020. In some scenarios this surplus growth could retire the whole national debt, with enough left over to invest in vast stretches of the private sector—*de facto* socialization of much of the economy.

Chile's social-security reforms, on the other hand, were really reforms. In 1981 workers there were allowed to leave the government-run system and make monthly tax-deductible contributions, equal to 19.5 per cent of their wages, to any of 12 private investment companies specifically created to manage individual retirement accounts. Those who made the switch were fully compensated for the contributions they made to the old system. Participation in the private system is mandatory for workers entering the work force since 1981.

Under the old system, which dated from 1924, payroll taxes had risen to 26 per cent of wages, with employers paying more than half. At these rates many employers simply stopped hiring. Tax evasion was widespread, as workers colluded with their employers not to report all of their wages. To make matters worse, government bureaucrats proved inept at managing the few surplus funds the system managed to accumulate. By 1980 the payroll-tax shortfall had grown so large that 28 per cent of the system's benefits had to be covered by general revenues.

Chile's new system resembles our IRAs in that private companies are allowed to compete for worker contributions, and workers are allowed to switch companies with little advance notice. Companies are required to invest pension contributions in a diversified portfolio of stocks, mortgages, bank CDs, and corporate bonds, as well as government bonds. So far, the real rate of return on these investments has greatly exceeded the 4 per cent rate deemed necessary to meet the goal of providing retirement benefits equal to 70 per cent of final salary. The old Chilean system, despite the high tax rate, paid only half of final salary on average.

By all accounts the Chilean reforms have been a smashing success. More than 90 per cent of workers opted for private plans when they were first offered, and within just four years funds invested in these accounts had grown to about 10 per cent of GNP. In recent years these funds have accounted for almost 50 per cent of the growth of the country's private savings. By expanding the pool of investment funds, social-security reform also increased the government's ability to sell off other heavily subsidized enterprises to the private sector.

The largest advantage of social-security privatization may not be quantifiable, however. The average worker has much more of a vested interest in the success of the private sector, and is therefore more willing to support policies that enhance economic growth rather than those that simply redistribute income.

Japan's Saving Graces

March 19, 1990

Numerous studies have tried to explain why Japanese households routinely save 15 to 18 per cent of their after-tax income while Americans save only 3 to 5 per cent. Tax incentives are prominently mentioned.

Under the *maruyu* ("tax free") system, which was in effect for most of the postwar period, interest income from savings accounts was completely tax-exempt and available to savers without limitation. Largely for this reason, the average Japanese household had $66,000 in savings in 1988, about ten times the American average. (By comparison, the Bush Administration's Family Savings Plan would limit the tax exemption to interest on $2,500 of savings each year, and require a seven-year waiting period for withdrawal.) Although a 1988 tax reform limited the *maruyu* system to individuals 65 or older, the handicapped, and families headed by women, widespread tax evasion reportedly keeps as much as 70 per cent of all Japanese personal savings tax-free.

Capital gains, for years not taxed at all, have been subject to a 20 per cent tax since April 1989. However, investors have the option of waiving the capital-gains tax in favor of paying a 1 per cent tax on the entire transaction. Dividends need not be declared on income-tax returns provided they do not exceed Y500,000 (about $3,500) from a single corporation.

Neither mortgage nor credit-card interest is deductible. Japanese banks normally require mortgage down-payments of 25 to 33 per cent of the purchase price, compared to the 10 to 20 per cent typically required by banks in the United States. Nearly half of Japan's personal savings rate is attributable to home down-payments, according to a McKinsey & Co. analysis.

The impact of Japan's system of lifetime employment is less clear. Other things being equal, one would expect that workers guaranteed a job and predictable salary increases over their entire careers would save less, since the rainy-day motive is largely absent. But the mandatory retirement age for most "lifetime" jobs is 55. Private pensions are usually paid out either as a lump sum or as an annuity lasting for a fixed period, usually about ten years. The resulting uncertainty provides a powerful incentive to save during the working years, as well as to take a second job after "retirement."

Are cultural differences responsible for the savings gap between the U.S. and Japan? This argument conveniently overlooks the fact that high savings rates are relatively new to Japan. During the fifty years prior to World War II, Japan's gross savings rate averaged 11.7 per cent of its GNP, while the comparable figure for the United States was about 19 per cent. Japan's postwar savings boom was motivated by a desire to rebuild the capital stock damaged by the war, and although the savings rate continued rising long after the damage was repaired, it appears to have peaked. Since hitting 23 per cent in 1974, the personal savings rate has drifted downward, reaching 15 per cent in 1988.

The Economic Wall

December 22, 1989

International economic comparisons are always tricky, especially when planned economies are compared with capitalist ones. Take these figures, from the CIA's *Handbook of Economic Statistics, 1989*:

Table 1-40. Two Systems Compared	West Germany	East Germany
GNP, 1988 (billions U.S.)	$870.0	$207.2
GNP per capita	$14,260	$12,480
Population (millions)	61.0	16.6
Population change, 1960–87 (millions)	+5.6	–0.5
Autos per 1,000 persons	446	209
Auto production, 1987	4,430,000	217,000
Life expectancy (years)	76	73
International Trade Data (1988, billions U.S.)		
Exports	$323.4	$30.7
Imports	250.6	31.0
Trade balance	72.8	(0.3)

Source: Central Intelligence Agency, *Handbook of Economic Statistics, 1989.*

The per-capita GNP figure, for example, shows only a 14.3 per cent advantage for West Germany. The actual gap in living standards is many times larger, since East German central planners channel the bulk of GNP into heavy industry, chemicals, and other exports, while giving short shrift to consumer products.

The East German economy is now believed to be in far worse shape than portrayed above. The recently departed finance minister, for example, disclosed a hitherto unacknowledged budget deficit of about $70 billion—roughly one-third of GNP. Industrial productivity, always a problem, has reportedly sunk by almost 50 per cent over the past nine years. Despite frequent attempts to "rationalize" production, East German factories still use two and a half times as much coal and twice as much steel per unit of output as their West German counterparts.

114

Inflation, theoretically impossible in a centrally planned economy, is now acknowledged to be well into double digits, although the exact figure is unknown. Debt owed to Western creditors totals $20 billion, putting East Germany in about the same position as Poland and Hungary on a per-capita basis.

Still, East Germany is far and away the economic class act of Eastern Europe. Its per-capita income in 1988 was estimated by the CIA to be 2.3 times that of Rumania, 1.7 times that of Poland, and 1.4 times that of Hungary. East German exports exceed those of Poland, a country nearly three times as populous. It is the only Eastern Bloc nation to export significant amounts to the West.

That this (relative) success occurred without any real attempt at *perestroika* is a tribute to the efficiency of the East German worker. Indeed, despite losing perhaps 100,000 skilled workers over the past few months, the East German labor force remains a big potential draw for Western businesses seeking investment opportunities. There are, according to the CIA, 8.9 million workers in the population. By comparison, West Germany's labor force is put at 28.1 million, or 46 per cent of the population.

Unify East and West Germany and you would have a nation with 78 million people, more than 660,000 of them under arms, and a GNP (assuming that the East Germans are brought up to West German levels) of $1.2 trillion, about two-thirds that of Japan.

The Birth Dearth Confirmed

May 5, 1989

In projecting the slowest rate of population growth in our history after 1995, and a declining population after 2038, the Census Bureau has merely confirmed that the demographic trends of the past thirty years are not likely to be reversed. Since 1973, American women have been having babies at less than the 2.1-per-lifetime rate needed to keep population constant. The current fertility rate—1.8 births per woman—is 50 per cent below the baby-boom peak reached in 1957, and is unlikely to change in the foreseeable future.

A number of factors argue against our becoming alarmed at this, however. For one thing, these "best guesses" have in the past been notoriously wide of the mark. Both the baby boom and the baby bust were missed in previous Census Bureau prognostications, and many uncertainties surround the current forecast also. The spread of AIDS to the heterosexual population, for example, could produce an earlier and sharper population decline than currently anticipated, but it seems at least as likely that the heightened *fear* of AIDS will produce more and earlier marriages and, ultimately, higher fertility rates and population growth.

Second, our economic competitors are, if anything, more beset by demographic woes than we are. The population of Germany, for example, has already started to fall. Fertility rates in most of Europe are in the range of 1.4 to 1.8 births per woman. Between 1990 and 2000 the working-age population (15 to 64) of the United States will increase at an average of 0.8 per cent per year versus only 0.3 per cent in the 23 other OECD countries; Japan, Germany, and Italy will actually have smaller working-age populations in the year 2000 than they do now.

Third, and perhaps most important, productivity, not population, seems to be the key to national power these days. The United States, with 4.9 per cent of the world's population, produced 28.4 per cent of global GNP in 1985; India with 16 per cent of the world's people, accounted for only 1.4 per cent. Since 1950 the share of the world's population living in the developed nations of the West (including Japan) has fallen from about 22 per cent to 15 per cent, with no discernible decline in power.

However, by 2035, according to Ben Wattenberg, only 8 per cent of the world's population will reside in the Western community; by 2085, only 5 per cent. Although Western productivity successfully bridged the gap between 22 per cent and 15 per cent of total world population, it may not be able to offset a decline from 15 per cent to 5 per cent, and at some point higher population growth may be required to maintain the relative economic and political standing of the Western community.

The Poverty of Communism

February 24, 1989

"We don't have to talk late into the night about which form of government is better," George Bush said in his inaugural address, and statistics published in the *Wall Street Journal* the following week bore this out:

Table 1-41. Two Systems Compared

	U.S.	USSR	U.S./USSR
GNP (in billions), 1987	$4,436.1	$2,375.0	1.9×
Per-Capita GNP, 1987	$18,200	$8,360	2.2×
Average Annual GNP Growth, 1980–87	3.0%	1.8%	1.7×
Per-Capita Grain Production (kg.)	1,150	740	1.6×

Source: *Wall Street Journal.*

Of course, the Communist riposte might be that although the West is clearly better at producing wealth, the East is better at distributing it. However, a survey of 120 nations published by the American Political Science Association early last year found a high correlation between a nation's per-capita income and equality in the distribution of income, but no relationship between equality and the type of political system. Switzerland, with the highest per-capita income, was ranked the most egalitarian country, followed by the United States. Both were found to be considerably more egalitarian than the Soviet Union.

The Soviet claim to have eliminated poverty is also belied by official statistics released since Gorbachev took power. The infant-mortality rate, reported at thirty per thousand live births in 1985, puts the Soviet Union in the same league as Panama and Tonga; after adjusting for the high-risk newborns excluded by Soviet authorities from the tally, the rate climbs to nearly forty per thousand, about four times the comparably computed U.S. rate.

Life expectancy in the Soviet Union reportedly declined from seventy years in 1972 to 68 in 1983, before rising slightly (to 69) in the first half of 1986. At 69 years, life expectancy in the USSR is lower than what the World Bank ascribes to such places as Chile, Ghana, Panama, and Uruguay.

Excessive alcoholism is implicated in both trends. Per-capita consumption of hard liquor in the USSR is estimated to be twice as high as in Sweden, with urban families reportedly devoting the same proportion of their weekly budgets to alcohol that American families devote to food.

Backwardness confers ironic benefits. In West Germany, where the problem of a declining birthrate and an aging population is reportedly most acute, there will only be two people of working age (20 to 65) per each retiree (over 65) by the start of the next century. In the Soviet Union this ratio will be more like seven to one. Also, shortages of consumer goods have resulted in a marked increase in the Soviet personal-savings rate, something that has eluded the United States in recent years.

H. The Gulf War

The Enemy Within?

April 15, 1991

With the Gulf War over, another war—this one waged against America's oil companies—seems about to start. Emergency price-gouging legislation has been enacted in Connecticut and Massachusetts; forty other states have initiated special investigations or public hearings. The "Excess Oil Profits Tax Act of 1991," introduced by Senators Metzenbaum (D., Ohio), Lieberman (D., Conn.), and Cohen (R., Me.), would impose a 40 per cent tax on the "excess profits" of the larger oil companies.

The suspicion that oil companies can manipulate the price of oil was reinforced when gasoline prices began rising immediately after the August invasion, long before the higher-priced crude actually reached service-station tanks. By the end of October prices had risen 28 per cent; the net decline in world oil supplies was less than 2 per cent. The historical relationship between crude-oil supply and gasoline prices suggested that a rise of only 13 per cent, less than half the actual rise, was justified.

The perception of "gouging" was unavoidable—and wrong. The free-market price for oil properly reflects both the current supply and the probability of future supply disruptions. The market seems to have worked perfectly this time: once the air war started and it was clear that the Saudi oil fields were safe from Iraqi attack, prices fell sharply.

If oil companies do orchestrate prices, they are singularly inept at it. A recent study by the St. Louis-based Center for the Study of American Business shows that the real price of gasoline (in constant 1990 dollars) was $1.26 per gallon in 1960, or about 12 cents more than the level of this February. Over the long haul gasoline prices have not kept pace with market-basket inflation, yet no one accuses the food or newspaper or automobile industry of price "gouging."

Many believe that profits are a better indicator of market power than prices. The petroleum industry did, in fact, make money from the recent oil-price rise: the profits of the major oil companies rose a whopping 77 per cent in the fourth quarter of last year compared to the same period of 1989, according to the Department of Energy.

As with prices, however, there is less here than meets the eye. Net income for all of 1990 was up only 9 per cent from 1989's figure, which was depressed below that of 1988. Competition among refiners, marketers, and distributors prevented gasoline prices from rising as much as crude-oil prices, and as a result this end of the industry generated about 30 per cent less profit in the last quarter of 1990 than in the same period of 1989.

More important, when profits are measured against the investment made to earn those profits, oil companies are seen to be doing less well than other industries. In 1990, for example, the rate of return on stockholders' equity for the major oil companies (12.8 per cent) was less than the return for large non-oil manufacturing companies (13.9 per cent). In fact, the rate of return on oil-industry sales, assets, and equity has been below the average for U.S. industry in each of the past six years.

An excess-profits tax is seen by many as a better solution than energy price controls. Its economic effects would be equally disastrous, however. As currently envisioned the tax would be levied on the difference between the current year's net income and the company's average net income over the previous five years. Any rise in oil prices, even if below the rate of inflation, would produce "excess profits." Indeed, if the industry were merely to push its profit rate up to the average for U.S. industry, it would incur a massive excess-profits tax liability. At a time when oil-import dependence is a major concern, this tax would penalize those firms that invest heavily and successfully in domestic operations.

Sharing the Gulf Burden

February 25, 1991

A few days before the Gulf War began, the CBO released a study estimating possible costs for a war, based on two widely different scenarios; the lower figure came in at $28 billion, the higher at $86 billion. After two weeks of actual combat the assumptions behind both figures seem unreasonable.

The lower estimate, for example, is based on a 15-day air campaign followed by 15 days of the Army and Marine Corps fighting at half the intensity assumed for a war in Europe. The thirty days of fighting would leave 600 Americans killed, 2,400 wounded, and 100 tactical aircraft lost.

The $86-billion figure assumes an air war pursued at variable rates over a "long period," followed by a ground war fought at full intensity for thirty days, or at lower intensity for a longer period. We would take 45,000 casualties (7,800 killed), and lose 600 aircraft valued at $25 million each, 900 tanks at $3 million each, and 5 ships at $750 million each. Replacing lost aircraft and weapons, and spent ammunition, would account for about half of Desert Storm's costs under this scenario.

At this writing the White House is relying on an intermediate figure—$60 billion—as the expected cost, based on a three-month war costing $650 million per day. Allied pledges have already topped $50 billion.

While gratifying, the allied contributions fall far short of true burden sharing. The $60-billion figure reflects only the incremental costs of Desert Storm, costs over and above routine peacetime spending. It thus ignores the R&D costs incurred to develop the Patriot, Tomahawk, and Stealth technologies, as well as the costs of maintaining and training a standing army and reserves. Total defense spending as a percentage of GNP seems a far more meaningful indicator of the relative economic burdens associated with the Gulf War (see Table 1-42).

In 1988 (the latest year for which international defense-spending figures are available) the U.S. spent $296 billion, or more than the rest of NATO and Japan combined. The U.S. defense bur-

Table 1-42. National Defense Burdens, 1988
$ Billions

	Defense Spending	GNP	Defense as % of GNP
U.S.	$296	$ 4,847	6.1
Germany	35	1,158	3.0
UK	35	830	4.2
France	36	953	3.8
Rest of NATO	63	2,459	2.6
Japan	28	2,844	1.0
Allies	$493	$13,091	3.8

Source: U.S. Department of Defense.

den was six times Japan's, twice Germany's, and half again as great as the UK's.

True burden sharing would require that each nation's defense budget be set at the allied average of 3.8 per cent of GNP. For the U.S. this would mean a $100-billion *reduction* in defense outlays, based on the 1988 spending figures. Germany would be obliged to increase its defense budget by $9 billion, and Japan's defense contribution would rise by $78 billion, or by more than the entire projected cost of Desert Storm.

A full accounting for the economic costs associated with defense spending should also include its effect on the budget deficit, domestic interest rates, and the U.S. trade imbalance with these same allied nations.

Can Sanctions Work?

December 31, 1990

Defense Secretary Cheney says no. President Bush has lost patience with them. The *Wall Street Journal* reports that smugglers are flourishing along Iraq's borders with Turkey and Iran, undermining the UN's embargo.

But at least one group of economists thinks that this embargo has a far better chance of working than most. In the recently revised edition of *Economic Sanctions Reconsidered,* Gary C. Hufbauer, Jeffrey J. Schott, and Kimberly Ann Elliott of the Washington-based Institute for International Economics conclude that Iraq's GNP is likely to decline by 48 per cent as a result of the sanctions. By comparison, none of the 115 other sanctions in this century reduced the target country's GNP by even half that amount, and the average for success-ful sanctions has been only 2.4 per cent. (Sanctions imposed upon South Africa cost it less than 1 per cent of GNP, according to the study.)

The overall success rate for economic arm-twisting is not good, however. According to the Institute's historical analysis, only 34 per cent of previous sanctions succeeded in realizing specific foreign-policy goals. Since 1973 the success rate has been still lower, reflecting the declining economic dominance of the U.S., which has been by far the most frequent user of economic sanctions (77 of the 115 cases).

Of course, the post-cold-war environment has produced an unri-valed degree of unanimity: 100 per cent of Iraq's foreign trade is affected versus an average of 36 per cent of the target country's trade in previous successful sanctions. Countries whose support of the embargo might be expected to waver—Jordan, Yemen, Libya, and possibly Iran—accounted for a minimal portion of Iraq's pre-invasion trade.

Smuggling is unlikely to affect the outcome since smugglers do not give credit, and Iraq is short on cash. The seizure of Kuwait net-ted perhaps $400 million in gold and $10 to $15 million in foreign currency at the Kuwaiti central bank—enough to pay for about one month of imports. The big money was abroad, but Saddam failed to move fast enough: the foreign assets of both Iraq ($4 billion) and Kuwait ($100 billion) were frozen before he could transfer them.

Despite eight years of war, Iraq's ability to endure economic hardship has not been tested. Massive borrowing from abroad along with outright gifts from the Persian Gulf states that felt threatened by Iran—including Kuwait—cushioned the economy during the war. The U.S. chipped in with $8 billion in agricultural-export subsidies. The ready availability of cheap food imports (nearly half from the U.S.) along with two decades of collectivized agriculture under the socialist Baathist party has left Iraq dependent on imports for three-quarters of its food. Food reserves were reportedly lower than usual before the invasion, another sign of Saddam's failure to anticipate the international reaction.

"Success," as defined by the authors, is a relative term. Only five of the 41 "successes" were unqualified victories in which all demands were met. The rest were partial victories in which some goals were attained, possibly with the aid of factors other than sanctions. As for the current situation, the authors are "relatively optimistic that sanctions will contribute to a positive outcome—the withdrawal of Iraqi troops from Kuwait, the release of all hostages, and the restoration of a credible, independent government in Kuwait—but not the complete defeat of Saddam Hussein." The authors believe that some payoff to Saddam—perhaps the Rumalia oil field or the forgiving of Iraq's war debt—may be needed to resolve the dispute without bloodshed.

The Real Price of Oil

September 17, 1990

For those Americans who still feel taken advantage of by the oil companies, a few facts. Crude-oil prices started to rise well before the Iraqi invasion, going from $15.50 per barrel in mid June to $20 by the end of July. That translates to an increase of 12 cents a gallon. However, the wholesale (spot-market) price of gasoline rose only 3 cents per gallon, and retail gasoline prices did not rise at all during this period, according to data provided by the American Petroleum Institute.

Viewed from this perspective, the increase in gasoline prices in the days following the Iraqi *Blitzkrieg* was simply a delayed response to an earlier rise in the price of crude oil—not "price gouging" as many have charged. Further price hikes are expected, but the real price of oil is likely to stop far short of its historic high:

Table 1-43. U.S. Oil Prices and Their Effects

	Crude-Oil Prices (Current $)	(1989 $)	Oil Consumption per $1 Real GNP (1,000 BTUs)	Active Oil Rigs
1973	3.89	11.10	12.7	1,194
1974	6.74	16.19	12.5	1,472
1979	12.51	20.43	11.6	2,177
1981	31.77	41.66	9.8	3,970
1985	24.09	29.99	8.5	1,976
1986	12.51	16.05	8.7	970
1989	15.70	15.70	8.3	872

Source: U.S. Department of Energy.

U.S. wellhead oil prices averaged $31.77 per barrel in 1981, the equivalent of $41.66 in 1989 dollars. At its peak—in early 1981—crude oil was selling for the equivalent of $50.50 in today's dollars.

Over the past four years the price of crude oil, adjusted for inflation, has been less than half of its 1981 peak. Although energy efficiency (as measured by the BTUs of oil consumed per dollar of real GNP) did not deteriorate, it has virtually ceased rising. What small gains we've made during this period reflect the gradual shift from a manufacturing to a service economy rather than increased conservation efforts.

No matter what oil prices do over the next few months we will not see anything like the burst of exploratory-oil-rig activity of 1981. Oil prices were deregulated that year, and the rig count grew by 1,060, or by more than the total number of rigs active today. Many of those operators went out of business when oil prices fell, and the capacity to expand exploration and development activity today is about half what it was a decade ago.

The large oil companies will not step up domestic exploration in a big way until they are convinced that the invasion of Kuwait will have a long-term effect on oil prices—three years is the rule of thumb. But in some areas, large-scale production could begin tomorrow if state and local authorities would give the go-ahead.

The ultimate brake on the price of oil is the ability to substitute alternative fuels. Natural gas, more plentiful than oil in this country, has already supplanted oil as the primary energy source at many factories and electric utilities. If oil prices go above $36—and stay there—gasoline becomes cheaper to make from natural gas than through the standard oil-based refining process. Price controls on natural gas were phased out in 1985, but the needed expansion in pipeline capacity remains mired in a morass of federal regulations.

Call Up the (Oil) Reserves

September 3, 1990

"With Kuwait under its control, Iraq commands a fifth of the world's proven oil reserves and can more easily manipulate prices." *Time*'s apprehension over oil reserves was echoed throughout the media. In fact, oil-reserve figures are manipulated far more easily than oil prices:

	Iraq	Kuwait	Iran	Saudi Arabia	U.S.	World
1985	43.0	90.0	48.5	169.0	28.4	699.8
1986	44.5	89.8	47.9	168.8	28.4	700.6
1987	47.1	91.9	48.8	166.6	26.9	699.8
1988	100.0	91.9	92.9	167.0	27.3	889.3
1989	100.0	91.9	92.9	170.0	26.8	907.8
1990	100.0	94.5	92.9	254.9	25.9	1,001.6

Table 1-44. Proven Crude Oil Reserves
Billions of Barrels

Source: *Oil and Gas Journal.*

The *Oil and Gas Journal*'s authoritative estimates show that on January 1, 1988, global oil reserves were 190 billion barrels higher than on the same date in 1987, a staggering 27 per cent increase. In one year Iraq's reserves more than doubled, Iran's rose 90 per cent. Abu Dhabi (not shown above) started 1988 with official reserves of 92.9 billion barrels, 61.9 billion more than at the start of 1987.

Obviously these changes do not reflect newly discovered oil. Politics and economics, not geology, lie behind the drastic "revisions" of "proven" oil reserves. Both Iran and Iraq borrowed heavily to finance the war and subsequent reconstruction: higher estimated reserves of crude mean higher collateral for international lenders. Reserves are also one of the factors OPEC uses in allocating production quotas, so it's advantageous for all cartel members to fudge these figures upward.

All this may be of little solace to the United States, where proven reserves have fallen steadily since Alaska's North Slope was added to the total in 1970. At the start of this year U.S. crude reserves were sufficient to sustain only 9.2 years of production. Iraq, even before the recent "revision," had fifty years' worth of oil in the ground; Kuwait and Saudi Arabia each have more than 100 years' worth.

However, political considerations influence U.S. oil-reserve figures also. According to geologists there are three hundred billion barrels of unrecovered oil—more than ten times the official proven reserve figure—lying underneath the United States.

This vast potential remains untapped primarily because the current price of oil is too low to cover the costs of extraction. But misguided public policy has exacerbated the situation. The 1986 tax reform, for example, was especially hard on oil companies. The depletion allowance was severely curbed, and tax shelters, which had enabled many of the industry's tax advantages to be passed on to investors, were eliminated. Not surprisingly, the funds available for exploration fell: despite the recent increase in drilling activity there are 75 per cent fewer rigs in operation now than in 1981. At the same time, environmentalists have succeeded in prohibiting even strictly controlled exploration in many promising areas.

U.S. domestic oil production has fallen 22 per cent since 1986, not because we are "running out of oil," but because the price of oil is simply too low to cover the cost of expanding production in this country.

Iraq and Kuwait accounted for a combined 10.2 per cent of total U.S. oil imports in 1989, or about 5 per cent of all oil consumed here. Losing that is no small hit. But the U.S. oil stockpile, including the Federal Government's underground cache in Louisiana, is large enough to cover this shortfall for more than two years. Pledges by Saudi Arabia and Venezuela to increase their output, together with the increased conservation that will surely accompany higher prices, make a big drawdown in oil stocks unlikely.

I. Poverty/Homelessness

Welfare Reform, Again

February 1993

President Clinton's credentials as a "new Democrat" may well rest on what he does to reform the welfare system. After showing little growth for nearly two decades, the number of Americans on welfare has skyrocketed. About 13.5 million people currently receive Aid to Families with Dependent Children (AFDC), an increase of 21 per cent in little more than three years.

Well over half of AFDC recipients remain on welfare for ten years or longer. A two-year eligibility limit, recently proposed by Mr. Clinton, would be a welcome change in a system remarkably devoid of such sanctions. But the need for expensive new job training programs is far less clear, however.

In fact, workfare—the requirement that employable welfare recipients work, or at least look for work—has been incorporated into social legislation since 1967. At first there was a federal Work Incentive or WIN program, which focused on job training. The early workfare programs targeted males and unmarried females with older children. In 1981, however, President Reagan authorized states to require any able-bodied AFDC recipient to perform unpaid community service in exchange for the grants.

The success of these early, fairly inexpensive, programs is the dirty little secret of a welfare bureaucracy forever clamoring for more funding. But from 1984 to 1988, 61 per cent of all workfare clients found jobs immediately, according to New York University Professor Lawrence Mead. In Chicago workfare filled 130,000 jobs in just three years. The problem there wasn't a lack of jobs, but the unwillingness of many clients to take low-paying positions. In general, however, the reduction in welfare benefits more than paid for the cost of workfare programs.

So much for the liberal assertion that dependency reflects a lack of job opportunities.

By comparison, the 1988 welfare reform act, sponsored by Senator Moynihan, has been a failure. Billed as mandatory workfare, the law exempts half of all welfare mothers from participation and requires the states to enroll only 20 per cent of the remainder. Most states have been able to fulfill their enrollment quotas with volunteer mothers, many of whom would have left welfare even without such benefits.

As a result, the hard-core underclass remains virtually untouched by the rigors of workfare. Indeed, the very generosity of the 1988 act may have exacerbated the work disincentives facing dependent families. An AFDC mother considering a low-income job in a small firm, for example, would be understandably reluctant to give up the medical, child care, lunch, transportation, and clothing benefits she now gets while enrolled in workfare.

CBO estimates that the 1988 workfare "reforms" will cut welfare caseloads by 50,000 families this year—a reduction of only 1 per cent. Meanwhile, the decision to expand AFDC eligibility to two-parent families is expected to add 80,000 families to the welfare rolls, for a net increase of 30,000 this year.

Mandatory workfare, even if coupled with a two-year eligibility limit, will not eliminate dependency immediately. But by requiring beneficiaries to participate every day, at a specific time, in job training, schooling, or unpaid work programs, it can give structure to previously unstructured lives. After this major change in lifestyle, says Professor Mead, employment tends to follow.

Family Values and Growth

October 5, 1992

The Republican Party's preoccupation with moral issues has been portrayed as a politically inspired diversion from Topic A: the economy. A return to traditional family values could, however, help the economy more than the most potent growth package.

In 1991, for example, families headed by a woman with no husband present experienced a 5.4 per cent decline in real median income, to $16,692. This was much worse than the 1.4 per cent drop—to $40,995—in income of families headed by a married couple.

Although the poverty rate rose in 1991 to 14.1 per cent—the highest level since 1983—the rate for married-couple families remained unchanged, at 6 per cent. By contrast, the percentage of female-headed families living in poverty increased significantly, from 33.4 in 1990 to 35.6 in 1991.

Health, especially that of children, is also highly correlated with family structure. The mortality rate of babies born to unmarried white women in 1989 stood at 13.1 deaths per 1,000 single births, compared to 7.8 deaths per 1,000 single births to married white mothers. Among blacks, the comparable infant-mortality rates were 19.6 and 14.6 per 1,000 single births, respectively. Regardless of the race, age, or income of its mother, a child is more likely to die in infancy if born out of wedlock. Even a mother's education matters less than her marital status: infant-mortality rates are higher for children of unmarried mothers who are college graduates than of married high-school dropouts.

A sharp rise in out-of-wedlock births has occurred in most industrialized nations, with Japan the notable exception (see table). Male joblessness has been blamed for this trend in the U.S., although this fails to explain why both illegitimacy and divorce rates continued rising during the prosperous Sixties and Eighties. The rise in the percentage of wives who work outside the home and the rise in wage rates paid to women relative to men has also been implicated in the rise of female-headed families.

In the U.S., however, the decline of the traditional family increasingly reflects a deliberate choice to accept single parenthood.

Table 1-45. Percentage of Births to Unmarried Women in Selected Countries

	1960	1970	1980	1989
U.S.	5.3	10.7	18.4	27.1
Canada	4.3	9.6	12.8	23.0
France	6.1	6.8	11.4	28.2
W. Germany	6.3	5.5	7.6	10.2
Japan	1.2	0.9	0.8	1.0
Sweden	11.3	18.4	39.7	51.8
U.K.	5.2	8.0	11.5	26.6

Source: *Statistical Abstract, 1991.*

During the early Sixties (1960–64), 52.2 per cent of unmarried women 15 to 34 years old who were pregnant with their first child married before the child was born. By 1985–89, the percentage had fallen by nearly half, to 26.6.

The ready availability of AFDC, Medicaid, and other welfare programs targeted to fatherless families undoubtedly explains much of this trend. But welfare cannot explain the sharp rise in illegitimacy among never-married white women over 24 years of age. At least some of them are choosing an untraditional remedy for the ticking away of their "biological clock."

More than half (55 per cent) of these Murphy Browns reported in 1988 that they deliberately set out to conceive a child at the time of their pregnancy—up from just 16 per cent in 1982. By contrast, only 44 per cent of the unmarried black mothers age 25 and over had intended to get pregnant.

Why the Poor Stay Poor

June 8, 1992

Bill Clinton blames the L.A. riots on "12 years of denial and neglect." The alleged "neglect," however, is not evident in federal spending trends of the Reagan/Bush years:

Table 1-46. Federal Social Spending
Billions of 1987 Dollars

	Transfer Payments	Grants to States and Cities	Total	Total as % of Budget	GDP
1981	$420.5	$72.4	$492.9	56.3	12.9
1989	490.8	50.3	541.1	51.6	11.5
1991	542.6	53.8	596.4	53.9	12.7
1992E	593.1	56.7	649.8	54.1	13.6
Percentage Change					
1981–89	16.7	–30.5	9.8		
1989–92	20.8	12.7	20.0		

Source: Congressional Research Service.

Federal social spending rose by nearly 10 per cent in real terms during the Reagan years, and another 20 per cent during the first three Bush years. Throughout the 1980s these programs accounted for more than half of all federal spending.

Of course, not all such spending is directed exclusively to the poor—notably Social Security. But according to the non-partisan Congressional Research Service, the fastest-growing segment of social spending is precisely the "safety net" programs, including AFDC, Medicaid, Food Stamps, and housing subsidies. Funding for the 38 programs targeting poor children and their families increased 18 per cent during the Reagan years, from $104 billion (1989 dollars) in 1981 to $123 billion in 1989.

In the wake of Los Angeles, the *New York Times* bemoaned "slashed federal assistance to cities." Federal grants to state and local governments did fall 31 per cent, in real dollars, between 1981 and

1989. A "war against the poor"? Hardly. One of these programs terminated under Reagan, Urban Development Action Grants, had helped local contractors build glitzy hotels and health spas; Community Development Grants had gone to such underprivileged cities as Greenwich, Palo Alto, and Houston at the height of the oil boom; the enormous fees paid to Job Corps contractors meant it would have been cheaper to send participants to Harvard for a year.

Why, then, did the inner-city poverty rate remain so high? Part of the explanation undoubtedly rests in the well known flaws (e.g., the failure to count non-cash benefits) in the poverty-rate calculation itself. But the rapid dissolution of black families offers a far more compelling explanation.

Table 1-47. Black Families with Children

| | Married couples | | Single Parents | |
	Number (Mils.)	Poverty Rate (%)	Number (Mils.)	Poverty Rate (%)
1980	2.154	15.5	2.311	54.1
1988	2.181	12.5	2.829	54.4
1990	2.104	14.3	2.965	53.5
Percentage Change, 1980–90				
	−2.3	−1.2	+28.3	−0.6

Source: Congressional Research Service.

Intact black families did well during the Reagan years. A booming economy lifted their real median income by 15.9 per cent between 1982 and 1989, compared to a 15.4 per cent gain registered by their white counterparts. By 1990 half of black husband-wife families had incomes above $33,393.

If the rising tide failed to lift female-headed black families, it was because they simply weren't in the water. In 1988 only 42 per cent of such mothers were employed even part-time; 13 per cent were unemployed, and 45 per cent were out of the labor force entirely. More ominous, boys born into such families are even less likely to be looking for work than their counterparts were twenty years ago.

135

How Many Homeless?

May 14, 1990

Advocates for the homeless are understandably annoyed at "shelter night," the Census Bureau's well-publicized effort to count the homeless population. For years these groups have traded on the figure of three million homeless—1.2 per cent of the nation's population. The media generally report this figure. Politicians and celebrities cite it. Yet every systematic survey of homelessness since 1984 has put the figure at between 250,000 and 600,000, with the average at about 400,000. The only study to reach a seven-figure estimate, *Homelessness: A Forced March to Nowhere*, was published by activist Mitch Snyder in 1982, and was based on a phone survey of shelter operators across the country.

The tricky part of any attempt to count the homeless is to determine the ratio of street homeless to shelter homeless. We know there are approximately 275,000 beds in shelters throughout the country. A HUD survey conducted in January 1984 found only 70 per cent of shelter beds occupied. Even assuming full occupancy, and even defining each of the approximately 110,000 persons in public mental hospitals as "homeless," the street-to-shelter ratio would have to be 8 to 1 for there to be three million homeless. Advocates for the homeless insist that street people go to great lengths to hide themselves and are grossly undercounted, but most studies have found the average annual street-to-shelter ratio to be less than 1 to 1, far less in those cities, such as New York, where shelters are readily available.

Researchers generally agree that between 35 and 40 per cent of homeless individuals have severe drug or alcohol problems, and 50 per cent are disabled by mental illness. A 1988 Urban Institute study was the first to look at other characteristics, and found that 56 per cent had served five or more days in jail, while more than 25 per cent had served time in state or federal prisons, implying felony convictions. Almost 50 per cent never finished high school, and only 5 per cent had steady employment. This contrasts sharply with the image portrayed by the media: the Center for Media and Public Affairs reports that only 12 per cent of the homeless interviewed for the three networks' evening news shows were unemployed, and only 3 per cent were drug or alcohol users. Their survey covered 103 stories on homelessness broadcast over a thirty-month period.

To what extent, then, is homelessness strictly a housing problem? We might start with the 10 per cent of homeless households made up of families with children. These families are poor, but relatively few members are drug addicts or mentally ill. However, most of these families are headed by females—half of them never married—suggesting that even in this group few are homeless solely because of a lack of affordable housing.

In New York City an average of 12,000 families are homeless over the course of a year. Surely the city's housing supply—1.9 million rental units—could be stretched to accommodate a less than 1 per cent rise in inhabitants. Where rents are not controlled this is accomplished by means of upward migration: affluent tenants move to better apartments, their old units are acquired by those just below them on the housing ladder, eventually freeing up the least desirable units for the poor and homeless. But one of the strictest rent-control laws in the nation induces New Yorkers to hold onto their apartments long after their incomes have risen, their families have grown, and, in many cases, they themselves have left town.

Losing More Ground

May 19, 1989

The persistence of poverty in the United States despite massive federal spending to alleviate that condition is quantified in data recently released by the House Ways and Means Committee:

Table 1-48. Impact of Federal Transfer Payments, 1987		
	Number of Poor People (Millions)	Poverty Gap ($ Billions)
Before Transfers	49.7	124.2
After Transfers	29.0	40.4
Change	(20.7)	(83.8)
Percentage Change	(41.6%)	(67.5%)
Source: House Ways and Means Committee.		

In the absence of federal transfer programs, 49.7 million people—one out of every five Americans—would have been poor in 1987, according to Ways and Means. Federal transfer expenditures of $413 billion that year succeeded in raising the incomes of 20.7 million of these erstwhile poor people to levels above the officially decreed poverty line, but at a cost of $19,950 *per person*, or roughly 72 per cent more than the poverty threshold income for a family of four.

The data also show that the 29 million people who remained poor after receiving federal transfer payments were made considerably less poor because of them. Thus, while the number of poor persons was cut by only 41.6 per cent, the poverty gap, which is simply the amount of additional income required to raise every poor person up to the official poverty line (i.e., the cost of eradicating poverty), was 67.5 per cent smaller after federal transfer spending.

Why does poverty persist in a country where transfer expenditures are more than three times the amount needed to eradicate poverty? For one thing, Social Security and Medicare, which together account for nearly 70 per cent of all federal transfer spending, are not means-tested and therefore cannot be considered anti-poverty programs, although they have dramatically reduced the incidence of poverty among the elderly. Even the programs specifically designed to combat poverty (AFDC, Food Stamps, housing subsidies, etc.) often miss their target, as evidenced by the $150 per year in means-tested benefits reportedly received, on average, by the wealthiest 20 per cent of families in 1987 (average income $52,600).

Whether the anti-poverty programs themselves induce increased dependency is still an open question, although the circumstantial evidence is compelling. Charles Murray points out in *Losing Ground* that the number of poor people before government transfer payments are taken into account, which he calls the "latent poor," started to rise in 1968, just as the Great Society programs were coming on stream. Up until then, increasing numbers of people had been able—and willing—to make a living that put them above the poverty line. Although the number of latent poor has declined recently, falling from 52.7 million in 1983 to 49.7 million in 1987, this is not nearly the decline one would have expected given the 11 million new jobs created during that time.

What is clear is that even a modicum of employment greatly reduces the probability of being poor. In 1987, 93.3 per cent of female-headed families in which no one worked were poor, but the poverty rate for those families where someone worked at least three-quarters of the year was only 14.8 per cent.

J. Distribution of Income

The Rich Poor

July 29, 1991

We are told that the poor got poorer during the Eighties. Virtually all sources show that the real income of poor families rose sharply until the mid Seventies, fell sharply under the Carter-engineered inflation of the late Seventies and early Eighties, rose again during the Reagan boom, but has not yet reached its Seventies peak.

But when economists look at what poor families actually *spend* rather than what they report as income, a very different story emerges, as a recent study by sociologists Susan E. Mayer of the University of Chicago and Christopher Jencks of Northwestern University shows:

Table 1-49. Income vs. Spending of the Rich and Poor

	1961	1973	1985	Percentage Change 1961–73	Percentage Change 1973–85
Per-Capita Income					
Poorest 10%	$ 1,243	$ 1,800	$ 901	44.8%	−50.0%
Richest 10%	18,688	29,240	32,382	56.5	10.7
All Families	6,504	10,017	10,313	54.0	3.0
Per-Capita Spending					
Poorest 10%	$ 1,653	$ 2,829	$ 4,545	71.1%	60.7%
Richest 10%	11,749	13,991	16,965	19.1	21.2
All Families	5,265	6,657	7,745	26.4	16.3

Source: Susan E. Mayer and Christopher Jencks, "Recent Trends in Economic Inequality in the United States: Income vs. Material Well-Being," 1991.

While the reported income of the poorest families plunged 50 per cent between 1973 and 1985, their real expenditures rose a whopping 60.7 per cent over the same period. Indeed, real per-capita spending of poor families grew nearly three times faster than that of wealthy families over both the 1961–73 and 1973–85 periods. Expenditure inequality shrank even as income inequality appeared to grow.

J. Distribution of Income

There may be perfectly legitimate reasons why poor families spend more than their reported income. Many of them get money from sources that the federal surveys do not ask about, such as savings, loans, gifts, payments by boarders, subsidized housing, and Medicaid.

Most of the discrepancy, however, reflects the underreporting of income by poor families. People are increasingly reluctant to answer questions about income (response rates for federal economic surveys dropped from 95 per cent in 1948 to 72 per cent in 1985), and the volunteered answers are rarely honest. Mayer and Jencks cite a study of fifty Chicago welfare mothers that found not one was living entirely on her AFDC benefit or was reporting all her outside income to the welfare department. The unreported income was as large as the welfare benefit.

The link between reported income and living standards is tenuous, especially for the poor. More than half of the poorest tenth of all families owned a home in 1985, and decennial Census surveys show poor families were more likely to have a car, a telephone, an air conditioner, and a complete bathroom in 1980 than in 1970 despite stagnant or declining real income over this period.

The authors do not deny that material deprivation persists: survey data suggest that more families go hungry at some point in the year than lack a television. But this reflects the perverse priorities of consumers rather than the indifference of government.

The Quota Fallacy

July 8, 1991

Do blacks need preferential treatment to share in the fruits of economic growth? Census Bureau statistics suggest not:

Table 1-50. Black/White Income Trends
1989 Dollars

	Median Family Income		Families with Incomes:			
			Under $5,000		Over $50,000	
	White	Black	White	Black	White	Black
1975	$32,885	$20,234	2.1%	6.3%	22.3%	8.3%
1982	31,614	17,473	3.2	11.4	22.9	7.3
1989	35,975	20,209	2.6	11.2	30.9	13.8
Percentage Change						
1975–82	–3.9	–13.6	52.3	81.0	2.7	–12.0
1982–89	13.8	15.7	–18.7	–1.8	34.9	89.0

Source: Bureau of the Census.

During the Reagan boom, 1982 to 1989, the median black family's income increased 15.7 per cent compared to a 13.8 per cent rise for the median white family. Those blacks with sufficient skills and education to garner incomes of more than $50,000 (1989 dollars) did particularly well. The share of black families in this category increased 89.0 per cent between 1982 and 1989, or more than twice the 34.9 per cent rise for whites.

Unfortunately, the percentage of black families with incomes below $5,000 rose dramatically during the late Seventies and early Eighties and was virtually unaffected by the subsequent boom. Obviously an income below $5,000 means nobody in the family worked full-time throughout the year. Indeed, the labor-force-participation rate for black males—the fraction either employed or actively looking for work—declined throughout the Eighties.

Does racial discrimination explain why black men drop out of the economic mainstream during periods of record job creation? The Urban Institute recently tested this proposition with scientific precision. In the summer of 1990 ten black–white pairs of applicants were sent on 476 carefully monitored job searches. The two members of each pair of applicants were matched as to job qualifications, experience, and demeanor; each pair answered the same entry-level job ad.

Lo and behold: in 85 per cent of the cases the black applicant received a job offer comparable to or better than the one his white counterpart received; in only 15 per cent of cases did the white get a job denied the black. In only 5 per cent of cases did the potential employer steer the black applicant to a less desirable position than his white counterpart, and even this was partially offset by the 3 per cent of whites steered to less desirable positions than blacks.

The Urban Institute study supports (inadvertently perhaps) what conservatives have long asserted: family disintegration, not racial discrimination, accounts overwhelmingly for the relatively large number of blacks in the lowest income bracket. The fraction of poor blacks who live in female-headed families increased from 48 per cent in 1970 to 60 per cent today. Although income differences between intact black and white families are fairly manageable (a black college-educated married couple averaged $52,020 in 1989 versus $57,224 for its white counterpart), median incomes of black *female-headed* families are not much more than half of their white counterparts'. Clearly, the principal economic drag on black families is a welfare system that encourages family breakups and nonemployment.

Wrong Data

May 13, 1991

The use—and abuse—of economic statistics to influence policy peaks during the spring, with the release of the House Ways and Means Committee's *Green Book.*

Among last year's 1,495 pages was a table showing the sources of income of the wealthiest American families:

Table 1-51. Average Income of the Top 1 Per Cent *1990 Dollars*			
	1977	**1990**	**% Change, 1977–90**
Wages and Salaries	$ 95,553	$198,452	107.7
Business Income	46,697	60,601	29.8
Capital Gains	64,704	175,536	171.3
Interest & Dividends	69,769	102,901	47.5
Other Income	6,020	11,480	90.7
All Income	$282,743	$548,970	94.2

Source: House Ways and Means Committee, *Green Book* (1990).

According to the table, the wealthiest 1 per cent of American families saw their average real income expand 94.2 per cent between 1977 and 1990, to $548,970. Capital gains appears to be the fastest growing source, up a whopping 171.3 per cent over a period when stock-market averages, as measured by the Standard & Poor's composite stock index, grew only 58 per cent in real terms.

How did the wealthy do it? It turns out they had some help from the Congressional Budget Office, which provides the data for the *Green Book.* By the CBO's reckoning, someone selling an asset for $150,000 in 1990 that he purchased for $100,000 in 1980 has a capital gain of $50,000, even though in real terms the asset is worth less than when originally purchased. By failing to adjust purchase prices for inflation, the CBO vastly overstates real-income growth of the top group.

Another, more subtle, statistical oversight enables the CBO to exaggerate the extent to which gains are concentrated in the upper-income brackets. In any given year many families find themselves in the top 1 per cent solely because of non-recurring capital gains. But income swelled by once-in-a-lifetime events such as the sale of a business or a home is obviously not an accurate reflection of a family's long-term economic circumstances. Had the CBO simply taken capital gains out of income when ranking families, the distribution of gains would have appeared far less concentrated among the "wealthy."

Because CBO data are used to "score" or estimate the cost of policy changes, statistical coverups can have wide-ranging effects. Representative Dick Armey (R., Tex.) recently brought to our attention the case of a former chairman of the Education and Labor Committee who, in 1988, requested that the CBO study the impact of a 50 per cent increase in the minimum wage. The CBO's preliminary report indicated that such an increase would eliminate as many as half a million jobs. The chairman then requested that this finding be deleted from the final report; the CBO graciously obliged.

Sometimes the political spin is so obvious that it works against the perpetrators. Mr. Armey recalls that in 1989 Senator Bob Packwood (R., Ore.) asked the Joint Committee on Taxation to estimate how much revenue could be raised by subjecting everyone earning more than $200,000 to a 100 per cent tax rate. The committee staff, apparently not believing that tax rates have any effect on human behavior, told the senator that this would generate $204 billion in 1990, and nearly $300 billion by 1993. Mr. Packwood then mockingly assured his colleagues on the Senate floor that American workers "will work forever and pay all of their money to the government . . ."

The outlook for statistical spin-doctors remains bullish: one of the first moves House Democrats made this session was to reassert the CBO's responsibility for scoring spending programs, thereby reneging on an agreement made during last fall's budget summit.

Hold the Malaise

December 3, 1990

"Social pundits" from Rep. Joe Kennedy, II (D., Mass.), to Kevin Phillips have convinced many Americans of the ravages inflicted upon working-class people by Reagan-era policies. Less well publicized is the latest Census Bureau survey, showing continued income growth among people of modest means:

Table 1-52. The Income Gap
Average Real Income (1989 Dollars)

	Poorest 20 Per Cent	Richest 20 Per Cent	Ratio: Richest/Poorest
1978	$6,769	$71,793	10.6
1980	6,494	70,056	10.8
1983	6,291	71,983	11.4
1985	6,470	76,466	11.8
1988	6,777	82,554	12.2
1989	6,994	85,529	12.2

Source: Bureau of the Census.

After falling during the late Seventies, the average real income of the poorest fifth of the population increased 11 per cent between 1983 and 1989, and is higher now than any year since the government began measuring the distribution of income in 1967. Still, the income gap between rich and poor is greater now than ever.

The "populists" assert, without proof, that Reaganomics tilted the economic playing field in favor of the rich via tax and budget cuts. However, economists with no political axe to grind are reporting a universal increase in income disparity, not just between rich and poor, but among professionals, college graduates, and blue-collar workers. Demographics, the changing economic returns to education, and foreign competition—not Reaganomics—are responsible for this trend.

For example, during the Seventies the labor market was inundated with young, college-educated workers. Their supply outstripped the demand for their skills, resulting in a decline in the ratio of wages paid to college graduates relative to those paid to the typical high-school graduate. Not surprisingly, this contributed to a narrowing of the rich/poor and black/white income differentials during the 1970s.

Things changed in the 1980s. Although the educational level of new workers continued to rise, the numbers rose far less quickly, resulting in an increased wage premium for college graduates. Marvin Kosters of the American Enterprise Institute calculates that male college graduates of all ages and levels of work experience were paid 61 per cent more than high-school graduates in 1988, nearly double the 32 per cent difference in 1980. The sharp rise in the economic returns to education is a major reason for the larger gap between rich and poor, offsetting transfer payments and other redistributionist public policies.

Of course, years of education say nothing about the quality or relevance of that education. Employers are increasingly paying workers on the basis of demonstrated skills rather than educational credentials. Ten years ago, for example, young pension lawyers of similar age and education could expect to land jobs paying comparable salaries in New York; today the spread ranges from $110,000 for top talent to $42,000 for the average. Similarly, young electrical engineers working in the computer industry earned within $12,000 of each other in 1980. The spread has grown to $25,000, far outstripping inflation, with the high end now at $65,000.

The waning power of unions is one factor often cited to explain the widening wage spread. Deregulation and increased international competition may also have persuaded many U.S. companies to pay more for top talent and pay lower wages to marginal employees.

Whatever the cause, it's clear that improving the quality of education is the key to improving the economic well being of lower-income workers. While many such workers may bemoan the loss of what appears to have been a de facto private-sector safety net, in the long run economic growth and their own standard of living will be better served.

The Rising Tide

December 8, 1989

Recently released Census Bureau data for 1988 show the number of poor persons declined by 500,000 last year. The poverty rate—13.1 per cent—was the lowest for any year since 1981, and real per-capita income was a record $13,120, up 19.2 per cent from 1982.

To the *Washington Post*, however, this was "bad news," further evidence that "the economy famous for lifting all boats no longer does so." The *Post*'s editors go on to assert that "Real per-capita income was up, but . . . this broadest measure of economic well-being is an average. As in other recent years, for the richest two-fifths of families median income and income share rose; for the poorest two-fifths, they declined."

A preoccupation with the distribution of income has led the *Post* to an important misstatement of fact. The Census data for families are as follows:

Table 1-53. Income Levels and Shares
1988 Dollars

| | The Poorest 40% | | The Richest 40% | |
	Income Share	Average Income	Income Share	Average Income
1978	16.8%	$15,310	65.6%	$59,783
1980	16.7	14,370	65.9	56,705
1982	15.9	13,347	67.0	56,243
1985	15.5	14,035	67.7	61,302
1986	15.4	14,513	67.7	63,800
1987	15.4	14,661	67.8	64,546
1988	15.3	14,768	68.0	65,634

Source: Bureau of the Census.

True, the data show a declining *share* of income going to the poorest 40 per cent of families over the past decade. However, income growth during the Reagan recovery more than compensated for the declining share: average real income of this group increased 11 per cent between 1982 and 1988, and is now higher than it was in

1980. Unfortunately, the bottom 40 per cent of families have yet to recover fully from the income losses incurred during the last two Carter years.

Furthermore, the degree of income inequality between "rich" and "poor" families is considerably less than suggested by these figures. For one thing, the Census Bureau counts cash income only, ignoring more than $150 billion in non-cash benefits (Food Stamps, housing subsidies, Medicaid, etc.) targeted to low-income families. The medical benefits alone have an estimated market value of more than $3,000 per year.

Low-income families are generally smaller than wealthier ones, and are more likely to be headed by individuals either under age 25 or over age 65. Not surprisingly, they have considerably fewer full-time workers. In 1986, for example, among the lowest two-fifths of households there were, on average, only 36 full-time workers per each 100 households; among the most affluent two-fifths there were 119 workers per each 100 households—three times the number found among the less affluent group.

Can we say that a retired couple with a $10,000 pension is really only one-third as well off as a middle-aged family of four with both parents employed and with total income of $30,000? Yet that is exactly the type of comparison implicit in the Census figures.

But no matter how carefully we adjust the income distribution to reflect these factors, it will still mislead as to the true degree of economic "fairness." Income mobility is a far better indicator: in any one year, many families at the bottom of the income distribution are there because of abnormal economic misfortune rather than chronic poverty. Conversely, many people at the top are there because of exceptional, non-recurring circumstances.

The fact that the bottom two-fifths of families received only 15.3 per cent of total income last year, or any year, is unimportant in an economy as dynamic as ours.

Income Disparity

June 24, 1988

A few months ago the Treasury Department released two typewritten pages showing that the share of income taxes paid by the wealthiest 1 per cent of taxpayers had risen from 18.1 per cent to 26.1 per cent between 1981 and 1986, while that of the bottom half had fallen to 6.4 per cent from 7.5 per cent.

The Op-Ed-page response was predictable: Sure, the rich are paying a larger percentage of all taxes, but their income grew considerably faster than their taxes, not to mention faster than that of the bottom half of taxpayers.

Both assertions happen to be correct. The share of total income going to the top 1 per cent rose 45.7 per cent over the period, a point or so higher than the 44.2 per cent rise in their tax share. Thus, the average tax rate (taxes as a percentage of income) of the top group fell 9.1 per cent. Over the same period, however, the average tax rate of the lower half of taxpayers fell by 15.2 per cent, a fact largely ignored in the press.

Income earned by the bottom half of taxpayers rose 10.9 per cent, in constant dollars, between 1981 and 1986, but this didn't keep pace with the top half; the bottom half's share of total income fell 6.7 per cent.

An increase in income disparity is exactly what one would expect given the pattern of tax reductions over this period: marginal tax rates on the highest incomes were cut by twenty percentage points, compared to a cut of three percentage points for the bottom bracket.

It's clear that work incentives have increased more for the upper incomes. This trend, however, has resulted in increased economic mobility in this country. More than ever before, wealthier taxpayers are likely to have gotten that way by virtue of their own work rather than via inheritance or income from capital.

In 1960, for example, the wealthiest 2 per cent of taxpayers derived more than two-thirds (69.3 per cent) of their income from dividends, interest, and capital gains, only 30.7 per cent from wages and salaries. The top marginal tax rate that year was 91 per cent. By

1975 the top rate on wages had been cut to 50 per cent, and the share of this group's income derived from wages and salaries had risen to 48.3 per cent. In 1988, with the top rate down to 28 per cent, 60.7 per cent of the income of the wealthiest 5 per cent of families will be derived from wages and salaries, according to the Congressional Budget Office.

The public debate on income distribution still proceeds from the assumption that "the rich" and "the poor" are fixed groups over time. But a University of Michigan study that tracked the year-to-year economic vicissitudes of five thousand representative American families found that only 48.5 per cent of the families who were among the wealthiest 20 per cent in 1971 were still there in 1978; 3.5 per cent of them had fallen into the lowest 20 per cent bracket. Conversely, 44.5 per cent of the families in the poorest fifth in 1971 were no longer there seven years later; 6 per cent had actually risen all the way to the highest fifth—suggesting that economic inequality is a good deal less pronounced than the commonly used statistics indicate.

K. Mario Cuomo/New York State

Mario Explains

August 20, 1990

We have before us a four-page letter from New York Governor Mario Cuomo, apparently sent to editors of several publications, in which he seeks to "clear up some misconceptions that I have encountered in the wake of this year's budget process."

Mario Cuomo: "We keep a close watch on spending in the so-called 'General Fund' ... because all the money in this Fund is raised by taxes and the more that is spent, the higher taxes are likely to be. For 1990–91 the General Fund will be nearly $30 billion. That is an increase of less than 2 per cent over last year."

Right Data: The General Fund isn't the whole story. Since Cuomo took office, many state agencies have been shifted out of the General Fund in order to give the *appearance* of spending restraint. Spending from all funds will be $49.8 billion this year, up 7.5 per cent over 1989. The governor had sought a 10.5 per cent rise in total spending.

MC: "It may surprise you to learn that the rate of growth in all General Fund spending in New York State since 1983 has been *below the national average and the averages for states in the Northeast and for the largest states.*" (Emphasis in original.)

RD: Again, the governor focuses attention on an arbitrary slice of total spending—the General Fund. His comparison also ignores New York's below-average population growth rate. Commerce Department data show that New York's per-capita state spending from all funds increased 55.8 per cent between 1983 and 1988; the nation as a whole experienced a 38.2 per cent increase during that period.

MC: "And this year, after all the talk about austerity, the legislature added $150 million in spending and revenues to the budget after the conclusion of three-way negotiations."

RD: In truth, the legislature added many spending items and deleted many others during a prolonged and acrimonious series of negotiations. The bottom line was a $1.6 billion *reduction* from the governor's original spending request. In any event, the governor of New York can veto spending he deems excessive. Governor Carey used this weapon to overturn $900 million of appropriations during his last year in office. Mr. Cuomo vetoed only $7 million of state bills this year.

MC: "New York now ranks *19th in the nation for total State taxes per $1,000* of personal income." (Emphasis in original.)

RD: True. But Albany mandates an inordinate amount of spending at the county- and local-government levels. As a result, New Yorkers pay an average of $164 in combined state, county, and local taxes per every $1,000 of personal income, the highest overall tax burden in the nation.

MC: "Our historic tax cuts reduced New York's top income-tax rate by about one half, and improved our ranking from the state with the highest income-tax rate down to the *12th* highest today." (Emphasis in original.)

RD: Marginal tax *rates* have come down, but not enough to offset the broadening of the tax base under tax reform. In 1988 New Yorkers paid an average of $42.28 in state income tax per every $1,000 of personal income, highest of all the states, and 11.1 per cent more than in 1983. Delaware's state-income-tax burden, at $35.14 per $1,000, was ranked second; the national average was $21.34 per $1,000, or about half New York's level.

MC: "While it has been suggested that New York has more state employees per capita than anywhere else, the fact of the matter is that New York ranks *27th* among all the states . . . for full-time-equivalent employees per ten thousand population." (Emphasis in original.)

RD: A 1988 survey of public-sector employment found New York had 634 state-and local-government employees per ten thousand population. The rest of the nation got by with 494 government employees per ten thousand population. Only Wyoming and Alaska—atypical states with low populations and large amounts of severance tax revenues exported to residents of other states—employed more public-sector workers relative to population.

153

Fiscal Meltdown

April 1, 1990

"I don't think we have told our story as well as we might," Governor Cuomo admitted in a recent interview, adding "there are many misimpressions about our condition and what we are doing about it." That "condition" is the fiscal meltdown in New York. Within the past four months the deficit projected for fiscal 1990 has risen by a factor of four, to $1.1 billion. The governor's budget office warns of a $3-billion shortfall for 1991 unless policies are changed. The governor's story is that the state has exhausted every possible opportunity to cut spending, and finds that austerity alone can no longer do the job. A weak economy and slow revenue growth make a tax hike unavoidable, Mr. Cuomo says. Specifically, he proposes closing next year's budget gap with $1.4 billion in new taxes and fees (including a permanent freeze on the state's income-tax cut), $1 billion in one-shot revenues, and $300 million in spending reductions.

Lost among the details is one overriding fact: total state spending would rise by 9.3 per cent under this "austerity" budget for 1991. Medicaid reimbursement rates would rise, as would unemployment-insurance benefits and AFDC benefits (already the highest in the nation). The state would hire 171 environmental regulators and pay for them with stiff regulatory fees. Two one-thousand-bed drug-treatment campuses would cost taxpayers $80 million. The Museum of the American Indian will get $5.5 million. A health-insurance system for children will cost $30 million the first year. All in all the governor is requesting a $4.4-billion rise in state spending for 1991, the largest dollar increase in the state's history. Contrast this to the situation in bordering states—Massachusetts, Connecticut, and Pennsylvania—all of which released 1991 budgets shortly after New York did. While each of them acknowledges economic difficulty, no other governor in the region requested a penny of additional taxes. Instead, each of them proposed that spending growth be brought into line with the current level of revenues. In Massachusetts, Governor Dukakis proposed that state spending be cut by 1.6 per cent in 1991. The governors of Pennsylvania and Connecticut called for spending increases of 1.9 per cent and 5.8 per cent, respectively.

Excessive spending, not insufficient revenues, is the cause of New York's problem. During Cuomo's eight years in office, state spending has increased 104.4 per cent, more than three times as much as inflation. In 1988, the latest year for which uniform data are available, New York spent $2,816 per capita—42 per cent more than the national average. If Albany cut its per-capita spending to the level of the next highest state, Delaware, it would save $3 billion. If New York's state and local governments cut per-capita spending to Massachusetts' level, taxpayers would save $19 billion per year.

The governor of New York can wield both a line-item veto and broad impoundment authority—levers for spending control that George Bush can only dream about. Mario Cuomo's predecessor employed those powers with telling results. Between 1975 and 1983 state spending increased 79.5 per cent, versus inflation of 95.8 per cent. While Hugh Carey was governor, the rest of the nation increased spending at a faster clip than New York. Unfortunately, Mr. Cuomo seems determined to secure New York's reputation as the nation's highest-spending state.

L. Miscellaneous

Reinventing Congress

October 4, 1993

Al Gore's plan to cut federal employment may have missed the area of government responsible for most of the problem: congressional staffs. Over the past twenty years the number of people employed by the House and Senate has almost doubled, while the total federal workforce has remained nearly constant.

Table 1-54. Big Government; Bigger Congress				
	Number of employees			% Increase
	1970	**1980**	**1992**	**1970–92**
Senate	4,105	6,995	7,820	90.5
House	7,022	11,406	12,236	74.6
Total Federal Gov't.	2.10 mil.	2.18 mil.	2.20 mil.	4.8

Source: Office of Personnel Management.

In 1970 it cost $343 million to run Congress. By 1980 it cost $1.2 billion. Congress is now a $2.8 billion-a-year operation, manned by 20,000 House and Senate staffers plus an additional 18,000 employees assigned to CBO, GAO, the Library of Congress, and other legislative agencies. In 1992 the average congressman had a staff of 28 people. As recently as 1960, congressmen got by with staffs that averaged only 9.

Some lawmakers insist that they need large staffs to match the resources available to the executive branch. Yet most new staff are assigned to district offices where they perform "constituency service," a euphemism that covers everything from helping the lady who didn't get her Social Security check to helping local businessmen procure federal contracts. In 1972 one out of eight Senate staffers, and fewer than a quarter of their counterparts in the House, were based in the home state. By 1990 more than a third of Senate staffers and more than 40 per cent of House staffers were based in the home state. More than any other factor—including the disproportionate share of PAC money going to incumbents—constituency service has killed competition in congressional races.

The staff infection has caused other major problems. In the name of oversight, a growing number of Washington-based staff spend their days meddling in the affairs of executive agencies. Subcommittees routinely order Cabinet agencies to hire more workers in a particular location, even when the district manager says they are not needed. The Veterans Administration, with more than 200,000 employees, needs congressional approval to fire just three workers. Committee staffs write detailed rules for federal programs, and insert exceptions for particular individuals and businesses.

When the political pressure to cut costs becomes inexorable, Congress slows things up with paperwork. The Pentagon, for example, is bombarded with more than 100,000 official written congressional inquiries each year. In the late 1970s four subcommittees wrote defense legislation; today 24 committees and 40 subcommittees oversee defense.

While handcuffing opponents, Congress exempts itself from most oversight. Neither OMB nor Al Gore can make any recommendations regarding the $2.8 billion legislative budget. Likewise, the Freedom of Information Act and key provisions of the Ethics in Government Act apply only to the executive branch of government.

Meanwhile, the Washington-based staff seems abysmally ignorant of vital policy issues. A recent survey of 100 congressional offices conducted by syndicated columnist Matthew Lesko found that 71 were unaware of existing federal health-care programs available to the uninsured, such as the Hill-Burton program which requires hospitals and nursing homes to provide free care to those who have trouble paying their bills.

Congressional staff has become so big that it doesn't know what it is doing—or what it has already done.

Buck(ley)ing the Trend

April 1993

The past few years have not been good ones for the magazine industry. Paid circulation of U.S. magazines, after growing from 280.7 million in 1980 to 366.1 in 1989, has slumped for the first time in twenty years. Magazine advertising has lost ground to radio, TV, and direct mail. After adjusting for inflation, ad revenues reported by magazine publishers were lower in 1992 than they were in 1989. Postal rates and paper costs are higher.

The key word in this $8 billion industry is *shakeout.* In recent years *Psychology Today, Manhattan Inc.,* and Condé Nast's *Woman* have closed for lack of advertising. Media directories show that the number of weekly and bi-weekly periodicals plummeted from a peak of 2,258 in 1987 to 837 in 1992. Total periodical employment has shrunk from an all-time high of 130,800 in November 1990 to 124,400 at the end of 1992.

National Review's performance stands out against this bleakness:

Table 1-55. National Review: An Increasing Presence

	Average NR Circulation	NR Subscribers per 100,000 U.S. Households	Subscription Price (12 Months) Current $	1993 $
1980	89,828	111	$24.00	$41.45
1989	134,018	144	39.00	44.78
1990	148,645	159	38.00	41.39
1991	153,075	162	57.00	59.56
1992	165,325	174	57.00	58.70
1993	201,138 *	209	57.00	57.00

* First three months.

Source: Audit Bureau of Circulation.

From 1989 to the first quarter of this year, NR's circulation grew by 67,000, a rise of exactly 50 per cent. By comparison, real GDP grew by a paltry 3.1 per cent, and the number of U.S. households—the universe of potential NR subscribers—was up only 3.7 per cent over the same period. At present 209 of every 100,000 households gets NR. If circulation continues growing at its first-quarter rate, within thirty years half of all households will be NR subscribers.

What's good for NR may not be good for the country, however. Traditionally, we have done best while opposing the policies of liberal Presidents. "People look to us for the real story, as an alternative to the left-wing media bias that gets worse when we have a Democrat in the White House," says NR's publisher, Ed Capano. This might explain why circulation grew rapidly during the Sixties and so far this year.

But what about the 1980s? "Ronald Reagan made conservatism a respectable political position for middle-America, and broadened our appeal tremendously," according to Capano. Reagan also touted NR as his favorite publication, thus helping raise the magazine's reputation beyond the conservative ghetto. President Reagan's popularity, of course, was augmented by a robust economy and low inflation rate—all of which helped NR. By contrast, the reverse-Reaganism and economic malaise of the Bush years made us an opposition organ once again, albeit with even happier circulation results than during previous liberal Administrations.

Politics doesn't explain everything, however. In recent years *National Review* has discovered mass marketing. NR commercials featuring William F. Buckley Jr. and Charlton Heston are aired nightly on CNN. A direct mail blitz soliciting 500,000 potential subscribers in January and February netted a 2 per cent-plus rate of return.

Political magazines were recently characterized by the publishing industry magazine *Folio* as "a difficult field for publishers— circulations are low, and most of the products are subsidized." At least on the Right this is wrong.

Punitive Damages

November 4, 1991

Vice President Dan Quayle this summer questioned whether the nation really needs 730,000 lawyers—70 per cent of the world's total—or 18 million new civil cases each year—one case for every ten adult Americans. He may have had the economy in mind.

A study conducted by University of Texas finance professor Stephen P. Magee found that predatory litigation reduced GNP by 10 per cent below its potential during the 1980s—a cost of about $1 million per lawyer. Only a fraction of this—some $80 billion—reflects legal fees, damage awards, and higher liability-insurance premiums. Most of the costs are indirect: the time wasted fighting spurious claims; the loss of potential engineers, doctors, and scientists to the legal profession; and the withholding of new products or technology from the marketplace to minimize legal exposure. The "tort tax" allegedly accounts for about 30 per cent of the price of a stepladder and 95 per cent of the price of childhood vaccines.

Surprisingly enough, scientists and engineers outnumber lawyers 4.8 to 1 in the U.S. In other nations—especially Japan—the ratio is considerably higher, as is economic productivity as measured by the increase in output per hour.

Table 1-56. The Case of Lawyers vs. Productivity

	Lawyers per 100,000 Population	Scientists & Engineers per Lawyer	Output per Hour (Avg. Ann. Growth, 1973–90)
Japan	11	115.5	4.4%
UK	82	14.5	3.3
Germany	111	9.1	2.8
U.S.	281	4.8	2.5

Source: Stephen Magee, University of Texas.

It's absurd to blame our sub-par productivity growth solely on a surfeit of lawyers. However, Magee's study found a universal tendency for economic growth to be negatively related to lawyers. At one extreme are Japan, Hong Kong, and Singapore—countries where lawyers comprise less than 1 per cent of the workforce. At the other extreme in his sample of 24 countries were Chile, Uruguay, and the U.S.—nations where lawyers account for nearly 5 per cent of white-collar workers, and where per-capita GNP grew at less than 2 per cent per annum between 1960 and 1985.

The legal profession has become increasingly engaged in redistributing property and income rather than protecting it. Punitive-damage awards are fingered by the White House Council on Competitiveness as a prime suspect. Once limited to cases of criminal intent, awards that exceed actual damages are now routinely bestowed in negligence and lesser civil cases. A survey of 24,000 jury trials found that the average award increased (in constant dollars) from $43,000 in the period from 1965 to 1969, to $729,000 in the years between 1980 and 1984—a jump of 1,500 per cent.

Pre-trial discovery, in which lawyers request obscene amounts of documents from the other side, has become a thinly disguised form of economic terrorism, forcing the less well endowed party to end the proceedings. One result is that when jury awards are made, the lawyers are the big winners: successful claimants receive only 15 per cent of litigation costs. To stymie these abuses the Council proposes that the initial round of discovery be "free," punitive awards be capped, and losers in certain suits pay the costs incurred by the winner. Magee proposes that a 20 per cent federal tax be imposed on the "excessive claims" of predatory claimants.

The prospects for reform are not good. About 42 per cent of the House, 62 per cent of the Senate, and an overwhelming majority of the judiciary are attorneys.

Charity or Suicide?

September 9, 1991

If Americans went on a spending binge during the 1980s, then charity seems to have been one of the most sought-after baubles. Charitable donations by individuals rose from $64.7 billion (1990 dollars) in 1980 to $102 billion in 1989, an increase of 57.7 per cent. At the same time, notes Richard McKenzie of the Center for the Study of American Business in St. Louis, real consumer spending rose a mere 33 per cent, and consumer borrowing—universally perceived as excessive during the decade—rose 48 per cent.

Moreover, after declining relative to national income during the Seventies, charitable donations rose from 2.1 per cent of income in 1979 to a record 2.7 per cent in 1989. McKenzie is unable to explain exactly why the charitable impulse grew. His statistical model finds, not surprisingly, that charitable donations rise along with per-capita income (people have more to give), with tax rates (the government, in effect, subsidizes a larger share of the tax-deductible donation), and with population (more potential donors and beneficiaries). Yet after taking these factors into account, Americans still gave $28 billion more in 1989 than would have been predicted based on earlier statistical relationships. Some other factor must have been responsible—perhaps a resurgence of religion.

Do Americans get what they pay for when they give to charity? A detailed study of the 1987 budgets of three health charities—the American Cancer Society, American Heart Association, and American Lung Association—found that less than one-quarter of their collections is used to fund medical research. Up to 33 per cent of their income is diverted to management salaries and fundraising, while other funds are used to amass real-estate, stock, and bond holdings, according to a June 1990 report of the Capital Research Center. In the case of the Lung Association, only four-tenths of 1 per cent of total income actually went to help people afflicted with disease.

Individuals are understandably taken in by some charities. Corporations, on the other hand, seem knowingly to give large sums to organizations that are clearly anti-business. In *Patterns of Corporate Philanthropy: The "Suicidal Impulse,"* economist Thomas DiLorenzo examines donations given by 146 major corporations to public-policy research organizations. DiLorenzo ranked these organizations from radical Left, defined as those favoring "government ownership and control of industry, wage and price controls, and industrial planning," to classical liberal, defined as groups that advocate "a minimal role for government, unrestricted free enterprise within the rule of law."

Of the total $28.2 million donated to policy groups in 1988, $17.5 million, or 62 per cent, went to left-of-center organizations. In the area of energy and environmental policy, left-of-center groups received $57.38 for each $1 going to conservative groups. While most businesses profess support for increased competition and parental choice in education, all but $72,600 of the $537,600 donated by corporations to policy groups in this area went to liberal groups.

In a foreword to the study, Pete duPont speculates on possible motives. Corporations may regard left-of-center institutions as more predictable, and therefore "safer," to support. Giving to such groups may reduce the chances that one's corporation will be singled out for criticism—a kind of "hush money." In the end the perverse giving may simply reflect ignorance on the part of executives, many of whom are oblivious to policy nuances. Since there are more think tanks on the Left than on the Right, even random donations will produce a left-of-center bias.

The Vanishing Voter

November 19, 1990

According to a poll taken four weeks before election day, only 27 per cent of the American people think Congress is doing a good job, and two-thirds believe it's time to throw the rascals out. But if recent history is any guide, few congressmen need worry about their re-election prospects:

Table 1-57. Voters and Incumbents

| | Percentage of Voting Age Population Casting Votes | | House Incumbents | |
	For President	For Repre-sentatives	Number Defeated	Percentage Re-elected
1974		35.9	48	87.7
1976	53.5	48.9	16	95.8
1978		34.9	24	93.7
1980	52.6	47.4	37	90.7
1982		38.0	39	90.1
1984	53.1	47.7	19	95.4
1986		33.4	8	98.0
1988	50.2	45.0	7	98.5

Source: Bureau of the Census; *Congressional Quarterly.*

Only seven incumbent congressmen—1.5 per cent of those seeking re-election—lost in 1988. Five were involved in issues of moral turpitude, leaving at most two rejected on the basis of policy issues.

In fact, winning votes seems to be less important here than strengthening institutions that make voters irrelevant. Creative redistricting on the part of state legislatures has given rise to the "safe seat": one in four House members will be unopposed by a major-party candidate this year, as will four senators. Thanks to gerrymandering, Democrats were able to win 60 per cent of House seats in 1988 with only 53 per cent of the total vote.

Re-election science took a quantum leap forward in 1974. That year's campaign-finance law limited individual campaign contributions to $1,000, sharply restricting the ability of political unknowns to raise funds. Political-action committees, supposed to neutralize the role of money in political campaigns, have instead tilted the playing field further in the incumbents' favor. In 1986, for example, PAC money represented 26 per cent of the campaign funds of the average Democrat, versus 10 per cent for the average Republican.

To limit PAC influence Congress seems inclined to have congressional campaigns partly or wholly financed by tax money. Unfortunately, neither spending limits nor public financing will deprive incumbents of a massive edge. Congressmen already receive public financing in the form of franked mail and staff support worth more than $1.5 million in this election cycle (1989–90), according to the Heritage Foundation. The postal privilege alone will cost taxpayers $136 million ($311,000 per congressman), dwarfing the $102 million donated by PACs and exceeding the $130 million contributed by individuals to all House candidates during the last election cycle. The average incumbent spends more on postage than the average challenger spends on his entire election campaign.

In the long run the biggest threat to political competition is voter apathy. During the last off-year election two-thirds of potential voters stayed at home. Of course, that was before the S&L scandal, a weakening economy, and "read my lips." If 1982 is any indication, the bad times will bring forth a significantly larger voter turnout. Unfortunately, there is no guarantee that that will change appreciably the rate at which incumbents are returned to office.

Crime Pays

June 25, 1990

Drugs, demographics, poverty, unemployment. Each undeniably plays a role in fostering criminal behavior. But according to the economic theory of crime, criminals are essentially rational individuals. They chose a career in crime only after weighing the expected benefits against the expected costs.

The cost of crime to criminals, as measured by the likelihood of imprisonment, has fallen dramatically over the past three decades. A study by the Dallas-based National Center for Policy Analysis (NCPA) uncovers a political facet to this trend:

Table 1-58. Crime and Punishment

Administration	Annual Average		Probability of Imprisonment
	Felony Crimes	Imprisonment	
Eisenhower	2,567,398	81,643	3.18%
Kennedy	3,783,223	90,140	2.38
Johnson	5,430,226	80,570	1.48
Nixon	8,211,400	99,784	1.22
Ford	10,938,290	120,936	1.11
Carter	11,879,100	131,835	1.11
Reagan	12,677,135	184,828	1.46

Source: National Center for Policy Analysis.

The odds started to tilt dramatically in favor of criminals during the Johnson years, when the number of people sent to state and federal prison actually declined. Nixon made law and order a political issue, and by the Ford Administration annual imprisonments were 50 per cent higher than the average for the Johnson years. The rise in imprisonments slowed during the Carter years.

An abrupt change for the better occurred during the Reagan years. Between 1981 and 1986 (the latest figures available), the rate of growth of serious crimes fell slightly, while the number of criminals going to prison increased by more than 37 per cent. Overall, criminals faced a 32 per cent higher probability of incarceration during the Reagan years than during the Carter or Ford years. Still, the probability of doing time for criminal activity today is less than half what it was during the Eisenhower years, and, to make matters worse, prison overcrowding has resulted in shorter prison sentences. The NCPA study calculates that after taking into account the probabilities of arrest, prosecution, conviction, and imprisonment, a perpetrator of a serious crime in the United States today can expect to spend about eight days in prison. In 1950 criminals could expect to spend 24 days in prison. The revolving door is spinning three times as fast now.

We are unlikely to reduce the crime rate to the level of the 1950s without first raising the expected cost of crime to criminals to the levels prevailing then. This invariably will require more prison space. America is already in the midst of the biggest prison construction boom in history: at the end of 1989 prisons held 235,000 more convicts than six years earlier, a rise of 53.5 per cent. One out of every 364 Americans is now in prison, and with another 296,000 in local jails, 362,000 on parole, and 2.4 million on probation, one out of every 69 Americans is currently in the purview of the corrections establishment.

With prison construction costs averaging $50,000 per bed, financially strapped states are likely to resist further expansion. A short-sighted policy, considering that crimes committed by each released prisoner are estimated to cost society about $430,000 in losses to the victims.

Cold Fusion and Property Rights

June 16, 1989

It would have been nice, but the odds were against it from the start. Most technological change is evolutionary, the product of many small accretions of knowledge rather than a single quantum leap forward such as the Utah fusion experiment originally appeared to be. And if data on patents issued in this country are any indication, new technologies are increasingly likely to be spawned abroad rather than in the United States:

Table 1-59. U.S Patents Granted, by Country of Inventor

	U.S.	Japan	All Other Countries	Foreign Share (%)
1971	55,984	4,029	18,304	28.5
1980	37,356	7,124	17,339	39.6
1983	32,871	8,793	15,196	42.2
1987	47,711	17,288	24,386	46.6
1988	44,570	16,984	22,718	47.1

Source: National Science Foundation.

In 1983 there were 23,000 fewer patents granted to U.S. nationals than in 1971, a 40 per cent decline, and although there has been a recovery during the last five years, the figure remains well below its earlier peak. Meanwhile, the share of U.S. patents going to foreign inventors, which had been as low as 18.6 per cent in 1963, approached 50 per cent last year.

The decline in patents granted to U.S. inventors does not mean we are devoting less of our resources to basic research and development. In fact, R&D spending in 1983, the low year for U.S. patent grants, was 40 per cent higher in real terms than in 1971, the peak year for patents. R&D spending continues to rise, with last year's $126 billion representing a 24 per cent real increase from 1983; this country now spends more on R&D than Japan, West Germany, France, and the UK combined, according to the National Science Foundation.

L. Miscellaneous

To a great extent the patent decline reflects shortcomings of the patent system itself, particularly its failure adequately to protect the intellectual property rights of U.S. innovators. A loophole in our trade laws, for example, allows foreigners to use patented U.S. production processes without the approval of the American patent-holder. Domestic competitors can also violate the property rights of the patent-holder by going abroad to use the patented technology, and shipping the goods back to the United States. The laws of virtually every other major industrialized country, including Japan, forbid this practice.

In theory, patent laws allow inventors to make their ideas public without relinquishing the economic benefits, conferring upon them the right to exclude others from making, selling, or otherwise using their invention or discovery for 17 years. In practice the cumbersome and often expensive patent-review process prevents many patented ideas from reaching the marketplace before well over half of the 17 year period has gone by. Understandably many firms and individuals are opting to keep new processes secret rather than to reveal them via the patent process, thereby denying society access to bits of technological knowledge, some of which, if made available to the right people, might make the next fusion experiment a success.

They Never Learn

October 28, 1988

In the mid Sixties a group headed by Professor James Coleman, then of Johns Hopkins University, administered standardized intelligence and achievement tests to approximately 605,000 elementary- and secondary-school children in schools spread throughout all fifty states and the District of Columbia. Coleman and his collaborators had expected to be able to explain the great differences in average test scores between white and minority-group students by differences in the quality of their schools. He found, instead, that black schools did not spend significantly less than white schools and did not have larger classes, fewer or less adequate textbooks, less qualified teachers, etc., etc.

More important, the Coleman Report found no tendency for students from a given socio-economic background to perform significantly better in newer schools with high per-pupil expenditures than in older schools with low per-pupil expenditures.

These findings—although corroborated in subsequent studies done in this country and Europe, as well as in a second Coleman Report (1981), which found that, on average, students in private schools achieve more, even with larger classes and fewer resources, than those in public schools—are still hotly disputed by the public-education establishment.

The most recent salvo was fired by Albert Shanker, who accused the Department of Education of fudging numbers in a chart that showed steady growth in elementary- and secondary-school expenditures on one side, and a steady decline in SAT scores on the other. Mr. Shanker complains that the expenditures were in current dollars, not adjusted for inflation, while the SAT scores, which go from 400 to 1,600, were displayed on a graph that went only from 800 to 1,000.

Unfortunately for Shanker's argument, the negative relationship between expenditures and test scores persists even after these changes are made, and is more pronounced when outlays are viewed on a per-student basis. After peaking at 980 in 1963, average SAT scores fell steadily to a low of 890 in 1980, after which they rebounded to 906 in 1985 (Table 1-60).

170

Table 1-60. Elementary/Secondary Public Education Spending and Achievement

	Total (Billions)		Per Pupil,	Average
	Current $	1985 $	1985 $	SAT Score
1951	7.3	30.2	1,295	970
1963	21.3	75.1	1,971	980
1970	45.5	124.6	2,983	948
1975	70.6	138.4	3,329	906
1980	104.1	130.9	3,470	890
1985	147.6	147.6	4,051	906

Source: U.S. Department of Education.

Real per-pupil expenditures rose throughout this period, and in fact increased at a faster clip during the 1960s, when the decline in scores first became evident, than during the 1950s, when scores were generally on the rise. Interestingly, the rate of decrease in average test scores abated somewhat during the 1975–80 period, just when the rate of increase in real per-pupil expenditures was also declining.

Public-school enrollment fell by more than 6.5 million students between 1970 and 1985, and the ratio of pupils to teachers fell from 22.3 to 17.9.

So, teachers might argue that they are able to provide considerably more individualized attention in today's smaller classes than their counterparts in 1960, and that the quality of the learning experience has improved. This assertion is belied by the decline in SAT scores, as well as a recent Department of Education report showing that average class size in Japan is approximately 35, about twice the U.S. level, and yet Japanese students do much better than Americans in math.

In 1950, public schools educated 16.6 per cent of the U.S. population at a cost of 2.2 per cent of the nation's GNP; in 1985 it took 3.7 per cent of a much larger GNP to educate the same proportion of the population. The reasons behind the test-score decline are obviously more complex than just the financial resources being applied to education.

M. Federal Regulations

The Re-regulation President

September 14, 1992

In July, a House committee passed a bill requiring that all cans, jars, bottles, and other containers used in the food industry be recyclable. The Resource Conservation and Recovery Act (RCRA) would cost consumers some $30 billion a year to rectify a problem that, even the EPA admits, "presents relatively low environmental risks."

Even without RCRA George Bush will, in four years, have undone the Reagan Administration's eight-year effort to reduce government regulations:

Table 1-61. Regulations and Regulators

	Cost of Administering Federal Regulations (Billions of 1987$)	Regulatory Employees	Pages in the *Federal Register*
1970	$ 2.322	69,946	20,036
1980	8.780	121,708	87,012
1988	9.558	104,360	53,376
1992	11.276	124,994	67,716

Source: Center for the Study of American Business.

After falling by 17,000 during the Reagan years, the number of federal employees devoted to issuing and enforcing regulations will hit an all-time high of 124,994 this year. Under Bush the cost of administering federal regulatory programs has risen 18 per cent, in constant dollars. An additional 14,000 pages of the *Federal Register* are required just to list the rules and regulations added since George Bush's inauguration.

More important, the total cost of federal regulations, including the indirect costs borne by business and consumers, is between $430 billion and $562 billion, according to the latest Federal Budget. By comparison, income-tax revenues in fiscal 1991 totaled $468 billion.

172

Part of the blame rests with particular individuals. EPA Administrator William Reilly, for example, expanded the scope of the "wetlands" designation within days of assuming his position. A Heritage Foundation study reports that land under water for as little as seven days a year, as well as land that is dry at the surface but moist 18 inches down, is subject to federal control, preventing many farmers from planting their own land.

Similarly, Bush appointees at the Department of Justice and the Federal Trade Commission are pursuing far more activist agendas in areas such as civil rights and anti-trust than their Reagan-era counterparts.

The 1990 Clean Air Act will eventually add $25 to $35 billion to the $100 billion that business already spends on pollution controls, according to Murray Weidenbaum. Another 1990 law, the Americans with Disabilities Act, requires businesses, landlords, and public transportation to make their premises accessible to disabled individuals. Robert Genetski, an economic consultant, estimates that the physical modifications required at office buildings and hospitals alone will cost $65 billion. Economic regulations, including international trade barriers, farm price supports, the remaining regulation of airline travel, and the (recently raised) minimum wage, cost as much as $256 billion each year, in the form of lower output due to the regulations, plus the redistribution of wealth from those harmed by regulations to those who are made richer because of them.

Most regulations either do not achieve the results claimed by their supporters, or have unintended (negative) consequences. Occupational Safety and Health Administration regulations, for example, have not lowered accident or illness rates in the workforce, according to most studies. The law requiring that all auto manufacturers meet a federal fuel-economy standard (27.5 mpg in 1991) has forced auto manufacturers to make lighter cars, thereby increasing automobile fatalities by 2,200 and 3,900 per year. When regulations do save lives, they do so at exorbitant cost: as much as $5.7 *trillion* per premature death for certain Consumer Product Safety regulations.

With pro-growth tax legislation held hostage to election-year politics, regulatory relief may be the economy's only hope.

Getting Hot in Rio

June 22, 1992

As complicated as the matter is, it appears that magnetic storms on the sun may have more to do with the earth's climate than the build-up of greenhouse gases on earth, according to a recent study by scientists at the George C. Marshall Institute.

Rising solar activity recorded over the past 100 years is consistent with a 0.7 per cent brightening of the sun—enough to explain the entire 0.5°C global warming over this period. The sun's pervasive influence is also confirmed by analysis of the amount of Carbon-14 in ancient tree rings. The isotope, known to fluctuate with solar activity, rises and falls by substantial amounts every 200 to 300 years, invariably presaging major changes in climate.

The greenhouse model, meanwhile, cannot explain the rapid rise in global temperature in the decades prior to 1940, or why average temperature dropped between 1940 and 1970, a period of rapid growth in CO_2 emissions but declining solar activity. This suggests that the worst-case scenario—a doubling of CO_2 and other greenhouse gases over the next century—would raise global temperatures by less than 1°C, and maybe less than 0.5°C.

The lack of hard greenhouse evidence hasn't stopped participants in the Rio "Earth Summit" from pushing for caps on CO_2 emissions. (See Table 1-62.) The world's advanced nations, with less than 25 per cent of world population, produce roughly 60 per cent of annual CO_2 emissions. If the UN, in its infinite wisdom, were to

Table 1-62. Share of Global Emissions
Population, and GNP, 1986

	U.S.	Other Industrial Nations	Less-Developed Countries
CO_2 Emissions	23%	37%	30%
Population	5	18	77
GNP	26	58	16

Source: Brookings Institution.

174

distribute CO_2 quotas on a per-capita basis, the industrialized nations would have about a third (the U.S. less than one-quarter) of what is needed to produce at current levels.

The less developed countries (LDCs), on the other hand, could reap a cash windfall by selling their excess CO_2 entitlements to developed nations. The market price for such quotas, according to a recent study, could reach $25 to $75 per ton, implying a transfer of up to $200 billion annually from the developed to the developing world. (Foreign aid from the OECD nations to LDCs is, by contrast, a mere $50 billion.)

A prudent policy would weigh economic costs against likely environmental benefits. A 20 per cent reduction in CO_2 emissions, favored by many Greens, would require that gasoline prices increase by $1.30 per gallon (1990 dollars), oil prices by $60 a barrel, and electricity rates double. According to the Department of Energy, this would cost the economy nearly $100 billion by the end of the decade.

Global Warming or Hot Air?

April 29, 1991

If we do nothing, global warming will eventually transform the nation's midsection into a desert, and put many of our coastal cities under water—at least that is the scenario proffered by environmental groups and the media.

Recent studies show, however, that a potentially dangerous cooling trend has been under way for most of the earth's history: there was five to ten times more carbon dioxide in the atmosphere one hundred million years ago, and the average temperature was 9°F to 18°F warmer than now. Fred Singer, a professor of environmental sciences at the University of Virginia, suggests that the "climate optimum" occurred around 1100 A.D., when Greenland was indeed green, and the area the Vikings called Vinland (thought to be Labrador) was warm enough for grape growing. The 0.9°F rise in average global temperature recorded since 1880 may simply be a return to normal following the "Little Ice Age" of 1600 to 1860.

In any event, it's not at all clear that man is responsible for the warming trend. Although carbon dioxide accounts for about half of all greenhouse gases, human activity accounts for only 5 per cent of all carbon dioxide. If economic activity caused global warming, the temperature rise should be accelerating, but it isn't. A recent study by Kent Jeffries of the Competitive Enterprise Institute shows that almost all warming in this century took place in the 1920s and 1930s, long before most of the emission of trace gases by humans. The earth cooled off from 1940 to the mid-Seventies, and got hotter from 1975 to 1980. Despite the recent string of abnormally warm years, the Eighties as a whole exhibited no discernible temperature trend.

Systematic global measurements suggest that any rise in temperature is occurring mainly at night, in the winter, and in the northern hemisphere. If this pattern persists, it will mean longer growing seasons, fewer frosts, but no increase in the likelihood of drought.

To the chagrin of environmentalists, the scientific community has largely retracted its earlier apocalyptic warnings. During the record heat of 1988 theorists were predicting that a doubling of carbon dioxide would raise global temperature by 8.1°F to 10.8°F. The scientific consensus is now below 2.7°F. Polar ice caps, far from melting, appear to be growing. So while most climatologists in 1980 were predicting a thirty-foot rise in future sea levels, that estimate had fallen to three to five feet by 1988, and to 12 inches in the current worst-case forecast, according to Jeffries. The dearth of hard evidence attesting to human culpability has not deterred those who think a little suffering is in order. A UN panel has urged international action to reduce greenhouse gases, and several bills in Congress would force U.S. industry to cap or roll back its carbon-dioxide emissions unilaterally via the imposition of a "carbon tax."

Even the most draconian restrictions would do little to halt an inevitable increase in greenhouse gases, most of which is occurring outside of the United States. Professor Singer believes that at best we might delay the doubling of these gases by five years—from 2040 to 2045—but at the cost of a trillion dollars in lost output.

There are far less costly ways of dealing with this problem. U.S. forests, for example, already consume more carbon dioxide each year than U.S. industry emits. Only a *growing* forest consumes this gas, however, so opening up more federal lands for private logging and reforestation would cleanse the atmosphere even more. Creating similar property rights in Brazil and other Third World countries could end the indiscriminate slashing and burning of Third World forests that some scientists believe is the leading source of greenhouse gases.

Our understanding of the link—if any—between economic activity and global warming will be substantially improved in a few years. In the interim there are sensible, free-market responses, which make sense even if no link is found.

Onward and Upward

June 11, 1990

Has airline deregulation worked? Proponents point to the great popularization of commercial aviation since 1978: the number of passengers nearly doubled, reaching 456 million in 1988, while air fares per passenger mile have declined 20 per cent in constant dollars. In 1971, half of all Americans had never flown; by 1988, 75 per cent had. And despite the airline-industry shakeout, consumers enjoy more choice now than a decade ago. DOT figures show that airline passengers could choose from two or more airlines for 89 per cent of their trips in 1988, up from 69 per cent in 1978. Air travelers can choose among five or more airlines for 29 per cent of their trips, a variety unheard of before deregulation.

Unfortunately, problems at certain hub airports are giving airline deregulation a bad name. While the nation's largest airline—Texas Air's combine of Continental and Eastern—accounts for only 16 per cent of total U.S. market, many hub airports are virtually monopolized by a single carrier. U.S. Air, for example, has 84 per cent of all flights out of Pittsburgh, TWA has 82 per cent out of St. Louis, and Northwest has 80 per cent out of Minneapolis. Passengers embarking from such "fortress hubs" are increasingly at the mercy of a single airline, and pay fares that have been found to be as much as 50 per cent higher than the "Standard Industry Fare Level." The apparent price gouging has led even Alfred Kahn, the father of airline deregulation, to recommend re-regulating fares on certain hub routes.

The hub-spoke route configuration per se is not the problem. On the contrary, feeding flights into a central hub where people can change planes enables the airlines to serve more cities with more frequent flights, using fewer planes. Although hubbing increases the possibility of having to change planes, the old two-, three-, and four-stop flights passengers used to endure are a thing of the past. Average travel time has decreased. And because airlines can choose the appropriate size of plane to fit the traffic between each pair of cities, a higher percentage of seats is now filled—which helps to explain why fares have declined.

In theory deregulation allows any airline to enter any market. Excessive fares at hub airports should attract a swarm of competitors, driving the fare level down. In practice the supply of airport gates and landing and take-off slots at hub airports is far smaller than the demand, with the incumbent airlines often wielding veto power over proposed expansion. As explained in a recent study by the Reason Foundation's Robert W. Poole, the veto power often derives from long-term leases signed by the airlines with local airport authorities during pre-deregulation days. Airport operators were perfectly willing to give airlines long-term leases—as long as fifty years—with clauses stipulating that a majority of the existing tenants could veto the issuance of bonds backed by lease revenues to finance airport expansion. Back when the Civil Aviation Board (CAB) restricted airline competition, those clauses were of little importance. Now airlines use them to maintain their monopolies.

What we have is not a failure of airline deregulation but a failure to deregulate airports. Poole believes the artificial shortage of airport capacity could best be remedied by allowing cities to privatize their airports. A profit-making airport would have every incentive to respond to excess demand by increasing the supply of gates and landing slots, financing these additions by charging passengers, airlines, and concessionaires.

The cities would also reap financial benefits. The nation's largest airport, Chicago's O'Hare, has an estimated market value of at least $1.7 billion, which would generate $29.5 million in annual property-tax payments. All in all, Poole says, privatizing the top fifty airports could generate nearly $24 billion in one-time revenues for local governments, and increase property-tax revenues by $391 million each year.

Clearing the Air

March 5, 1990

The Environmental Protection Agency reports that emissions of sulphur dioxide—the substance implicated in acid rain—fell 35 per cent between 1978 and 1987. Airborne lead declined 88 per cent during that period; carbon monoxide 32 per cent; dust, soot, and particulate matter 21 per cent; and ground-level ozone, the main constituent of smog, declined 16 per cent.

Why, then, is the environment perceived to be in such bad shape? Environmentalist jargon may be partly responsible. We are told, for example, that 89 million Americans live in "non-attainment areas"—cities where air quality does not meet the national ozone standard. "Non-attainment" occurs when the level of "volatile organic compounds" (VOCs)—fumes emitted by gasoline, paints, solvents, etc.—exceeds 0.12 parts per million for at least one hour on as few as four days over a three-year period:

Table 1-63. Five Worst Cities Based on EPA Ozone Standards

1986–88

	1987 Population (Millions)	VOC Level (Parts per Million)	Percentage above Standard
Los Angeles	8.3	0.34	183
New York City	8.5	0.22	83
Chicago	6.2	0.20	67
Houston	3.2	0.19	58
Baltimore *	2.9	0.18	50

* Tied with six other cities.

Source: Center for the Study of American Business.

But a far different picture of air quality emerges when you look at a more representative set of facts (see Table 1-64). Angelenos obviously live in the area with the poorest air quality, but they breathe air that meets ozone standards 97.3 per cent of the time. Almost all other "non-attainment" areas actually meet federal ozone standards more than 99.4 per cent of the time.

Unfortunately, federal policy in this area is designed as if the exceptionally bad conditions that may obtain for a few hours over a

Table 1-64. Five Worst Cities Based on Percentage of Time
Ozone Standards Were Not Met

Percentage of Monitored Hours

	Above 0.12 ppm	At or Below 0.12 ppm
Los Angeles	2.67	97.33
Houston	.53	99.47
Atlantic City	.49	99.51
New York	.36	99.64
Providence	.33	99.67

Source: Center for the Study of American Business.

three-year period were typical. The Administration's Clean Air Bill would tighten tailpipe standards, reduce gasoline volatility, and require automakers to sell by 1997 at least one million cars that run on methanol. Senate amendments would go considerably further, subjecting the entire nation to the same emission standards recently adopted by California. These provisions could cost U.S. industry $34 billion per year on top of the $17 billion already spent to comply with ozone-control laws.

Is this overkill? Consider that if we stuck with current laws, most "non-attainment" cities would probably reach attainment within five years. That's because most ozone comes from pre-1983 cars, which make up less than half the current fleet. As these cars are replaced, VOC emissions could fall another 20 per cent by 1995.

Killer Regulations

November 24, 1989

Here, in no particular order, are a few laws and regulations without which more of us could live:

1. *Tort Law.* The fear of lawsuits forced 50 per cent of U.S. vaccine manufacturers to cease production between 1965 and 1985, according to liability expert Peter Huber. By 1986 the nation depended on a single supplier for vaccines against polio, rubella, measles, mumps, and rabies. The unbridled right to sue for accident damages has stymied innovation in medicine, pesticides, contraceptives, hazardous-waste disposal, small planes, and cars, while costing Americans at least $80 billion per year in direct payments and insurance costs, according to Huber.

2. *Average Fuel Economy Standards.* In response to a perceived energy crisis, Congress mandated that each car company increase the average fuel efficiency of its fleet—to 26.5 miles per gallon in 1989. Since compliance is based on the average car sold, automakers have simply raised the prices of big cars, forcing consumers to purchase the more efficient, less safe smaller cars. By one estimate the 1989 standards will cause between 2,200 and 3,900 additional fatalities, along with 10,000 to 20,000 serious injuries. As for energy conservation, each gallon of gas saved will end up costing us four dollars.

3. *The DDT Ban.* DDT was misused. It probably did, as the environmentalists charge, thin the eggshells of eagles and peregrine falcons. But it was the one cheap pesticide available, credited with stopping typhus in Europe, controlling malaria in the Third World, and increasing agricultural production throughout the world. And the newer pesticides are considerably more toxic to man: in 1985 the number of accidental poisoning incidents involving pesticides was 14 per cent higher than it was in 1973 when DDT was in use, according to a study published in the *American Journal of Public Health.*

4. *FDA Regulations.* Under pressure from AIDS sufferers and others, the Food and Drug Administration (FDA) has relented somewhat on its screening procedures for new drugs. But not nearly enough. Last December, for example, the FDA completed a high-

priority review of the ulcer drug misoprostol in "only" nine months. More than seven thousand Americans died of gastric-ulcer bleeding during this period, almost all of whom would probably have been saved by the drug.

5. *Proposition 65.* California's Proposition 65, passed in 1986, requires warning labels on over two hundred "carcinogens," defined so broadly as to include chemicals that would put individuals at risk only if exposure had been maintained for an entire lifetime. The possible effects on other, more likely modes of dying are overlooked. For example, chlorine, listed as carcinogenic, is used to prevent a much more relevant danger, the risk to children of food poisoning from nonchlorinated milk.

Doomsday Again

August 4, 1989

Greenhouse effect got you down? The ozone hole? Acid rain? AIDS? In fact, doomsday scenarios have been the rage for at least ten thousand years, according to Texas A&M economists Charles Maurice and Charles Smithson. In *The Doomsday Myth* (Hoover Institution Press, 1984) they recount mankind's uncanny ability to benefit from the seemingly disastrous raw-material shortage, health crisis, or climatic shift.

One of the most momentous and, as it turns out, fortunate economic transformations in history—the shift from nomadic hunter-gatherer to food producer—was made necessary by the retreat of the ice sheet circa 8000 B.C. Had this ancient warming trend not occurred, had part of the population not been forced to specialize in the production of food, mankind would never have achieved the manpower surplus needed to develop manufacturing, trade, and the arts. Total world population, according to some estimates, would have topped out at twenty to thirty million.

An equally profound revolution was catalyzed by the Black Plague, which killed from 35 to 65 per cent of Europe's population between 1348 and 1350, 80 per cent of the deaths coming within three days of contracting the disease.

Table 1-65. Estimated European Populations

In Millions

	1300	1400	% Decline
England	3.7	2.3	37.8
France	17.5	11.5	34.3
Germany	17.0	12.0	29.4
Italy	8.5	6.0	29.4

Source: Charles Maurice and Charles Smithson, *The Doomsday Myth* (Hoover Institution Press, 1984).

Labor suddenly became a scarce commodity. In England the initial response was a series of laws freezing wages and restricting the right of peasants to migrate to higher-paying occupations in the towns. Eventually real wages rose more than three-fold, forcing most landowners to raise sheep, which required little labor, instead of grain, which had been harvested using labor-intensive techniques unchanged from Roman times. Water power replaced manpower in the mills that turned wool into cloth, and England, a net importer of cloth before the Black Plague, was suddenly competitive enough to export to the rest of Europe.

Teddy Roosevelt's environmentalism was a reaction to the "inexorable" depletion of the nation's timber supply, a problem remediable only by reforesting the nation's commercial timberlands, according to the U.S. Forest Service. In fact, the timber gap became a timber glut long before any of the Forest Service's seedlings bore fruit. Skyrocketing timber prices induced the railroads, which had been the largest consumer of timber, to season and preserve the wood used for railroad ties, to shift from wood to metal cars, and to substitute iron, steel, or concrete for wood in bridges. Timber prices fell, and reforestation proved to be the Synfuels project of the early 1900s.

The U.S. petroleum industry was created by private entrepreneurs in response to the imminent depletion of whales and their oil. U.S. tire manufacturers began using synthetic rubber in 1940—after Japan conquered regions producing 98 per cent of all natural rubber, but before the inevitable U.S. Government project. The Iron Age supplanted the Bronze Age not because iron was deemed the superior metal, but because the supply of tin used in the manufacture of bronze was suddenly cut off.

Economic or ecological disaster is always possible, of course. The point is that when free to act in their own self-interest, individuals will minimize that probability.

Regulation Redux

March 18, 1988

Economic and social deregulation was a cornerstone of President Reagan's pledge to get the government off our collective backs. After a number of early successes, including the dismemberment of the Civil Aeronautics Board, deregulation of trucks, buses, and railroads, and cutbacks on expensive but ineffectual regulatory activity in the area of consumer and occupational safety, regulatory spending and staffing are again on the upswing.

Spending at the Federal Government's 52 major regulatory agencies will exceed $10 billion for the first time ever in 1988, a 31.2 per cent rise from 1984; during the first term, real regulatory spending fell 5 per cent. There are today more than 118,000 federal staff members, a group equal in number to the population of Peoria.

But budget outlays are only the beginning of the true economic burden of federal regulations. The Center for the Study of American Business estimates that each dollar Congress appropriates gives rise to an additional $20 of compliance costs borne by the private sector, either by requiring more costly ways of doing business, or in paperwork costs for filling out the torrent of regulatory forms and questionnaires. So we are talking about an aggregate economic burden of about $220 billion from federal regulations, nearly 5 per cent of GNP.

This might be acceptable if we could show a commensurate flow of benefits, but unfortunately the measurable benefits, if they can be found at all, fall far short of the costs. In attempting to restrict air pollution, for example, EPA now requires that costly scrubbers be used in new coal-burning electric plants regardless of the sulphur content of the coal used—a change that has produced more sulphur dioxide emissions than the previous, less costly (by $3.4 billion) alternative of mandating the use of low-sulphur coal as a means of controlling pollution.

Human lives are priceless, of course, and any regulation that saves even one is worth the cost, but the point here is that we can save more lives at less cost by spending a little more on enforcing those regulations that have lower costs per life saved, while eliminating those that are the least cost-effective. A recent study showed that the average cost per life saved varies across regulations, from as little as $100,000 for the National Highway Traffic Safety Administration's steering-column protection rule, to $132 million for the FDA's ban on DES in cattle feed. EPA's proposed restrictions on the disposal of dioxins are estimated to cost $3.2 *billion* per life saved.

Individuals can mitigate or eliminate many of the most serious risks they face by exercising personal discretion. The fatality rate from smoking, for example, is 26 times greater than the probability of dying from a job-related accident and 462 times greater than the risk of dying from air pollution. A stiff increase in the federal tax on cigarettes would likely save more lives than all federal regulatory activities combined.

N. Debt & the Economy

Some Junk!

August 9, 1993

Only a few years after they were allegedly discredited as a "Ponzi scheme" supported by the machinations of Michael Milken and Drexel Burnham, "junk" bonds are again in vogue. Investors are clamoring for high-yield corporate debt as an alternative to the rock-bottom interest rates currently paid by CDs and passbook accounts. In 1992, two years after Drexel's demise, a record $40 billion worth of new junk-bond issues were brought to market.

How have investors fared with junk bonds? For the period 1980 through 1992 the Merrill Lynch High Yield Index averaged a 13.7 per cent annual rate of return, outperforming intermediate Treasuries (12.3 per cent). The higher yield, of course, is necessary to compensate investors for the higher risks associated with these securities. Indeed, junk-bond defaults hit a record $18.9 billion (10.3 per cent of all outstanding principal) in 1991, as federal regulators forced

Table 1-66. Junk Bond Renaissance

	Number of New Issues	Principal Amount (Billions)	Junk as % All New Corp. Debt	Default Rate
1980	45	$ 1.4	3.9%	1.5%
1985	175	15.7	19.5	1.7
1986	226	33.3	21.3	3.5
1987	190	30.5	24.2	5.8
1988	160	31.1	23.1	2.7
1989	130	28.8	20.1	4.3
1990	10	1.4	1.3	10.1
1991	48	10.0	4.8	10.3
1992	245	39.8	12.5	3.4

Source: Merrill Lynch.

S&Ls and insurers to dump their junk-bond portfolios. Yet despite continued congressional overkill, default rates fell by two-thirds last year, to 3.4 per cent.

The relative riskiness of junk bonds is best measured by the "spread" between the yields of junk bonds and U.S. Treasury bonds with similar maturities. During the junk-bond debacle of 1990 and 1991, the spread was as much as 11 percentage points; in June of this year it was only 4 percentage points.

The politically inspired vendetta against junk bonds and their purveyors has obscured their considerable economic merits. Corporate restructurings usually produce smaller, less diversified, and more efficient corporations. When managers become owners, their self-interest suddenly shifts from building wasteful corporate empires to maximizing company profits. Harvard Professor Michael Jensen, in a recent article in the *Journal of Applied Corporate Finance*, estimates that stockholders gained $650 billion as a result of takeovers, mergers, LBOs, and divestitures over the period 1976 to 1990. This figure represents gains to the "sellers," or owners of the acquired company, in such transactions; it omits the allegedly "obscene" profits accruing to the "buyers"—corporate raiders.

Critics warned that higher interest costs would force highly leveraged companies to lay off workers. Research shows that although there was a loss of jobs among top management and corporate staff, the overall job growth in restructured companies was six times higher than industry averages during the 1980s. We were also told that junk-bond interest would crowd out R&D spending. In fact, real R&D expenditures reached new highs in each year of the 1975 to 1990 period.

Unfortunately, the recent surge in junk-bond issuance may not portend more economically beneficial restructurings. Federal regulations now restrict banks from funding such transactions, and state anti-takeover laws have significantly decreased the chances of successful hostile takeovers and thus the chances of a more enterprising U.S. economy. The new bonds are simply being used to refinance existing bonds at generally lower rates of interest.

Balance-Sheet Recession

January 20, 1992

Why is this recession different? Most economic downturns since World War II have been triggered by a build-up of unwanted inventories, the result of too much production relative to consumption. The current malaise, however, appears rooted in a glut of debt-financed real estate and industrial capacity. While excess inventories—and the debt incurred to finance them—can be worked off fairly quickly, it can take years for the economy to digest redundant office space, shopping malls, and industrial property.

A financial convalescence has been under way for some time. The annual growth rate of domestic debt peaked at 14.4 per cent in the last quarter of 1984, and is now below 5 per cent—the lowest rate since 1961. In 1991, for the first time since 1983, American corporations raised more money from new stock offerings than from debt. Similarly, households are liquidating auto and home-equity loans at record rates.

Most economists agree, however, that long-term growth requires more than just the repayment of old debts. A rise in the national savings rate—making more of our current income available for productive investment—is the *sine qua non* for higher living standards. Policies to increase the pool of available savings include the following:

1. *Reinstate Individual Retirement Accounts (IRAs).* The 1986 Tax Reform Act ended tax-deductible IRAs for families with incomes greater than $50,000. The results were dramatic: in 1987 IRA contributions plummeted by 60 per cent, and the personal savings rate hit a forty-year low of 3.2 per cent. Most IRAs were funded from current income, not by shifting pre-existing assets into the accounts, as many had feared. As evidence: of the taxpayers with assets of less than $2,000 who opened IRAs in 1982, 71 per cent contributed to IRAs in 1983, and 66 per cent in 1984. With such a low level of wealth to begin with, these people could never have continued funding IRAs by simply reshuffling assets. A recent study showed that economic activity stimulated by deductible IRAs would increase federal revenues by nearly $20 billion through the year 2000. But the Federal

190

Government, using a static revenue model, still views IRAs as a $6-billion "tax expenditure."

2. *Cut Capital-Gains Tax Rates.* The U.S. and Australia are the only countries in the world to tax capital gains at the same rate as ordinary income. Other developed nations, and most economists, have long since concluded that capital-gains taxes discourage investment by lowering the return. Moreover, while Australia indexes assets for inflation, the U.S. tax code ignores the problem entirely, thereby subjecting many long-held assets to affective tax rates of over 100 per cent. Such confiscatory taxation discourages investors from reinvesting accumulated gains revenues.

3. *Eliminate Double Taxation of Dividends.* By allowing corporations to deduct interest but not dividends, the current tax code encourages debt over equity, perhaps contributing to the current "balance-sheet recession." The double taxation of equity income is a major factor behind our high cost of capital *vis-à-vis* Japan—where dividends paid to individuals are not taxed. The anti-equity bias is especially burdensome for newer and smaller companies, many of which have only limited access to commercial banks.

4. *Restore Corporate Investment Incentives.* The 1986 Tax Reform Act shifted $120 billion in federal tax liability from individuals to corporations, mainly via higher taxes on industrial equipment and structures. As a result, investment spending slowed after 1986, well before the current recession. Restoring growth incentives means reinstating the investment tax credit (ITC), which allowed corporations to deduct a portion of their investment outlays, and eliminating the alternative minimum tax (AMT), which, in effect, punishes firms that make large capital investments.

The Bush Plan

March 18, 1991

A day after releasing the budget President Bush outlined his economic game plan to the Economic Club of New York:

George Bush: *"Encouraging economic growth means reducing federal borrowing . . . . That's why we sent Congress a budget proposal that holds spending growth below the rate of inflation—the lowest increase in five years."*

Right Data: Promises, promises. A year ago Mr. Bush also promised to cut spending. Now the Administration is saying that real federal spending will increase 6.8 per cent this year, the second largest increase in 15 years. And the war is not to blame: non-defense spending is expected to increase by a staggering 11 per cent. More important, federal spending as a percentage of GNP is expected to rise from 23.2 per cent in 1990 to 25.1 per cent this year, undoing all the gains made during the Reagan years.

GB: *"But thanks to the budget reforms that began last fall, the deficit will be virtually eliminated by 1995."*

RD: Five years ago Gramm-Rudman supposedly set us on a course for a zero deficit by 1991. If we're lucky—if the Administration's rosy economic scenario proves accurate—then the 1991 deficit will reach $318 billion, or nearly $100 billion above the previous high. The much-heralded spending caps in last fall's budget agreement are undermined by provisions that permit entitlements to rise without limit in response to changing economic conditions, budget "emergencies," or technical "re-estimates." And a recent study by the National Center for Policy Analysis concludes that the agreement's $166 billion tax hike will depress the economy far more than the Administration is willing to admit.

GB: *"To ensure economic growth, this Administration will also redouble its efforts to weed out counterproductive government regulations."*

RD: So far Mr. Bush's efforts have brought on the biggest increase in regulatory activism since the Carter years. The Americans with Disabilities Act requires companies with 15 or more workers to make extensive accommodations for disabled customers and employees. The new Clean Air Act adds $25 to $35 billion to the $100 billion already spent annually on pollution controls. The enlightened policies of the Reagan years have been replaced by something akin to trust-busting at the FTC. The headcount at federal regulatory agencies, after falling by 13,000 during the 1980s, is slated to increase by 7,500 this year, according to Murray Weidenbaum.

GB: *"When you look at what we put out there yesterday, you'll see that defense spending is down."*

RD: In fact defense spending has been falling, in real terms, since 1989; outlays for new weapons and R&D have been falling since 1986. Despite the war, defense spending is expected to account for only 21.2 per cent of total federal outlays this year, the lowest share since before World War II.

GB: *"We must also renew our investments in America's future. . . . And that means . . . investing in the infrastructure of our transportation system."*

RD: And that means millions spent studying magnetic levitation technology, intelligent vehicle/highway systems, bicycle-path planning, the effects of jet lag, and other "transportation-related" programs.

A Lively Corpse

May 28, 1990

Reports of a "collapse" in the junk-bond market are highly exaggerated. First Boston reports that during the first three months of 1990 the high-yield market grew by $4.2 billion, to $230.4 billion. This is far below the growth of recent years, but about in line with what's happening to total credit market debt, which is currently growing at the slowest pace in twenty years. Junk bonds now account for about 22 per cent of all corporate bonds outstanding; in 1985 they accounted for 14 per cent; in 1979, 4 per cent. Junk-bond prices have tumbled sharply over the past few months, what with the demise of Campeau and Drexel Burnham. But all security prices have suffered during this year's credit crunch. And because of the higher interest rates on junk bonds, their first quarter return of –2.6 per cent (based on First Boston's index of 349 issues) exceeded the return on ten-year Treasuries (–2.8 per cent) and the S&P 500 (–3.0 per cent). Yet no one speaks of a "collapse" of Treasury bonds or the stock market. The first-quarter standings are not anomalous. Over the past ten years junk bonds have produced a 13.0 per cent average annual rate of return, outperforming high-grade corporate bonds, U.S. Government bonds, and common stocks, while showing far less variability of return from year to year. In forcing S&Ls to sell off their junk-bond holdings Congress eliminated one of the few profitable investments the thrifts made.

Of course, the U.S. Government never defaults on its bonds. Junk-bond issuers do, to the tune of $8.1 billion in 1989. While many in the media interpreted this dismal performance as evidence of Drexel Burnham's weakened ability to prop up failing companies, junk-bond defaults are nothing new. In 1987 $9.1 billion of them went belly up, and the default rate—defaults as a percentage of total junk bonds outstanding—have exceeded 1989's 4 per cent level three times since 1970. Still, 1989 shook investors' confidence. Many are asking: "If junk-bond defaults are up now, what's going to happen when we're in a recession?" But corporate profits—from which interest payments are made—were at recession levels in 1989, slipping 13 per cent from 1988.

In any case, the inherent riskiness of these investments is well known to investors. The risk posed by a 4 per cent default rate is more than compensated for by junk-bond interest rates, which currently exceed those offered on U.S. Treasury bonds by more than eight percentage points. And defaulted bonds are not exactly worthless: senior obligations of the Campeau corporation trade at more than fifty cents on the dollar.

If junk bonds are a good long-term deal for investors, what about for corporations? The traditional view is that higher interest payments siphon off corporate cash that would otherwise have gone for R&D, new-product development, and other research yielding long-term results. But this paradigm is based on a fanciful notion of what corporations actually do with their spare cash. Harvard economist Michael Jensen argues that a heavy load of debt is good, precisely because it leaves managers little slack. Spare cash is often frittered away on perks, managerial salaries, and investments aimed at increasing sales (on which managers' salaries are based) rather than profits. A financial structure that keeps companies on the edge of default forces managers to focus on efficiency and profits. Financial markets seem to agree with his analysis, as evidenced by the sharp subsequent increase in share prices of companies taken over in LBOs.

More than two thousand companies have issued junk bonds. Thirty-three of them defaulted last year. For every Campeau and Resorts there are hundreds of successful, growing concerns like Compaq Computers, Calvin Klein Industries, Safeway Stores, and Computerland, that still do not have the financial strength to be classified investment grade and so must issue high-yield bonds. These companies and their bonds are anything but junk.

Who Owns America?

August 18, 1989

The Commerce Department recently reported on the foreign stake in U.S. corporations and real estate:

Table 1-67. Foreign Investment in the U.S.
$ Billions; Year End

	1987	1988	% Change
UK	$ 79.7	$101.9	27.9
Japan	35.2	53.4	51.7
Netherlands	49.1	49.0	(0.2)
Canada	24.0	27.4	14.2
West Germany	20.3	23.8	17.2
All others	63.5	73.4	15.6
Total	$271.8	$328.9	21.0

Source: U.S. Department of Commerce.

While growing too fast not to be of some concern, foreign investment does not loom large relative to the total economy: at $328.9 billion, it represents only 6 per cent of tangible corporate assets in this country. British corporations are by far the largest foreign investors, although if the growth rates of the past year persist, the Japanese will assume that role within four years.

However, these figures understate the amount of foreign acquisition activity in this country because they reflect only that part of foreign investment financed by the inflow of capital from abroad. When you include the domestically financed portion, total assets of foreign-owned U.S. corporations came to $926 billion at the end of 1987 (the latest figure available), or more than three times the Commerce Department's figure for direct foreign investment. On this basis Japan is the biggest investor ($196 billion), followed by the UK ($156 billion), Canada ($140 billion), and Switzerland ($74 billion).

The truth is we don't know what the actual level of foreign involvement is. Two dozen federal agencies collect data on foreign investment, but the reporting requirements range from lax to non-

196

existent. The Commerce Department, usually cited as the most reliable source of foreign-ownership information, admits to overlooking
at least $223 billion in foreign capital entering the country between
1981 and 1987, referring to this in its publications as a "statistical discrepancy." According to some experts, as much as 50 per cent of all
foreign investment goes unreported.

National origin is also easily obscured. The Department of Agriculture, for example, is prohibited by law from investigating beyond
three levels of incorporation. Thus the 270,000 acres of Texas farm-
land registered with dummy corporations located in the Netherlands
Antilles—one acre for every man, woman, and child living in that
country—may, for all we know, belong to drug dealers or agents of a
hostile nation.

Similarly, the Federal Reserve requires foreign banks, but not
foreign individuals, to report bank acquisitions, a loophole that enabled the Soviet Union to acquire four Silicon Valley banks during
the 1970s. This sale, aborted only because a CIA agent happened to
recognize the Singapore businessman acting as a front for the
Soviets, would have given them access not only to U.S. technology
but also to the financial structure of the computer industry, allowing
them to identify those computer-industry executives most susceptible
to financial pressure.

The most glaring information gap is in urban and residential
real estate. No federal agency collects or analyzes these data,
although private studies suggest that foreigners own nearly half of
the prime commercial real estate in Los Angeles, 40 per cent in
Houston, and 33 per cent in the Washington, D.C., area.

A bill sponsored by Representative John Bryant (D., Tex.) would
require foreign investors to register and disclose holdings accounting for 5 per cent or more of a U.S. business, or real estate worth
more than $5 million. Lobbying by some of the more than one hun-
dred PACs formed by foreign-owned American companies helped
sink the Bryant bill when it was first introduced last year.

Now for the Good News

April 1, 1988

The unemployment situation continues to amaze. Only a few years ago economists were saying that 7 per cent unemployment was the point below which inflationary pressures would start to build. February's 5.7 per cent marked the twentieth consecutive month of sub-7 per cent unemployment, and yet inflation forecasts are being revised steadily downward.

Not a small amount of credit for this happy confluence must go to the reductions in personal-income-tax rates, which have resulted in both an increased demand for labor and a lowering of unit labor costs.

The official unemployment numbers actually overstate the true dimensions of the problem. Only 3.2 million of the seven million people counted as unemployed last month actually lost their jobs. The rest either left work voluntarily (961,000), recently re-entered the labor force (1,951,000), or are looking for their first job (864,000).

Although the perception exists that job quality has deteriorated, with menial service jobs replacing high-paying manufacturing positions, the data show that 52 per cent of all jobs created between 1979 and 1985 paid 150 per cent or more of the median wage.

Youth and minority unemployment rates are still high in this country, but they are falling and—surprise!—we do a much better job of keeping our youth employed than do some countries in which you might not expect to find youth or minority problems. The OECD reports 1987 youth unemployment at 11.3 per cent in the U.S. versus 23 per cent in France, 17.8 per cent in the UK, 37 per cent in Italy, 14.5 per cent in Australia, and 14 per cent in Canada.

Germany and Japan had lower youth unemployment rates, respectively 8.4 per cent and 5.8 per cent, but the trend since 1980 has been sharply upward in those nations, while here, Reaganomics and all, the rate is more than two points lower now than it was in 1980.

We also do a much better job at keeping the duration of unemployment under control. The long-term unemployed (defined as those out of work for more than 12 months) typically constitute 30 to 50 per cent of the total unemployed in the major European countries, and more than 70 per cent in Belgium, while the proportion in the U.S. is about 8 per cent.

In the not-too-distant future our primary labor-market problem will be a shortage not of jobs but of workers—this bringing its own set of problems, including an increased risk of high inflation and higher tax burdens on workers.

PART TWO

THE REAL REAGAN RECORD

National Review, *August 31, 1992*

PREFACE

Ronald Reagan inherited an economy that was in the midst of its worst crisis since the Great Depression. In January 1981 the unemployment rate stood at 7.4 per cent, on its way up to 10 per cent. Persistent double-digit inflation had pushed interest rates to an unbelievable 21 per cent. Real pre-tax income of the average American family had been dropping since 1976, and—thanks to bracket creep—after-tax income was falling even faster. The supply of oil and other raw materials seemed precarious. The outgoing President warned of a bleak economic future.

That era, roughly coinciding with the Carter Administration, was the last time liberal policies held sway over the economy.

Two years into Ronald Reagan's Presidency the economy began to recover. By most conventional indices the recovery was strong and sustained, outlasting Mr. Reagan's Presidency by nearly two years. And yet it was widely felt that the recovery was illusory—"smoke and mirrors," as Mario Cuomo memorably put it—and that the stock market crash in 1987 was merely the foretaste of the post-1990 recession. We propose to examine these claims in detail in the balance of this section.

—Edwin S. Rubenstein

A. The Reagan Boom

Upstarts and Downstarts

Alan Reynolds

Mr. Reynolds is Director of Economic Research at the Hudson Institute in Indianapolis.

The economic policies presided over by Ronald Reagan were stunningly successful—except to informed opinion, as represented by the academy and the major media. The principal charge against Reagan has become almost a chant: The rich got richer, the poor got poorer, and the middle class was squeezed out of existence.

A key player in the campaign to popularize this view has been Sylvia Nasar of the *New York Times*, who relied on statistics concocted by Paul Krugman of MIT, who, in turn, garbled some already disreputable estimates from the Congressional Budget Office (CBO).

The purpose of the crusade was obvious. Mr. Krugman has been advocating that we somehow double tax collections from those earning over $200,000, so as to increase greatly federal spending. Miss Nasar openly boasted about "supplying fresh ammunition for those . . . searching for new ways to raise government revenue." Governor Clinton immediately seized upon the Krugman-Nasar statisics as the rationale for his economic plan to tax us into prosperity.

Since the question is what happened in the 1980s, after the Carter Administration, it makes no sense to begin with 1977, as Mr. Krugman and Miss Nasar do, or with 1973, as the Children's Defense Fund does. Real incomes fell sharply during the runaway inflations of 1974–75 and 1979–80. Median real income among black families, for example, fell 15 per cent from 1973 to 1980, then rose 16 per cent from 1982 to 1990.

Table 2-1 shows the actual real income of households by fifths of the income distribution, for the most commonly cited years. There is no question that *all* income groups experienced significant income gains from 1980 to 1989, despite the 1981–82 recession, and were still well ahead of 1980 even in the 1990 slump. For all U.S. households, the mean average of real income rose by 15.2 per cent from

Table 2-1. Average Household Income
In 1990 Dollars

	Lowest Fifth	Second Fifth	Third Fifth	Fourth Fifth	Highest Fifth	Top 5%
1990	7,195	18,030	29,781	44,901	87,137	138,756
1989	7,372	18,341	30,488	46,177	90,150	145,651
1980	6,836	17,015	28,077	41,364	73,752	110,213
1977	7,193	17,715	29,287	42,911	76,522	117,023

Source: Bureau of the Census, *Money Income of Households, Families & Persons: 1990*, p. 202.

1980 to 1989 (from $33,409 to $38,493, in 1990 dollars), compared with a 0.8 per cent *decline* from 1970 to 1980.

This table shows that the "income gap" did not widen merely between the bottom fifth and any "top" group, but also between the bottom fifth and the next highest fifth, the middle fifth, and so on.

A common complaint about these figures is that they exclude capital gains and therefore understate income at the top. However, the figures also exclude *taxes.* Average income taxes and payroll taxes among the top fifth of households amounted to $24,322 in 1990, according to the Census Bureau, but capital gains among the top fifth were only $14,972. To add the capital gains and not subtract the taxes, as some CBO figures do, is indefensible. Indeed, all CBO estimates of income gains are useless, because they include an estimate of capital gains based on a sample of tax returns. Since lower tax rates on capital gains after 1977 induced more people to sell assets more often, the CBO wrongly records this as increased income. It also ignores all capital losses above the deductible $3,000 and fails to adjust capital gains for inflation.

The Middle-Class Boom
One thing that we know with 100 per cent certainty is that *most* Americans—far more than half—did very well during the long and strong economic expansion from 1982 to 1989. In those fat years, real after-tax income per person rose by 15.5 per cent, and real *median* income of families, before taxes, went up 12.5 per cent. That

means half of all families had gains *larger* than 12.5 per cent, while many below the median also had income gains, though not as large. Many families had to have gained even more than 12.5 per cent, since the more familiar *mean* average rose 16.8 per cent from 1982 to 1989. Even if we begin with 1980, rather than 1982, median income was up 8 per cent by 1989, and mean income by 14.9 per cent. And even if we end this comparison with the slump of 1990, median family income was still up 5.9 per cent from 1980, and mean income was up 12 per cent.

In *U.S. News & World Report* (March 23, 1992), Paul Krugman claimed that "the income of a few very well-off families soared. This raised average family income—but *most* families didn't share in the good times" (emphasis added). Mr. Krugman apparently does not understand what a rising median income means.

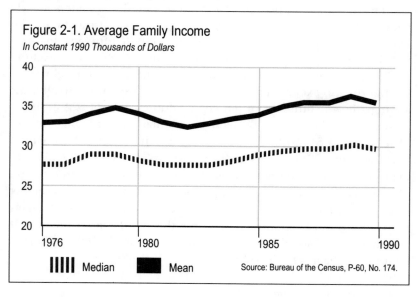

Figure 2-1. Average Family Income
In Constant 1990 Thousands of Dollars

Median | Mean | Source: Bureau of the Census, P-60, No. 174.

The whole idea of dividing people into arbitrary fifths by income ignores the enormous mobility of people in and out of these categories. What was most unusual about the Eighties, though, was that the number moving *up* far exceeded the number moving *down*. A Treasury Department study of 14,351 taxpayers shows that 86 per cent of

206

those in the lowest fifth in 1979, and 60 per cent in the second fifth, had moved up into a higher income category by 1988. Among those in the middle income group, 47 per cent moved up, while fewer than 20 per cent moved down. Indeed, many more families moved up than down in every income group except the top 1 per cent, where 53 per cent fell into a lower category. Similar research by Isabel Sawhill and Mark Condon of the Urban Institute found that real incomes of those who started out in the bottom fifth in 1977 had risen 77 per cent by 1986—more than 15 times as fast as those who started in the top fifth. Miss Sawhill and Mr. Condon concluded that "the rich got a little richer and the poor got much richer."

This remarkable upward mobility is the sole cause of "The Incredible Shrinking Middle Class," featured in the May 1992 issue of *American Demographics.* Measured in constant 1990 dollars, the percentage of families earning between $15,000 and $50,000 fell by 5 points, from about 58 per cent to 53 per cent. This is what is meant by a "shrinking" middle class. We know they didn't disappear into poverty, because the percentage of families earning less than $15,000 (in 1990 dollars), dropped a bit, from 17.5 per cent in 1980 to 16.9 per cent in 1990. What instead happened is that the percentage earning more than $50,000, in constant dollars, *rose* by 5 points—from less than 25 per cent to nearly 31 per cent. Several million families "vanished" from the middle class by earning much more money!

It is not possible to reconcile the increase in median incomes with the often-repeated claim that low-wage service jobs ("McJobs") expanded at the expense of high-wage manufacturing jobs. Actually, there were millions more jobs in sectors where wages were rising most briskly, which meant competitive export industries but also services. From 1980 to 1991, average hourly earnings rose by 6.8 per cent a year in services, compared with only 4.8 per cent in manufacturing. The percentage of working-age Americans with jobs, which had never before the 1980s been nearly as high as 60 per cent, rose to 63 per cent by 1989.

The Myth of Low-Wage Jobs

An editorial in *Business Week* (May 25, 1992) claimed that, "according to a just-released Census Bureau study, the number of working poor rose dramatically from 1979 to 1990." This is completely false. In fact, the report shows that the percentage of low-income workers who are in poverty *fell* dramatically. Among husbands with such low-income jobs, for example, 35.7 per cent were members of poor families in 1979, but only 21.4 per cent in 1990.

Low incomes, in this report, were defined as "less than the poverty level for a four-person family" ($12,195 a year in 1990). Yet very few people with entry-level or part-time jobs are trying to support a family of four. Husbands now account for only a fifth of such low-income jobs, which are instead increasingly held by young singles and by dependent children living with their parents. Wives had 34 per cent of such jobs in 1979, but fewer than 28 per cent in 1990. That reflects the impressive fact that the median income of women rose by 31 per cent in real terms from 1979 to 1990.

It is true that the absolute *number* of low-income jobs increased in all categories, but that increase was not nearly as large as the increase in medium- and high-income jobs. All that the rise in low-income jobs really shows is that students living with their parents and young singles found it much easier to find acceptable work. The only reason fewer young people had low-income jobs back in the glorious Seventies is a larger percentage of them had no jobs at all! Only 51.4 per cent of single males had full-time jobs in 1974, but 61.8 per cent did by 1989. Young people always start out with low earnings, if they get a chance to start out at all.

In his new book, *Head to Head*, Lester Thurow writes that "between 1973 and 1990, real hourly wages for non-supervisory workers . . . fell 12 per cent, and real weekly wages fell 18 per cent." Yet these averages include part-time workers, which is why *average* wages appeared to be only $355 a week in 1991, even though half of all full-time workers (the *median*) earned more than $430 a week. Because many more students and young mothers were able to find part-time jobs in the Eighties, that diluted both the weekly and the hourly "average" wage. It most definitely did not mean that the wages of the "average worker" went down, but rather that otherwise unemployed part-time and entry-level workers were able to raise their wages above zero. The increase in part-time jobs also does not mean that families are poorer; rather, they are richer. Out of 19.3 million part-time workers in 1991, only 1.2 million were family heads, and only 10 per cent said they were unable to find full-time work.

The Rich Work Harder

Although the vast majority clearly had large income gains in the Eighties, Mr. Krugman and Miss Nasar nonetheless assert that those at the top had even larger gains, and that this is something that ought to provoke resentment or envy. Yet the figures they offer to make this point are grossly misleading. Moreover, the whole static routine of slicing up income into fifths is bound to show the highest percentage increases in average (mean) incomes among the "top" 20 per cent or 1 per cent. *That is because for top groups alone, any and all increases in income are included in the average, rather than in movement to a higher group.*

In his *U.S. News* article, Krugman first claimed that CBO figures show that "Ronald Reagan's tax cuts" boosted after-tax income of the top 1 per cent "by a whopping 102 per cent." That figure, though, is based on a "tax simulation model" that estimates "adjusted" incomes as a multiple of the poverty level. The top 1 per cent supposedly earned less than 22 times the poverty level in 1980, but 44 times the poverty level in 1989—hence the gain of 102 per cent. Yet this is a purely relative measure of affluence, not an absolute gain in real income. As more and more families rose further and further above the unchanged "poverty line" in the Eighties, thus lifting the income needed to be in the "top 1 per cent," the CBO technique had to show a "widening gap."

Furthermore, the share of federal income tax paid by the top 1 per cent soared from 18.2 per cent in 1981 to 28 per cent in 1988, though it slipped to 25.4 per cent in 1990. Indeed, this unexpected revenue from the rich was used to double personal exemptions and triple the earned-income tax credit, which was of enormous benefit to the working poor.

By the time Mr. Krugman's alleged 102 per cent gain at the top had reached the *New York Times*, it had shrunk to 60 per cent. However, the CBO wrote a memo disowning this estimate too, noting that "of the total rise in aggregate income . . . about one-fourth went to families in the top 1 per cent." By fiddling with "adjusted" data, the

CBO managed to get that share of the top 1 per cent up to one-third. Whether a fourth or a third, these estimates still begin with 1977, not 1980. Between 1977 and 1980, the CBO shows real incomes falling by 6.6 per cent for the poorest fifth. The top 5 per cent fared *relatively* well before 1980, because everybody else suffered an outright drop in real income.

Even if the Krugman-Nasar figures had been remotely accurate, the whole exercise is conceptually flawed. In every income group except the top, many families can move up from one group to another with little or no effect on the average income of those remaining in the lower group. Above-average increases in income among those in the lower groups simply move them into a higher fifth, rather than raising the average income of the fifth they used to be in. Only the top income groups have no ceiling, as those in such a group cannot possibly move into any higher group. A rap star's first hit record may lift his income from the lowest fifth to the top 1 per cent, with no perceptible effect on the average income of the lowest fifth. But two hit records in the next year would raise the total amount of income counted in the top 1 per cent, and thus raise the average for that category.

Nobody knows exactly how much income is needed to be counted among the top 1 per cent, because the Census Bureau keeps track only of the top 5 per cent. Census officials argue that apparent changes in the small sample used to estimate a "top 1 per cent" may largely reflect differences in the degree of dishonest reporting. When marginal tax rates fell from 70 per cent to 28 per cent, for example, more people told the truth about what they earned, so "the rich" *appeared* to earn much more.

One thing we do know, though, is that the minimum amount of income needed to be included among the top 1 per cent has to have risen quite sharply since 1980, because of the huge increase in the percentage of families earning more than $50,000 or $100,000. This increased proportion of families with higher incomes pushed up the income ceilings on all middle and higher income groups, and thus raised the floor defining the highest income groups.

While $200,000 may have been enough to make the top 1 per cent in 1980, a family might need over $300,000 to be in that category a decade later. Clearly, any average of all the income above $300,000 is going to yield a much bigger number than an average of income above $200,000. The CBO thus estimates that average pre-tax income among the top 1 per cent rose from $343,610 in 1980 to $566,674 in 1992. But this 65 per cent increase in the average does *not* mean that those specific families that were in the top 1 per cent in 1980 typically experienced a 65 per cent increase in real income. It simply means that the standards for belonging to this exclusive club have gone way up. That is because millions more couples are earning higher incomes today than in 1980, not because only a tiny fraction are earning 65 per cent more.

Sylvia Nasar totally misreported the CBO's complaints with her first article, and audaciously quoted her own discredited assertions in a later *New York Times* piece (April 21). This front-page editorial changed the subject—from income to wealth. It claimed a "Federal Reserve" study had found that the wealthiest 1 per cent had 37 per cent of all net worth in 1989, up from 31 per cent in 1983. Paul Krugman, writing in the *Wall Street Journal,* likewise cited this "careful study by the Federal Reserve." Yet the cited figures are from a mere *footnote* in a rough "working paper" produced by one of hundreds of Fed economists, Arthur Kennickell, along with a statistician from the IRS, Louise Woodburn. It comes with a clear warning that "opinions in this paper . . . in no way reflect the views of . . . the Federal Reserve System."

At that, all of the gain of the top 1 per cent was supposedly at the expense of others within the top 10 per cent, not the middle class or poor. In any case, the figures are little more than a guess. The authors acknowledge that they "cannot offer a formal statistical test of the significance of the change."

"The 1983 and 1989 sample designs and the weights developed are quite different," they write. "The effect of this difference is unknown." Their estimated range of error does not account for "error attributable to imputation or to other data problems." Yet it is nonetheless within that range of error for the share of net worth held by the top 1 per cent to have risen imperceptibly, from 34.5 to 34.6 per cent. This is why Kennickell and Woodburn say their estimates merely "suggest that there may have been an

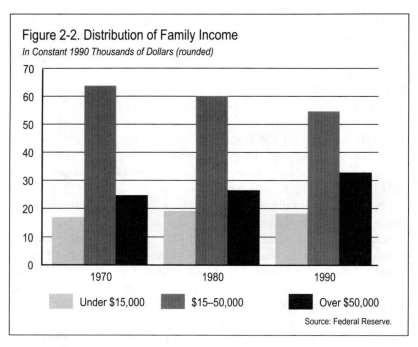

Figure 2-2. Distribution of Family Income
In Constant 1990 Thousands of Dollars (rounded)

Under $15,000 $15–50,000   Over $50,000

Source: Federal Reserve.

increase in the share of wealth held by this top group in 1989." Or maybe not.

The actual, official Federal Reserve study tells a quite different story. It shows that real net worth rose by 28 per cent among 40 per cent of families earning between $20,000 and $50,000, but by only 6.6 per cent for the top 20 per cent, earning more than $50,000. Since this huge increase in net worth among those with modest incomes means their assets grew much faster than their debts, this also puts to rest the myth that the Eighties was built upon "a mountain of debt." It was, instead, built upon a mountain of assets, particularly small businesses.

Children without Fathers

What about the poor? There is no question that there has been a stubbornly large increase of people with very low incomes. However, annual "money income" turns out to be a surprisingly bad measure of ability to buy goods and services. In 1988, average consumer

212

spending among the lowest fifth of the population was $10,893 a year—more than double their apparent income of $4,942. That huge gap occurs partly because annual incomes are highly variable in many occupations, and many people have temporary spells of low income, due to illness or job loss. People can and do draw upon savings during periods when their income dips below normal.

Another reason why those in the bottom fifth are able to spend twice their earnings is that many in-kind government transfers (such as Food Stamps) are not counted as "money income." Census surveys also acknowledge that a fourth of the cash income from welfare and pensions is unreported. And, of course, very little income from illegal activities is reported. In CBO figures, incomes of low-income families are further understated by counting singles as separate families, as though young people stopped getting checks from home the minute they get their first apartment.

Despite such flaws in measured income, nearly all of the income differences between the bottom fifth and the top fifth can nonetheless be explained by the number of people per family with full-time jobs, their age, and their schooling. Among household heads in the lowest fifth, for example, only 21 per cent worked full-time all year in 1990, and half had no job all year. In the top fifth, by contrast, the average number of full-time workers was more than two.

> "Fully 80 per cent of [American] families are on a treadmill—they saw their net family income decline over the past decade or grow by a smaller percentage than did their hours of work. To merely maintain their standard of living, or to avoid falling further behind, they have had to increase their hours of work at the expense of their time with their family and community. Only the very top fifth of these families enjoyed clear gains in their standard of living."
> —Senator Paul Sarbanes (D., Md.)
> January 17, 1992
> (reporting on a Democratic Party-sponsored Joint Economic Committee study)

The May 25 *Business Week* editorial noted that "the percentage of Americans below the poverty line rose from 11.7 per cent in 1979 to 13.5 per cent in 1990." Yet this poverty rate is exaggerated, because it is based on an obsolete consumer price index that mismeasured housing inflation before 1983. Using the corrected inflation measure, the poverty rate was 11.5 per cent in 1980 and 11.4 in 1989, before rising to 12.1 per cent in 1990. That 12.1 per cent figure, though, is only one of 14 different Census Bureau measures of poverty, and not the most credible. Like income for the "bottom fifth," the usual measure of poverty excludes many in-kind transfer payments, as well as cash from the earned-income tax credit. By instead including such benefits, and also subtracting taxes, the Census Bureau brings the actual poverty rate down to 9.5 per cent for 1990, or to 8.5 per cent if home-ownership is considered (those who own homes need less cash because they don't pay rent).

"Tragically, during the 1980s, American families with children saw their incomes fall—by an average of $1,600. To top it off, their taxes went up while the taxes of the richest Americans were being cut—by an average of $42,000."
—Sen. Lloyd Bentsen (D., Tex.)
USA Today
October 23, 1991

Even by the conventional measure, the poverty rate among married-couple families dropped slightly, from 5.2 per cent in 1980 to 4.9 per cent in 1990, and poverty rates among those above age 65 have fallen quite substantially. On the other hand, among female household heads with children under the age of 18 and "no husband present," poverty rose from 37.1 per cent in 1979 to 39.9 per cent in 1980, and then to 41.6 per cent by 1990.

The poverty rate among fatherless families, then, is slightly higher now than it was in the previous decade, and is lower if these young women work. (Among female householders with children under the age of 6, the poverty rate among those with jobs dropped from 20.2 per cent in 1979 to 17.9 per cent in 1989, and the percentage of such mothers who worked full-time rose from 24.9 to 30.6 per cent.) But there are so many more female-headed households, and so few of these women work, that the net effect is nonetheless to keep the overall poverty rate from falling. The number of female-headed households with children under age 18 rose from 5.8 million in 1979 to 7.2 million in 1989. In too many cases, these mothers are so young that child-labor laws would not allow them to work in any case.

In March 1991, the average money income of female-headed families with children was only $17,500, and most of that money

214

(plus Food Stamps, housing allowance, and Medicaid) came from taxpayers. For married couples who both worked full-time, average income was $55,700 before taxes—about enough to put the *average* two-earner family in the top fifth. Taxing hard-working two-earner families to subsidize broken, no-earner families can only discourage the former, encourage the latter, and thus exacerbate the problems it pretends to solve.

To summarize what actually happened in the 1980s, the "middle class," and the vast majority by any measure, unquestionably experienced substantial gains in real income and wealth. With millions more families earning much higher incomes, it required much higher incomes to make it into the top 5 per cent or top 1 per cent, which largely accounts for the illusion that such "top" groups experienced disproportionate gains. The rising tide lifted at least 90 per cent of all boats. About 9 to 12 per cent continued to be poor, but this group increasingly consisted of female-headed households with young children. More and better jobs cannot help those who do not work, improved investment opportunities cannot help those who do not save, and increased incomes cannot help families whose fathers refuse to support their own children.

The CBO's Faulty Data

Ed Gillespie & Christopher Frenze

*Mr. Gillespie is Policy/Communications Director,
House Republican Conference. Mr. Frenze is a senior
economist for the Joint Economic Committee.*

Myth: The top 1 per cent of earners got most of the income gains of the 1980s.

> "We all know that there has been a redistribution of income in America. That redistribution over the last 12 years has been from average working Americans to the wealthiest 1 per cent in our nation." —Rep. Steny Hoyer (D., Md.), *Wall Street Journal*, April 8, 1992

> "Even Among the Well-Off, the Richest Get Richer—Data Show the Top 1 Per Cent Got 60 Per Cent of the Gain in the '80s Boom." —*New York Times* front-page headline, March 5, 1992

The Texas education establishment was rocked last year by the discovery of 230 mistakes in history books distributed in the state's schools. Among the interesting "facts" in these texts were that *Sputnik* was the Soviet Union's first intercontinental ballistic missile, that the United States easily settled the Korean conflict by using "the bomb," and that Japan attacked Pearl Harbor in 1942.

These errors were the results of innocent (albeit stupid) mistakes. The same cannot be said of the endless stream of newspaper accounts and "economic studies" purporting to show that, contrary to our best recollections, the decade of the 1980s was not a period of prosperity after all.

The CBO's figures are particularly suspect. Alan Reynolds details some of its errors in the preceding article; another is that reporting capital gains, it does not adjust the cost of the asset for inflation. The general effect of the CBO's methodology is to exaggerate the income of the affluent while understating that of middle- and lower-income groups. Net capital losses are capped and most partnership

216

losses are ignored, even though all capital gains and partnership income are fully counted. Furthermore, capital gains and other income accruing to the middle-income brackets in the form of pension funds (which amount to some $3 trillion) or home values are not counted.

The CBO also adopts a bizarre method of compiling income data. It assigns families to fifths with an adjustment for family size, but the income measured is not adjusted for family size. The CBO indicates that family income in the bottom three quintiles dropped between 1977 or 1980 and 1989. This is flatly contradicted by the Census Bureau, whose data show the average level of income in all quintiles rising between 1977 or 1980 and 1989. The bottom line is that middle-class real family income jumped 13 per cent during the 1982–89 expansion years.

Even if these faulty CBO data were taken at face value, they would place the era of greed, when the top 1 per cent of families had 100 per cent of net income growth, in the Carter years, 1977–80. The share of income gains going to the top 1 per cent of families was 160 per cent higher under Carter than under Reagan.

Adding at the Bottom

June O'Neill

Mrs. O'Neill is a professor of economics at Baruch College, City University of New York, and Director, Center for the Study of Business and Government.

The soundbite about the richest 1 per cent of the population is untrue in itself, as Alan Reynolds demonstrates above; it also lacks context, particularly the historical trends in the share of total income received by the richest 5 per cent of families.

Income was much more unequally distributed in the first half of this century. In 1913 the richest 5 per cent received about 30 per cent of aggregate income (excluding capital gains), and this share held until 1933, when it began a slow but steady decline, followed by a rapid decline during World War II. By 1947 the share of the top 5 per cent had fallen to 17.5 per cent of aggregate income; it declined further (to about 15.5 per cent) in the 1960s and 1970s but increased in the 1980s back to the neighborhood of 17.5 per cent. This small increase in the share of the rich is in sharp contrast with the soundbite's message of run-away inequality.

Should government attempt to reverse increases in inequality? Those who view any increase in inequality as horrendous are already proposing schemes for redistributing income. However, any response requires that we first know what caused the increased inequality, a relatively small change in historical perspective.

Many commentators attribute the change to the Reagan Administration's tax policies. But the changes in income distribution look quite similar whether based on pre-tax or post-tax income. Moreover, general increases in the inequality of earnings started a decade before the 1982 tax cut. So we must look to other causes.

Accumulating research shows that changes in the labor market have resulted in higher wages for college graduates and depressed wages for young men with lower levels of schooling. These shifts in relative wages are partly due to advances in technology, boosting productivity and increasing the demand for highly skilled workers. This trend occurred not only in the United States, but internationally.

A. The Reagan Boom

Within the United States, however, another trend is also at work: a huge wave of immigration has reduced the wages of low-skill workers. In the 1970s 4.5 million immigrants were legally admitted, and many more came illegally; in the 1980s legal immigration rose to 7.4 million, with additional millions of illegal entrants. The vast majority of immigrants from Central and South America (who make up about one-half of the total) have considerably lower levels of schooling than native-born Americans. (In 1980 Mexican immigrants on average had completed only seven years of school, five years less than the average worker in the U.S.) The most obvious effect in the U.S. is to add a new group of workers with lower skills who are available for low-wage work (by U.S. standards). This depresses *average* wages and income in the lowest brackets. The immigrants themselves typically enjoy large wage increases over what they were earning in their native countries. And while some low-skill native-born workers may find their wages lowered still more by this increased supply, many move up into higher brackets.

Not only have relative wages and incomes of Hispanics in the U.S. declined over the past 15 years as the Hispanic population has nearly doubled through immigration, but wage inequality among the Hispanic population has also increased, and this is probably due to the increasing diversity of that population. The earnings gap widened between native-born Hispanics, with higher education levels and English-speaking skills, and the new Hispanic immigrants.

In the past, waves of immigration caused transitional increases in wage and income inequality that faded as the immigrants' skills increased. The much greater levels of income inequality that existed early in this century were probably partly traceable to the very heterogeneous amalgam of immigrants and native-born Americans. We again appear to be moving through one of these transitional phases of increased inequality due to surges in immigration. Only this time we have an additional factor—increased demand for skilled labor due to technological changes and trade patterns—adding to inequality.

More Than "McJobs"

Edwin S. Rubenstein

Myth: Most of the jobs created during the Eighties were of the dead-end, burger-flipper variety.

"Caught between the lawmakers in Washington and the deal-makers on Wall Street have been millions of American workers forced to move between jobs that once paid $15 an hour into jobs that now pay $7.

"As a result, the already-rich are richer than ever; there has been an explosion in overnight new rich; life for the working class is deteriorating, and those at the bottom are trapped." —Donald L. Barlett and James B. Steele, "America: What Went Wrong," *Philadelphia Inquirer*, October 20, 1991

Contrary to what everyone knows to be true, 82 per cent of the jobs created during the Reagan recovery were in the higher-paying, higher-skilled occupations (technical, precision production, managerial, and professional). Many of these are "service" jobs, including positions in law, advertising, computers, and medicine. Only 12 per

Table 2-2. Job Creation in the Eighties

Job Category	Jobs Created, Jan. 1982–Dec. 1989 Number (Mils.)	Percentage Increase	1989 Median Earnings
Managerial/Professional	7.600	33.1%	$32,873
Production	2.194	19.0	25,831
Technical	6.630	21.8	20,905
Operators	1.374	8.2	19,886
Services	2.210	16.8	14,858
Farming	−0.116	−3.7	13,539
Total / Average	19.892	20.3%	$23,333

Source: Bureau of Labor Statistics (employment); Bureau of the Census (earnings).

cent of the increase in employment occurred in the lowest-paid, low-skilled service occupations such as retailing and fast-food restaurants.

Studies purporting to show an erosion of job quality are quite often flawed. In December 1986, for example, a report commissioned by the Democratic members of the Joint Economic Committee concluded that six out of every ten new jobs created during the expansion paid less than $7,000 per year. The study, however, failed to note the high-proportion of (voluntary) part-time workers among newly employed individuals.

B. Supply-Side Kept Its Promises

Debts, Lies, and Inflation

Paul Craig Roberts

Mr. Roberts, Assistant Secretary of the Treasury for Economic Policy in 1981–82, is Chairman of the Institute of Political Economy and a Distinguished Fellow at the Cato Institute.

The pro-entrepreneurial policies supported by Ronald Reagan and supply-side economics pose a massive threat to interests of the rent-seeking Democratic and Republican establishments, as well as to the ideological commitments of left-leaning media and academic pundits. It is not surprising, then, that the American public has been subjected to an unprecedented disinformation campaign against "Reaganomics." The campaign was carefully crafted to appeal to conservatives who have long been convinced that public debt is a certain road to national collapse. President Reagan was shown to have increased the public debt even more than the despised Jimmy Carter. President Reagan's policies had left Americans uniquely burdened with red ink, and the country was collapsing beneath the "Twin Towers of Debt." Only another tax increase could save us.

The twin towers of debt were budget and trade deficits, and the implication was that only Americans were burdened with these ills. As the result of them, we had been rendered economically uncompetitive, hopelessly in debt to foreigners, and at their mercy. The day the Japanese stopped buying our Treasury bonds, interest rates would skyrocket, and our economy would plunge over the precipice. Moreover, federal irresponsibility had encouraged corporate and household debt to explode as well. Wherever one looked, the U.S. was smothered in debt.

This story has been repeated relentlessly for a decade despite its lack of any factual basis. Throughout the disinformation campaign, the Organization for Economic Cooperation and Development (OECD) twice a year published internationally comparable statistics on public, corporate, and household debt that reveal nothing unique about U.S. debt levels. If we have too much debt, so do our competitors in the Group of Seven industrialized countries. If we are dependent on our G-7 partners to finance our debts, who is financing theirs?

As the information in Table 2-3 shows, U.S. public debt as a share of gross domestic product is below the G-7 average. U.S. corporate debt as a share of GDP is the lowest of the G-7 countries. And U.S. household debt as a share of GDP, while above average, is lower than Japanese and British household debt.

The OECD's measure of public debt, which includes federal, state, and local, reveals nothing unusual about the growth or level of U.S. public debt. During the 1980s, only Germany and France have had public-debt ratios consistently lower than the United States', and the difference is not large. The UK has had a lower ratio only since 1990, and Japan's ratio has been lower only since 1986. Italy and Canada have substantially higher ratios. The U.S. ratio has almost doubled since 1980, but Canada's has increased fourfold. All the public-debt ratios have increased except the Japanese and British, which fell during the second half of the decade—proof governments can bring debt under control. Moreover, the British ratio fell following the massive Thatcher tax-rate reduction—proof that tax-rate reduction does not cause debt to rise.

U.S. non-financial corporations may be over-leveraged and burdened with junk bonds, but their aggregate gross debt ratio is by far the lowest in the Group of Seven.

The gross household debt ratios suggest that if the American consumer is overburdened, so are the British, Japanese, and Canadians. It is Germany and Italy, with extremely low ratios, that are the anomalies.

Overall, there appears to be a rough balance of sorts. Countries with relatively high public-debt ratios tend not to have high corporate and household debt ratios also, and vice versa. But whatever we make of the figures, one thing is clear: The United States is not uniquely burdened with debt.

The Twin Towers of Debt argument was constructed by economists such as Martin Feldstein, who apparently lack the ability to read balance-of-payments statistics. According to their totally spuri-

Table 2-3. How Much Debt?

Household Debt as % of GDP:

	'80	'81	'82	'83	'84	'85	'86	'87	'88	'89	'90
U.S.	55	53	54	55	56	60	64	66	67	69	72
Japan	54	56	58	60	61	61	63	68	71	74	76
Germany	10	10	10	10	10	11	11	11	11	11	11
France	44	44	42	42	45	45	44	48	51	55	53
Italy	6	6	6	6	7	7	8	8	9	10	NA
U.K.	39	43	46	50	54	58	63	68	73	77	80
Canada	56	51	49	50	48	50	53	56	58	60	62

Corporate Debt as % of GDP:

	'80	'81	'82	'83	'84	'85	'86	'87	'88	'89	'90
U.S.	74	74	76	77	82	85	89	91	92	93	91
Japan	149	149	151	159	160	161	162	182	187	191	196
Germany	90	88	90	93	94	109	104	95	99	107	102
France	137	130	127	142	152	166	201	187	242	289	246
Italy	98	100	91	90	93	131	152	122	127	NA	NA
U.K.	94	96	105	112	124	128	147	152	159	183	168
Canada	174	179	176	169	168	169	170	170	167	168	169

Government Debt as % of GDP:

	'80	'81	'82	'83	'84	'85	'86	'87	'88	'89	'90	'91
U.S.	19	19	22	24	25	27	30	31	31	31	34	36
Japan	17	21	23	26	27	27	26	21	18	15	11	8
Germany	14	18	20	21	22	22	22	23	24	22	23	24
France	14	14	18	20	21	23	26	25	25	25	25	25
Italy	54	58	64	69	74	81	86	91	94	96	98	101
U.K.	47	46	46	46	47	46	45	43	36	31	30	30
Canada	12	11	17	23	27	33	37	38	37	40	43	48

Source: Organization for Economic Cooperation and Development;
percentages rounded to nearest percentage point.

ous argument, large budget deficits from the loss of tax revenues brought high interest rates. Lured by high interest rates, foreign money poured into the U.S., pushing up the dollar and causing the trade deficit. Thus, the two pillars of debt were both due to cutting tax rates. Between 1982 and 1983, when the U.S. became a net importer of capital, many academic economists joined Feldstein in putting out the story of foreign money pouring into America to finance over-consumption caused by the Reagan tax-rate reduction. Reaganomics was portrayed as an extreme form of Keynesianism that was causing America to disinvest and de-industrialize.

In fact, the official balance-of-payments statistics show no evidence of the foreign money that allegedly was financing excessive U.S. consumption. As Table 2-4 shows, between 1982 and 1983 foreign-capital inflow into the U.S. actually fell by $9 billion. The change in the capital account of the balance of payments resulted from a $71-billion fall in U.S. capital *outflows*. During 1982–84 there was no significant change in the inflow of foreign capital into the United States. However, U.S. capital outflows dropped from $121 billion to $22 billion—a decline of 80 per cent—throwing the U.S. capital account into a $100-billion surplus. It was this collapse in U.S. capital outflow that created the large trade deficit, which by definition is a mirror image of the capital surplus.

Table 2-4. U.S. Capital Account, 1980 to 1987

Billions of Dollars

	1980	1981	1982	1983	1984	1985	1986	1987
1. Capital inflow to U.S.	58	83	94	85	102	130	213	203
2. Less: Capital outflow from U.S.	86	111	121	50	22	31	96	64
3. Equals: Net identified capital inflow	−28	−28	−27	35	80	99	117	139
4. Plus: Statistical discrepancy and other inflows	26	21	36	11	27	18	24	22
5. Equals: Net capital inflow to U.S.	−2	−7	9	46	107	117	141	161
6. Current account balance	2	7	−9	−46	−107	−116	−141	−161

Source: U.S. Department of Commerce; + implies inflow, − outflow.

Why did American investors suddenly cease exporting their capital and instead retain it at home where it supposedly was subject to reckless policies of inflationary debt accumulation? After all, such a dangerous program as Reagan's was alleged to be should have resulted in capital flight. Why then the sudden preference of American capital for the U.S. as compared, for example, to West Germany, a country with an economic policy that everyone considered sound?

The answer is so obvious that the only mystery is how economists and financial writers missed it. The 1981 business-tax cut and the reductions in personal-income-tax rates in 1982 and 1983 raised the after-tax earnings on real investment in the U.S. relative to the rest of the world. Instead of exporting capital, the U.S. retained it and financed its own deficit.

The spectacle of almost every economist misinterpreting the source of the capital surplus is extraordinary. Economists looked at the net figure, ignored its composition, and, seeing what they wanted to see, erroneously concluded that the net inflow was foreign money financing American over-consumption.

After convincing themselves and many others on the basis of this fundamental error that the U.S. was dangerously dependent on foreign capital, economists began warning of the consequences. The inflow of foreign money to finance our consumption, they declared, was keeping the dollar high, thus wrecking the competitiveness of U.S. industry. Furthermore, our addiction to foreign capital meant that the U.S. would have to maintain high interest rates in order to continue to attract the money, thus undermining U.S. investment and de-industrializing America. If U.S. interest rates or the dollar were to fall, foreign capital would flee, depriving us of financing for the "twin deficits."

This doomsday scenario was picked up by journalists and kept international markets unnerved. U.S. economic policy came under ever-stronger criticism from our allies. America's "twin deficits" became the scapegoat for every country's problems.

Then, in the autumn of 1985, Secretary of the Treasury James A. Baker III engineered the political fall of the dollar, which plunged, along with U.S. interest rates, in 1986 and 1987. Remarkably, foreign capital inflows to the U.S. promptly doubled.

There's More . . .

The Twin Towers of Debt argument was also contradicted by the behavior of interest rates. As the budget deficit rose, interest rates fell. The high interest rates that retirees fondly recall *preceded* the large deficits. An inverted yield curve, with short-term rates above long-term rates, characterized the economy in 1979, 1980, and 1981. The inverted yield curve is a sign that high interest rates are caused by stringent monetary policy. The federal-fund rate, an overnight rate set by the Fed, was higher than the interest rate on long-term triple-A corporate bonds from October 1978 to May 1980, from October 1980 to October 1981, and from March 1982 to June 1982. The federal-funds rate exceeded the corporate-bond rate by 5.57 percentage points in April 1980 and by 5.69 percentage points in December 1980. In January 1981, when Mr. Reagan was inaugurated as President, the gap peaked at 6.27 percentage points. Overall, interest rates peaked in 1981, with the budget deficit unchanged from its previous year's level. Reagan's budget deficit peaked in 1986 at three times the size of the 1981 deficit, with the federal-funds rate only one-third as high as it was in 1981. By the summer of 1992, Bush's budget deficit was twice the size of Reagan's, and interest rates (long and short) had fallen to the lowest levels since the 1960s. None of the predicted financing problems of the debt have materialized.

But what about the debt? Isn't it historically high, and, unlike the past when we "owed it to ourselves," don't foreigners hold a dangerously high percentage? The answer to both questions is "no." The accumulated public debt today as a share of GNP is less than half what it was in 1946. We financed World War II by borrowing, and at the close of the war the public debt was 127 per cent of GNP. This huge debt overhang did not prevent the postwar expansion of the U.S. economy. Taxes were not raised to pay off the debt, and government spending was not cut. Government spending has grown consistently during the postwar period, as has the public debt. But the economy grew, too, and we grew out from under the debt.

During the 1980s, the ratio of public debt to GNP rose slightly, back to where it had been under John Kennedy. Under George Bush the ratio has risen further, due in part to his resumption of tax-and-spend policies and to a weak economy, but primarily to the negative impact the 1986 Tax Reform Act has had on real-estate values and insured financial deposits. Unless the bailout of insured deposits becomes an ongoing activity of the government, the deficit should decline again, both absolutely and as a share of GNP, as it did in the latter part of Reagan's second term.

As for foreign holdings of U.S. debt, the official U.S. statistics show they peaked in 1978 as a percentage of the total. The recycling of petrodollars had a bigger impact on foreign holdings of U.S. debt than the budget and trade deficits of the 1980s.

But what about investment? Isn't it true that investment measures show the U.S. to be in decline? The illusion of the U.S. as a disinvesting nation was created by incompetent economists measuring investment in net nominal terms, without adjusting for inflation and for shifts in the composition of investment. During the 1980s, prices of capital goods in the U.S. rose only about half as fast as the overall U.S. inflation rate. Unless an inflation-adjusted measure of investment is used, the decline in the relative price of capital goods can be misinterpreted as a fall in investment's share of GDP.

Measuring investment net of depreciation or replacement of the capital used in production has the same result. On the surface net investment seems to be a more reliable measure than gross investment. However, net investment fails to make any adjustment for the shift in the composition of investment from longer-lived assets, such as buildings, to shorter-lived assets, such as equipment, that generate more rapid depreciation. Net investment has been falling as a share of U.S. GNP for the past 25 years as a result of a rise in the depreciation rate corresponding to an increase in equipment's share of investment. By misinterpreting a change in asset mix as a decline in investment, economists painted a false picture of disinvestment. As Table 2-5 shows, real gross investment's share of GNP in the 1980s was unprecedented in the postwar era.

Prompted by criticisms from economists that U.S. Government statistics were failing to detect a weakening in the nation's industrial base, the Commerce Department undertook a two-and-a-half-year study of American manufacturing. The study, released in 1991, shows that the 1980s were years of an almost unbelievable revival by U.S. industry.

Table 2-5. Real Gross Business Fixed Investment as a Percentage of GNP

Years	Total	Structures	Equipment
1960–64	8.76%	4.05%	4.72%
1965–69	10.23	4.38	5.85
1970–74	10.36	4.12	6.24
1975–79	10.57	3.80	6.77
1980–84	11.51	4.52	6.99
1985–89	11.40	3.95	7.45
1959–90	10.44	4.11	6.32

Source: U.S. Department of Commerce.

In a front-page story that must have been galling for that paper's editorial writers, the *New York Times* reported on February 5, 1991, that the rate of growth in U.S. manufacturing productivity had tripled during the 1980s and now was on a par with Japan's and Europe's, and that manufacturing's share of GNP had rebounded to the "level of output achieved in the 1960s when American factories hummed at a feverish clip." Far from losing its competitiveness, the report revealed, the U.S. had experienced an unprecedented export boom.

Turning Japanese

On the rare occasion when they are confronted with facts, the purveyors of disinformation retreat to lesser theses. Foreigners, they say, can afford more debt than Americans because they save more. The high Japanese saving rate is invoked as proof of the failure of Reagan's tax cuts. If only we had not cut taxes, we would not have the deficits and, therefore, would be saving more.

But the high Japanese saving rate, used to deflate American economic success in the 1980s, is apparently another fable. In the spring 1989 issue of the *Quarterly Review* of the Federal Reserve Bank of Minneapolis, University of Pennsylvania Professor Fumio Hayashi points out that most of the "apparent savings-rate gap between Japan and the U.S. is a statistical illusion attributable to differences in the way the two countries compile their national income accounts."

The Japanese value depreciation at historical cost rather than at the higher replacement-cost figure that Americans use. As a result, Japanese accounting understates the value of assets used in production and makes Japanese investment look higher than it is. Another source of the saving-gap illusion is the U.S. practice of counting all government expenditures—including money spent on roads, schools, and warships—as consumption, whereas Japan counts such spending as investment. Once the accounting systems are put on an equal footing, Hayashi finds, the notoriously wide difference in the savings rate disappears.

Economists who look carefully at the subject have found that the gloomy view of the U.S. as a community of spendthrifts is without foundation. For example, Robert E. Lipsey of Queens College and Irving B. Kravis of the University of Pennsylvania studied savings and investment rates in industrialized countries and found that America's bad reputation is based on careless comparisons and narrow measures of investment. This is consonant with other distortions, for example the myth that Reaganomics was based on the belief in self-financing tax cuts and that the deficits prove its failure. In fact, all the official public documents setting out the Reagan program show that the tax reductions at the heart of the 1981–85 budget plan are based on the traditional Treasury static-revenue estimate that every dollar of tax cut would lose a dollar of revenue.

President Reagan's economic program was set forth in an inch-thick document, "A Program for Economic Recovery," made available to the public and submitted to Congress on February 18, 1981. Tables in the document make it unmistakably clear that the Administration expected the forthcoming tax cut to reduce revenues substantially below the amounts that would be collected in the absence of such a cut. Without the tax cut, revenues were projected to rise from $609 billion in 1981 to $1,159.8 billion in 1986. With the tax cut, they were projected to rise from $600.2 billion in 1981 to $942 billion in 1986. The total six-year revenue cost of the tax cut was thus estimated at $718.2 billion.

As the tax-rate reduction was expected to slow the growth of revenues, receipts as a percentage of GNP were expected to fall from 21.1 per cent in 1981 to 19.6 per cent in 1986. Accordingly, the document spelled out the necessity of slowing the growth of spending in order to avoid rising deficits. The Administration planned to hold the annual growth of spending to 6 per cent during 1981–84 and to 9 per cent during 1984–86. On this basis, the Reagan budget projected a rise in spending (including the defense buildup) from $654.7 billion in 1981 to $912.1 billion in 1986.

A summary fact sheet showing the expected revenue losses and planned spending reductions was put out for wire transmission. Months of testimony and debate followed, during the course of which the massive revenue losses were in the forefront. After the Economic Recovery Tax Act of 1981 was passed, the Treasury Department issued to the media a comprehensive report on the legislation, including a three-page table detailing the revenue loss for each of its provisions. (Between introduction and final passage of the bill, the estimated total six-year revenue cost had grown slightly, from $718.2 to $726.6 billion.)

The Reagan deficit forecast was off, not because of a "Laffer curve forecast," but because the inflation rate unexpectedly collapsed. This surprised almost everyone, especially the critics who had repeatedly claimed that the Reagan tax cuts would be inflationary. Since monetary policy was a "weak sister," pundits proclaimed that not even tight money (itself unlikely) could subdue the inflationary impact of such a large tax cut.

As any economist should know, a budget forecast is based on an assumption about the growth path of nominal GNP. If the inflation forecast is wrong, so will be the GNP, revenue, and deficit forecasts. The consumer price index tells the story: For 1981 the Reagan Administration forecast 11 per cent inflation versus 8.9 per cent actual; for 1982, 8.2 per cent versus 3.9 per cent; for 1983, 6.2 per cent versus 3.8 per cent; for 1984, 5.4 per cent versus 4.0 per cent. (In 1981 critics had derided what turned out to be a pessimistic inflation forecast as "optimistic," a "rosy scenario," and "not credible.") The unanticipated disinflation, together with the loss in real output from the 1981–82 recession resulted in GNP during 1981–86 being $2.5 trillion less than forecast—with an estimated loss of federal revenue of $500 billion, and higher real spending than intended. This is the cause of the budget deficits.

Lest we forget, supply-side economics was controversial because of its claim that worsening "Phillips curve" tradeoffs between inflation and employment were the product of a policy mix that pumped up demand while reducing incentives to supply. By reducing the growth rate of money while improving incentives, the economy could escape from its malaise.

Supply-side economics made good on its promise, and Ronald Reagan delivered both the longest peacetime U.S. expansion and disinflation. This achievement has been buried under a pack of lies told by people whose reputations exceed what their integrity warrants. They succeeded in their goal of pushing the Bush Administration away from successful policies and toward self-destruction.

C. Undertaxed? Overspent!

To Cut and to Please

Norman B. Ture

Mr. Ture, Undersecretary of the Treasury for Tax and Economic Affairs in 1981–82, is now President of the Institute for Research on the Economics of Taxation (IRET).

One of the standard allegations is that the very large budget deficits were caused by the Reagan tax cuts. As Representative Donald J. Pease (D., Ohio) put it (June 11, 1992): "Let us look at the big deficits we have and try to find out what caused them. . . . Fundamentally, our $4-trillion deficit or debt is caused by loss of revenue. The $4-trillion debt is caused by the 1981 tax cut and misguided supply-side economics." The facts give the lie to this charge.

The initial Reagan game plan, as detailed in the February 18, 1981, White Paper referred to by Paul Craig Roberts, projected a shift in federal budget outcomes from deficit to surplus occurring in fiscal year 1984. Although federal revenues as a percentage of gross national product were projected to fall from 21.1 per cent in 1981 to 19.3 per cent in 1984, the dollar amount of budget receipts was expected to increase from $600.2 billion in the former year to $772.1 billion in the latter. In the same period, federal outlays were to rise from $654.7 billion to $771.6 billion, although falling in relation to GNP from 23.0 per cent to 19.3 per cent. In essence, this budget policy represented an effort to bring receipts and outlays in relation to GNP more nearly in line with the average postwar experience.

The 1981–82 recession that had been developing in the late 1970s and in 1980 undid the Reagan plan. The revenue projections in the White Paper assumed prompt enactment and implementation of the proposed individual rate reductions and changes in depreciation provisions that would have raised the level and rate of growth of GNP. Although these tax changes were expected to reduce tax revenues compared to the amounts that would have been obtained under prior law, revenues in 1981 were nevertheless expected, at the

Table 2-6. Growth in Federal Outlays
Billions of Dollars

Fiscal Year	Real (1987 Dollars) Amount	% Increase	Current Dollars Amount	% Increase
1980	$ 832.1	6.4	$ 590.9	17.4
1981	867.7	4.3	678.2	14.8
1982	891.1	2.7	745.8	10.0
1983	921.1	3.4	808.4	8.4
1984	933.5	1.4	851.8	5.4
1985	1001.3	7.3	946.4	11.1
1986	1017.3	1.6	990.3	4.6
1987	1003.9	(1.3)	1003.9	1.4
1988	1027.1	2.3	1064.1	6.0
1989	1057.9	3.0	1144.2	7.5

Source: Budget of the United States Government, FY 1993, Supplement 1992, Table 1.3, Part 5.

higher levels of income produced by the tax changes, to exceed those in 1980 and to continue to grow each year thereafter.

In fact, under the influence of the recession and the unexpectedly sharp deceleration of inflation, budget receipts fell far short of those projected in the White Paper. Receipts were virtually the same in fiscal 1983 as in fiscal 1981 and were about $110 billion below the White Paper estimate. From 19.6 per cent of GNP in 1981, receipts fell to 18.1 per cent of GNP in fiscal 1983.

With the recovery beginning in late 1982, budget receipts expanded rapidly, on the average by slightly over 8 per cent a year, through fiscal 1990. By that year, budget receipts were 18.9 per cent of GNP. Whether the several substantial tax increases from 1982 through 1989—particularly the Tax Equity and Fiscal Responsibility Act (TEFRA) of 1982, the Deficit Reduction Act (DEFRA) of 1984, and the Tax Reform Act of 1986 (TRA86)—contributed to rather than retarded this growth in revenue is, at the least, debatable. Unless one believes, however, that tax increases necessarily lose revenue (a not entirely implausible proposition), there is no basis in fact for insisting that tax-policy developments were responsible for the budget deficits of the Reagan years.

A major element in the initial Reagan budget policy was a slow-down in the growth of federal outlays and a change in their composition. The White Paper contemplated total budget outlays rising from $654.7 billion in fiscal 1981 to $771.6 billion in fiscal 1984, an annual rate of increase of 5.6 per cent. Defense outlays were to increase from 24.1 per cent of the total to 32.4 per cent, and the so-called "safety net" programs were to increase from 36.6 to 40.6 per cent, while all other programs and interest were to fall from 38.3 to 27.0 per cent.

This part of the budget plan, too, was not realized. Although the growth in federal outlays, in both nominal and real terms, slowed materially from fiscal 1980 through fiscal 1989, total outlays substantially exceeded those proposed in every Reagan budget. As a result, even had the revenues projected in the White Paper been realized, the budget would have failed to come into balance in 1984, when actual outlays of $851.8 billion were $80 billion more than had been contemplated.

Table 2-7. Federal Budget Outlays, Proposed and Actual

Dollar amounts in Billions

Fiscal Year	Outlays Proposed	Outlays Actual
1981	$ 655.2	$ 678.2
1982	695.3	745.8
1983	773.3	808.4
1984	862.5	851.8
1985	940.3	946.4
1986	973.7	990.3
1987	994.0	1003.9
1988	1024.3	1064.1
1989	1094.2	1144.2

Source: Budget Message of the President, Fiscal Years 1981–89; Budget of the United States, FY 1993, Part Five, Table 1.3, pages 5–18. Proposed outlays for 1981 from the March 1981 FY 1982 Budget Revisions.

Federal spending growth slowed more in Reagan's second term under the constraints imposed by the Gramm-Rudman-Hollings deficit-reduction targets. Contrary to the widespread assertion that it failed of its purpose, G-R-H was amazingly effective in slowing the growth of federal outlays. From fiscal 1985 through fiscal 1989, total outlays, measured in constant 1987 dollars, increased at an average annual rate of only 1.4 per cent, just over one-third the annual rate of increase in fiscal years 1981–85. Even measured in current dollars, G-R-H slowed the growth of spending, from an annual rate of 8.69 per cent in fiscal years 1981–85 to 4.86 per cent over the next four years.

Had federal outlays in the ensuing fiscal years increased no more rapidly than the 4.86 per cent average rate of 1985–89, federal outlays in fiscal 1992 would have totaled $1,319.2 billion, $156.2 billion less than the amount projected in the February 1992 budget document. Even with the recession-depressed revenues projected in the budget for the current fiscal year, the 1992 deficit would be $243.5 billion, not the $399.7 billion forecast.

Despite the success of G-R-H until its emasculation by the Omnibus Budget Reconciliation Act of 1990, total federal outlays grew too rapidly to achieve anything like fiscally prudent budget results. Political memories are short, but surely neither Democrats nor Republicans have forgotten that the standard congressional response to the Reagan budget proposals was "DOA." The historical budget record documents the failure of Congress to curb its appetite for spending increases. With the single exception of fiscal 1984, actual outlays in each of the fiscal years 1981–89 exceeded the Reagan budget requests, by as much as $50 billion in fiscal 1989. Spending excesses, not excessive tax cuts, account for the sorry budget deficit record of the past decade.

Deliberate Deficits?

A related myth is that these deficits were deliberate, part of the Reagan Administration's effort to reduce social spending. As Senator Daniel Patrick Moynihan (D., N.Y.) put it (June 25, 1992): "Mr. Stockman, in his book, *The Triumph of Politics: Why the Reagan Revolution Failed*, describes this policy, this conscious policy of creating deficits, which in the White House and in the Office of Management and Budget at the time there was a term for it, it was called starve the beast . . . the Federal Government was the beast. It had to be starved."

The view that President Reagan, indeed any President, could have engineered the deficits of the last several years boggles the mind. Conceivably, this could occur if federal budget receipts and outlays were determined solely by the President, and if these fiats of the President were impervious to economic developments. David Stockman, Pat Moynihan, and everyone else who subscribes to this notion know it is patent nonsense.

Table 2-8. Distribution of Aggregate Revenue Loss
Relative to Prior Law

Millions of Dollars; 1981 Income Levels

Expanded Income Class *	Prior Law Tax Liability	1982 Total Reductions	1983 Total Reductions
Under $5,000	−157	−69	−109
$5,000–$10,000	6,381	−937	−1,479
$10,000–$15,000	16,317	−1,925	−3.287
$15,000–$20,000	22,987	−2,651	−4,675
$20,000–$30,000	58,558	−6,715	−12,349
$30,000–$50,000	85,708	−10,183	−18,923
$50,000–$100,000	51,631	−5,900	−11,002
$100,000–$200,000	24,125	−2,639	−4,437
Over $200,000	21,110	−3,588	−4,080
Total	286,659	−34,803	−60,341

* Expanded income equals adjusted gross income plus excluded capital gains and various tax preference items, less investment interest to the extent of investment income.

Source: Joint Committee on Taxation.

The initial Reagan fiscal agenda, as we have seen, called for spending slowdowns aimed at eliminating the budget deficit in fiscal 1984 and at producing budget surpluses thereafter. This agenda relied on the economic and budget projections for which David Stockman, as Director of OMB, was chiefly responsible. Stockman himself made determined efforts to come up with feasible proposals for slowing the growth of total outlays, while effecting the compositional shifts that were a basic part of the Reagan strategy. When he discovered the obstacles to achieving adequate cuts in increases in spending, Stockman sought to moderate the revenue losses in ERTA. And when the recession depressed tax revenues below the levels in his original projections, Stockman urged a shift to tax increases to moderate the deficits. It is astonishing that he would subsequently avow what would necessarily have been his own duplicity if the budget policies for which he was so largely responsible had, in fact, aimed at creating budget deficits.

As we have also seen, following ERTA, every tax bill proposed or supported by the Administration was a revenue raiser. It is impossible to reconcile this record of tax increases with the inane notion that the Reagan Administration's objective was to enlarge budget deficits.

The key to the deficits is the role of the Congress in budget making. Most of the budgets that President Reagan sent to Congress after 1981 were either rejected out of hand or very materially altered. Former OMB Director Jim Miller often recounts Reagan's asking him why he bothered to send a budget to Congress since the Budget Committee's standard reaction was to disregard it and to fashion its own.

Indeed, it may have been Congress's embarrassment over its role as the engineer of budget deficits that led most of its members to support G-R-H. And it is certainly reasonable to believe that deficit projections dampened congressional ardor for spending increases greater than those that actually occurred. But none of this places responsibility for the budget deficits on the Reagan Administration.

The Incentive Angle

According to the mythmakers, in addition to starving social spending, the Reagan policies were intended to favor the rich at the expense of the poor. As Governor Clinton's *Putting People First: A National Economic Strategy for America* (June 20, 1992) stated it: "For twelve years, the driving idea behind American economic policy has been cutting taxes on the richest individuals and corporations. . . ." The Governor has a fragile grasp of history, even that of the recent past.

For one thing, during the eight years of the Reagan Administration, only one tax bill, ERTA, reduced taxes for upper-income individuals and corporations. The central objective of the initial Reagan program, of which ERTA was a critically important part, was to reorient national economic policy. Instead of focusing on income redistribution and aggregate demand management of the economy, the Reagan policy aimed at reducing the Federal Government's intrusion into the nation's economic life. It sought to provide a policy climate in which individuals' incentives to pursue their own economic progress would not be frustrated by government tax, spending, regulatory, and monetary policies. ERTA's role in this economic strategy was to reduce the disincentives of high and steeply progressive individual tax rates and the biases they exerted against working, saving, and investing, and to provide more realistic and more nearly neutral tax treatment of investment in plant, machinery, and other depreciable property.

ERTA's core elements were a 25 per cent cut in individual marginal tax rates, phased in over three years, and the replacement of the archaic Useful Life depreciation system with the Accelerated Cost Recovery System. Another extremely important element in the Act was the indexing of the individual rate brackets, personal exemptions, and standard deductions. The indexing provisions sought to limit the bracket creep that, during the inflation-ridden 1970s, had escalated the real tax burdens of all taxpayers, but most severely hurt low- and middle-income individuals, for whom the tax brackets were very narrow.

ERTA reduced taxes for virtually all individual taxpayers, but the percentage reductions in tax liabilities for the lower- and middle-income taxpayers exceeded those for the rich. To be sure, the dollar amounts of the tax reductions for the well-to-do were greater; even Bill Clinton and his allies should have enough arithmetical savvy to recognize that a cut of one-tenth of one per cent in a $1,000,000 tax liability is ten times as many dollars as a 100 per cent cut in a $100 tax liability. If they troubled themselves to hunt up the data, they'd find that, according to the estimates of the staff of the Joint Committee on Taxation, the overwhelming bulk—more than two-thirds—of ERTA's individual tax cuts went to people with so-called "expanded" incomes of less than $50,000. Moreover, the percentage reductions in tax liabilities were greatest for people with expanded incomes of less than $10,000. People in the over-$200,000 class enjoyed tax reductions of 20.9 per cent, while the income taxes of those in the $5,000 to $10,000 range were reduced by 27.1 per cent.

Before President Reagan's signature on ERTA was dry, an effort to reverse the thrust of the Reagan tax policy got under way. The effort was undertaken both in Congress and in the Administration itself.

239

The Administration found itself in the late summer of 1981 looking at what it thought was the need for a drastic shift in fiscal strategy. The Democratic leadership in the Congress, smarting under its blistering defeat at President Reagan's hands in the enactment of ERTA, launched their own counterattack in the late summer of 1981. Its principal effort was to roll back the business-incentive provisions in ERTA, an effort that met with little resistance from the White House. The result was the grossly mislabeled Tax Equity and Fiscal Responsibility Act of 1982 (TEFRA). With this legislation, much of ERTA's tax savings and most of the positive incentive effects for business were eliminated.

The alleged centerpiece of the Reagan tax policy is the Tax Reform Act of 1986 (TRA86). The Act's attention grabbers were the dramatic revision in the individual-income-tax rate structure, eliminating all but two of the prior law's sixteen rate brackets, and the sharp cuts in the top rates of both the individual and corporate income taxes. Far more consequential and extensive, however, were the Act's so-called base broadeners. In this respect, TRA86 was the most thorough-going revision of the income tax since its inception— the culmination of the traditional, liberal tax reformers' "loophole"-closing efforts.

Some of these changes broadened the tax base, while others contracted it. The increases in the personal exemption and standard deduction had the effect of taking an estimated four million or more low-income individuals off the income-tax rolls altogether and of materially reducing the tax liabilities of millions of low- and middle-income individuals. Virtually all of the other base changes, on the other hand, increased the taxes of millions of other middle-income as well as most higher-income taxpayers.

According to estimates of the staff of the Joint Committee on Taxation, TRA86 would reduce individual income-tax liabilities by close to $122 billion over the five-year period 1987–91. Over the same period, it would raise corporate income-tax liabilities by $120.3 billion.

Estimated percentage changes in tax liabilities ignored entirely the huge increases (about $227 billion for the years 1987–91) in higher-income individuals' tax liabilities resulting from the hundreds of billions of dollars of base broadeners—effectively accentuating the double taxation of saving.

Welcome as were the changes in the statutory rate structure of the individual income tax and the cutback in the top statutory rate to 28 per cent, TRA86's base broadeners were an enormous price to pay. TRA86 can be perceived as conferring tax favors on the rich only if these base broadeners are ignored.

Additional tax increases, falling entirely on businesses and upper-middle and higher-income individuals were enacted in 1987 and 1988.

The cumulative effects of the tax legislation during the Reagan years has been a substantial increase in the share of federal income-tax liabilities paid by the wealthy. In 1981, the wealthiest—the top 1 per cent—paid 17.6 per cent of total federal individual income taxes; in 1988, their share had increased to 27.5 per cent.

Even a cursory review of the fiscal history of the Reagan years reveals that, with the sole exception of ERTA, all the tax changes enacted during that period were unmistakably anti-business and anti-rich individuals. If, contrary to fact, tax fairness were properly measured by the shares of total tax burdens borne by lower-, middle-, and higher-income individuals, one would have to say that the Reagan tax program was as fair as all get-out.

Decade of Neglect?

Edwin S. Rubenstein

Myth: Social spending was savaged under Reagan.

"[W]hile the numbers on welfare increased, the value of
assistance fell by more than 30 per cent. During the same
time, other federal spending in the cities also dropped. Subsidized housing fell 82 per cent. Job training, 63 per cent.
And programs to develop new business, down 40 per cent."
—Rebecca Chase, ABC News

Did the Reagan Administration deeply cut social spending? Total
federal payments for individuals—the broadest measure of transfer-
payment spending—rose from $344.3 billion in 1981 to $412 billion
in 1989 (1982 dollars), a 19.7 per cent increase. The conventional
wisdom insists this rise conceals two divergent trends: an enormous
increase in payments to the elderly (mainly Social Security and Medicare), offset by reductions in the "safety net" programs targeted to
the poor.

A detailed analysis shows, however, that spending on programs
that provide income, food, health care, housing, education and
training, and social services to poor families increased substantially
(in constant dollars) between 1981 and 1989.

An alternative way of measuring social spending is the percentage of GNP transferred by the Federal Government to poor people.

Table 2-9. Social Program Spending
Billions of 1989 Dollars

	Income Support	Health	Housing	Nutrition	Social Services	Educational/ Training	Total
1981	$39.7	19.1	8.3	17.1	7.7	12.3	$104.1
1989	$42.1	31.1	13.6	17.0	7.7	11.6	$123.1
Change	6%	63%	65%	0%	0%	–6%	18%

Source: Congressional Research Service.

C. Undertaxed? Overspent!

In the Carter years (1977–80) means-tested programs averaged 1.65 per cent of GNP; during Reagan's two terms, this share averaged 1.73 per cent.

Whether measured in real dollars or as a percentage of GNP, the Reagan years can hardly be called a time of declining commitment to the poor. The most persuasive proof of this is the decline in poverty itself. When Reagan took office the poverty rate had been rising from 11.4 per cent in 1978 to 14.0 per cent in 1981. Within 18 months the trend was reversed. After climbing to a high of 15.1 per cent at the end of the recession, the rate declined steadily—to 13.0 per cent in 1988. And, according to the Ways and Means Committee's *Green Book*, when food and housing benefits are taken into account, the 1988 rate was only 11.6 per cent.

The Tide Rose

Ed Gillespie & Christopher Frenze

Myth: The rich paid a larger share of taxes only because they had a larger share of income.

> "Economic research shows that if a wealthy family paid more taxes than its middle-class counterpart during the Reagan-Bush years it was only because the rich had bigger paychecks . . . It was all part of the 'Reagan Revolution,' during which federal income taxes of the wealthiest were reduced from a top rate of 70 per cent to a top rate of 28 per cent."
> —*Boston Globe*, October 14, 1990

Federal Reserve Board Governor Lawrence Lindsey, who served on the staff of Reagan's Council of Economic Advisors, lays waste to this notion in his 1990 book *The Growth Experiment.*

Lindsey, whose appointment to the Federal Reserve has been President Bush's greatest economic-policy achievement, notes the effect lower rates have not only on high-income taxpayers' willingness to work longer hours, but on "decisions about how to arrange their given financial condition, such as choosing taxable or tax-exempt bonds, or one stock over another, or more cash over fringes in salary negotiation, or how much to contribute to charity." In other words, how much income to shelter and how much to declare as taxable income, which is the data source for average-income comparisons.

"Consider the decision to buy a bond," Mr. Lindsey explains. "Suppose a taxable bond yields 10 per cent and a tax-exempt bond, issued by a state or municipal government, yields only 4 per cent. . . . For a taxpayer in the 70 per cent bracket, the taxable bond yields only 3 per cent after taxes. The tax-exempt bond is the better investment. On the other hand, if this taxpayer's tax rate is cut to 50 per cent, the after-tax yield on the taxable bond rises to 5 per cent, more than the tax-exempt bond. Thus one pecuniary effect of tax cuts is to cause investors to hold more taxable securities and fewer tax-exempt securities, producing more tax revenue."

C. Undertaxed? Overspent!

James Gwartney, an economics professor at Florida State University, notes that "the lower rates drew funds out of the tax shelters and reduced the attractiveness of pleasurable, tax-deductible, business-related expenses (e.g., plush offices, travel to nice places, and luxury automobiles). As a result the reported income—after deductions—from partnerships and Sub-S Corporations (two major vehicles used for tax-shelter investments) of the top 5 per cent of taxpayers rose from $12 billion in 1980 to $56 billion in 1988, a whopping 360 per cent increase. Similarly, the reported income from business and professional practice of the top earners skyrocketed during the 1980s."

More important, the lower tax rates are conducive to entrepreneurial startups and greater work effort. Lindsey, again: "Indeed, the evidence suggests that high tax rates help ossify the class structure rather than break it down. In 1960, when the top rate was 91 per cent, the income of the rich was drawn disproportionately from interest and dividends. The top 2 per cent of taxpayers received 48 per cent of interest and dividends but only 8.7 per cent of wage, salary, and entrepreneurial income. *By 1985, with a 50 per cent top rate, the share of interest and dividends received by this group was cut in half while the share of wage and entrepreneurial income had risen 28 per cent.* The real losers from soak-the-rich taxation are not the presently rich, but the would-be rich. High income-tax rates bar access to the upper class."

What Do the Wealthy Pay?

Edwin S. Rubenstein

Myth: The 1986 tax act was pro-rich.

"When Congress enacted the Tax Reform Act of 1986, law-makers hailed its alternative minimum tax provision as the most stringent ever, guaranteeing that nobody would ever escape paying at least some tax. . . . [But] passage of 'the toughest minimum tax ever' resulted in a 75 per cent drop in the number of people who paid the tax, and a 90 per cent drop in the amount they paid.

"On average, a millionaire in 1986 paid an alternative minimum tax of $116,395. Three years later, a millionaire paid $54,758. That amounted to a 53 per cent tax cut."

—Barlett and Steele, *Philadelphia Inquirer*, October 1991

This is a schoolboy howler of such proportions that if the authors had been correct on everything else, their reputations would still be in ruins. They note—correctly—that fewer millionaires pay the Alternative Minimum Tax today than before the 1986 tax reform, and that those who do generally pay less AMT than before the 1986 act. However, rather than indicating an "illusory" tax hike on the rich, lower AMT payments reflect a more progressive tax system.

AMT payments rise or fall in lockstep with the number of tax loopholes or "tax preferences" available to wealthy taxpayers. (The

Table 2-10. Personal Income Taxes Paid by the Wealthy				
	— Amount ($Bil.) —		— % of Total —	
Gross-Income Bracket	**1986**	**1989**	**1986**	**1989**
$100,000–$200,000	$37.3	$55.1	10.2%	12.5%
$200,000–$500,000	27.1	42.9	7.4	9.8
$500,000–$1 million	12.9	20.0	3.5	4.6
$1 million +	29.2	39.4	7.9	9.0
$100,000 +	$106.5	$157.4	29.0%	35.9%

Source: Internal Revenue Service.

minimum tax is designed to curtail the benefits of such exemptions.) The 1986 reform eliminated many of these loopholes, including passive real-estate tax shelters and the preferential tax treatment for capital gains. Thus while AMT payments fell after 1986, the total amount of personal income taxes collected from wealthy taxpayers rose dramatically.

Taxes paid by individuals earning $100,000 and above rose by more than $50 billion within three years of the 1986 tax act; their share of total income taxes rose from 29.0 per cent in 1986 to 35.9 per cent in 1989.

It follows that people earning less than $100,000 paid a smaller share of income taxes in 1989 than in 1986.

D. A Bigger Pie

High Yield or Junk?

Glenn Yago

Mr. Yago is Professor of Economics
at SUNY-Stony Brook and CUNY Graduate School.

In the search for simple causes of the nation's economic problems, corporate debt became a familiar scapegoat. The received opinion is that U.S. business accumulated excessive debt loads during the Eighties largely through takeovers, which also caused massive job loss. In this legend, corporate financial practice (particularly the reliance on junk bonds) was a matter of paper shuffling that produced no economic value. Debt distorted economic horizons, leading to chronic "short-termism," and the high-yield-bond market was a "Ponzi scheme" that led to an inevitable market collapse, causing major disruptions in the financial-services industry (e.g., the S&L crisis).

This near demonic view of corporate debt and high-yield securities dates from the takeover battles of the mid-1980s. As Robert Bartley notes, "Much of the concern over leverage, finally, is connected to the takeover wars, to the battle between those trying to protect old capital and those trying to build new capital."

Basically, no one heard a peep about excessive debt or takeovers prior to the mid Eighties. In fact, the Business Roundtable and Fortune 500 companies that promoted new regulations on credit access and ownership change in the Eighties had opposed restrictions on takeovers during the Carter years when they were the only companies that were able to finance large-scale acquisitions. But by the mid Eighties, when merger-and-acquisition departments on Wall Street had discovered high-yield financing as a means to launch takeover bids, old-money firms and their white-shoe investment banks sought protection not by offering a better deal to their shareholders, but by going to courts, legislators, and regulatory bodies.

How many big oil companies wanted to see another Boone Pickens, and how many Revlons wanted to see another Ron Pearlman preaching the doctrine of market efficiency? Moreover, corporate control was not the only area where entrenched and protected managers were losing ground. Market share in major industries was being eroded by entrepreneurial newcomers who deftly leveraged growth through what was then the lowest cost of capital—debt. How many more Bill McGowans and MCIs could AT&T stand? How interested were CBS and ABC/Capital Cities in seeing Ted Turner or TCI or MTV coming into their markets? Whether the assault on corporate power appeared in the form of a takeover bid or in the form of a new, more technologically and financially adept competitor, the main cause of concern for those holding on to their seats in the corporate suites was the new channels of capital access that had been carved into the securities markets.

Demythologizing Junk Bonds
Nowhere is the gap between empirical evidence and public perception greater than in the case of high-yield securities and the capital access created in the Eighties. To demythologize the changes that occurred, we need to examine each of the distorted propositions in turn.

Myth 1: Debt destroyed jobs.

> "Thousands of workers lost their jobs, companies loaded up with debt to pay for deals, profits were sacrificed to pay interest costs on the borrowings, and even so, many companies were eventually forced into bankruptcy."
> —James Stewart, *Den of Thieves*

When access to capital was opened up, the greatest period of job growth since World War II ensued. It is true that the largest firms eliminated jobs. However, while the 800 investment-grade firms decreased employment by 4 per cent, non-investment-grade firms increased employment by 24 per cent. Job loss in the Fortune 500 companies for the same period was around 2 million, while the overall economy added 12 million jobs. In my own research on high-yield companies, I found that job growth was six times higher among non-investment-grade companies than industry averages and that those companies exhibited one-third greater growth in productivity, 50 per cent greater growth in sales and about three times greater growth in capital spending than U.S. industry generally.

Simply put, businesses have two ways to sustain or increase profits—increase revenues or decrease costs. Generally, in the Eighties, smaller entrepreneurial companies in growth and emergent industries (e.g., cable, health care, restructured manufacturing, telecommunications) used the former strategy, while the largest established companies used the latter. Instead of focusing on R&D, new products, and new markets, larger companies focused on cutting costs, mainly by cutting their workforce.

In the Sixties and Seventies, in order to avoid being confined to their mature markets, large companies had diversified wildly, leading to industrial conglomeration. Defense companies went into mass transit and nearly out of business, steel companies went into oil, tire companies went into gas, and oil companies bought circuses and insurance companies.

The restructuring of the Eighties for the most part unwound the bad acquisitions of the previous decades, leading to a deconcentration of industries and deconglomeration of unwieldy units in unrelated lines of business. The widespread association of layoffs, shutdowns, and unemployment with this restructuring is spurious. Only 4.4 per cent of mass layoffs in the Eighties, representing 6.6 per cent of the total jobs lost in shutdowns, resulted from ownership change. In tracking 1,100 plants involved in 110 LBOs, my colleagues and I found that plants involved in management buyouts were substantially less likely to close than other plants.

Moreover, high-yield and restructured companies in sectors that were hard hit by import pressures and declining demand showed higher rates of job retention than the rest of the firms in their industry. Manufacturing companies such as Mattel, Seminole Kraft, and National Can actually restored jobs in plants previously threatened by closings. We found that productivity growth was about 14 per cent higher in plants that were either divested or restructured through buyouts than other plants in the same industry. In plants with significant management participation, the difference was even greater: 20 per cent.

This is not to say that there were not some poorly structured transactions that resulted in job loss. This was particularly true in those defensive LBOs where entrenched managers took on more debt to defend against takeovers (e.g., Fruehauf). Two-thirds of the distressed credits for the Eighties were issued in the last few years of the decade, when deal-hungry merger-and-acquisition departments overpriced issues in poorly structured, fee-driven transactions. Entrepreneurial buyouts that added strategic economic value became superseded in the LBO market by defensive, financially driven buyouts, in which failed management maintained its empire with an undercapitalized, overleveraged financial structure.

The lack of job growth in the Nineties is the consequence of too little credit available for new investment, not too much. Job creation halted abruptly at the end of the Eighties when regulatory and tax measures failed to keep growth alive.

Myth 2: Junk debt financed takeovers.

> "There's nothing wrong with mergers per se, except for the junk-bond, highly leveraged, bust-up type. But if you eliminated that kind of deal, then an unfriendly takeover offer is less hostile."
> —Martin Lipton, Wachtell Lipton

Takeover waves have gone on for decades. Earlier waves of mergers and acquisitions led to increased levels of economic and industrial concentration. At the turn of the century, horizontal acquisitions led to the formation of the great trusts. In the 1920s, vertical integration built large, monolithic corporations. In the late 1960s and early 1970s companies diversified into sprawling conglomerates. What was different about the merger wave that began in 1981 was the tendency toward deconcentration.

According to the Securities and Exchange Commission, high-yield debt represented 10 per cent of tender-offer financings in the 1980s, while banks provided 73 per cent. In hostile takeovers, bank

251

borrowing accounted for 78 per cent of the financing. Of the $215 billion raised in the high-yield market during the 1980s, 23 per cent was used to finance leveraged buyouts and repayment of LBO debt.

Most takeovers continued to be done by the largest companies, often without debt financing. The difference in the Eighties was that the largest firms now sometimes faced smaller competitors in these acquisition bids. However, LBO acquisitions never exceeded 25 per cent of the total value of merger-and-acquisition activity. Big companies made the majority of offers for other big and small companies.

Of the top 100 transactions of all time (hostile and friendly), only 14 per cent used high-yield financing; the rest were done by large domestic or foreign corporations with no debt financing. The first recorded hostile takeover was done in 1974 by International Nickel Co. of Canada under the financial advice of Morgan Stanley & Co. with no debt financing. By the early Eighties, law firms and investment banks saw new potential deal flow in takeovers.

Ironically, many of the most visible debt bashers came from these firms. Martin Lipton built a profitable practice in the takeover market by offering target firms the chance to pay his firm a pre-emptive retainer to ensure that his services would not be used by corporate raiders. Similarly, Felix Rohatyn (who referred to high-yield securities as "securities swill") and his firm, Lazard Frères, built an important practice defending against takeovers. By the end of the decade, Lazard was issuing junk bonds to fund a "White Squire" fund for the sole purpose of providing equity capital to managers facing potential takeovers.

Myth 3: Debt destroyed value.

"... an army of business buccaneers began buying, selling, and trading companies the way most Americans buy, sell, and trade knick-knacks at a yard sale. They borrowed money to destroy, not to build. They constructed financial houses of cards, then vanished before they collapsed."
—Barlett and Steele, *Philadelphia Inquirer*,
    October 20, 1991

D. A Bigger Pie

This myth has done a great deal to damage capital markets, companies, job creation, competitiveness, and communities in the Nineties. Based on misinformation about the past decade, regulators and financial institutions have redlined whole industries and communities, creating a credit crunch that caused and prolonged the recession and dampened the current cyclical recovery.

The origins of credit expansion in the Eighties go back to the last credit crunch of 1974, when companies learned that they could not take bank financing for granted. New industries in services, communications, health, and science needed money to grow. Older industries, such as automobiles, farm equipment, mining, and steel, needed huge sums to rebuild. Simultaneously, investors sought higher yields after disappointing results in the mid-Seventies. Unlike traditional lenders (such as banks and savings-and-loans), money managers in insurance companies and mutual funds were able to make investment decisions without the restrictions that come with government subsidy or guarantee.

In the convergence of corporate need for long-term, fixed-rate capital and investor need for higher returns, the non-investment-grade debt market emerged. Of the $215 billion of high-yield debt issued in the 1980s, 77 per cent was used for growing or rebuilding firms. Some of the most innovative and creative industries of the last decade were financed in this market, including home building, low-cost pharmaceuticals, health care, cable television, long-distance services, and cellular communications.

The use of traditional accounting standards that focus only on book values, original costs, and historical performance fail to reflect an enterprise's potential. According to U.S. Federal Reserve data, the market value of nonfinancial U.S. companies as of January 1, 1970, exceeded their debt by more than $300 billion. During the next five years, values would decline, so that by 1974, debt actually exceeded equity by nearly $20 billion, even though corporations weren't necessarily borrowing more. The recovery of stocks, which began in 1975, stimulated equity values to rise $180 billion relative to debt over the balance of the Seventies. Still, by the end of the decade, equity exceeded debt by only $160 billion, well below the level of the previous decade.

The recovery of equity securities in the latter half of the 1970s laid the groundwork for a tripling of stock-market values in the 1980s, from $1 trillion to more than $3.2 trillion. This dramatic turnaround resulted in equity exceeding debt by over $1.2 trillion in nonfinancial companies, a near eightfold increase from $160 billion in 1979.

The perception of excessive debt comes from confounding historical book/cost accounting measures that are snapshots of the past with market values in a dynamically growing marketplace. Traditional and conventional methods measured cost, not value—yesterday, not tomorrow. During the Eighties, investors purchased over $6 billion in securities from companies in the fields of cable, cellular communications, entertainment, and health care. By the end of the decade, the combined equity market value of those firms was over $15 billion, even though they collectively had reported no net income. Such investments were based on the promise of the future.

Examples of value-creating business strategies abound also among firms that faced rebuilding. Northwest Industries was an investment-grade company that was purchased in 1985 through a leveraged buyout by Farley Industries and subsequently downgraded. In 1987, its Fruit of the Loom subsidiary was taken public in a $553-million stock and bond offering. Fruit of the Loom increased its debt, but the additional capital allowed it to expand capital spending, create new jobs, and increase sales by $2 million.

In 1988, Duracell was the battery division of Kraft Inc., a AAA-rated company. That year Duracell was sold to a group that included management and outside investors. Duracell found itself a leveraged, non-investment-grade company that no longer enjoyed ready access to inexpensive capital through Kraft. But Duracell's president realized that it wasn't debt that had inhibited the company's growth, it was being owned by a cheese company. Through innovation in new products and marketing, Duracell was able to increase annual pre-tax earnings nearly sixfold, from $39 million at the time of its buyout to $226 million by the end of 1990.

As Michael Milken once put it, "The true test of any financier is not to structure securities for companies in good times, but to help

find solutions to problems for companies in tough times." In manufacturing and energy industries hit by the collapse of prices in the
early Eighties, exchange offers allowed companies to swap high-
coupon debt issues for lower-coupon debt issues or equity. Access to
interest-rate and currency swaps, futures, and options also afforded
new opportunities in debt management. Regrettably, tax-code and
regulatory changes in the late Eighties began to restrict these
financial innovations and reduced the capacity of companies to
adapt to changing market conditions.

**Myth 4: Innovative debt instruments were wampum; the market was
a "Ponzi scheme."**

> "Evidence now suggests that Mr. Milken's theory was
> wrong—and that he was far from the genius he seemed to
> be about junk bonds. . . . When the past decade is taken as a
> whole, junk bonds appear to have been a mediocre invest-
> ment."
> —*Wall Street Journal*, November 20, 1990

During most of the post-World War II period, inflation was low and
interest rates were stable. Financial innovation was largely unnecessary.

With increased global competition and volatility of interest rates,
currencies, and equity prices, companies required flexibility to
change their corporate capital structure for varying conditions.
Investors also needed flexibility in their portfolio management.
While most people think of finance in binary categories—either debt
or equity—the 1980s saw a broad spectrum of innovative securities.
Examples included zero-coupon bonds used by McCaw Cellular to
build up its network and convertible preferred bonds issued by War-
ner and Chrysler.

But the best known innovation is high-yield debt securities.
According to the dominant media perception, the securities were
the province of a small network of financiers, who "controlled" and
"manipulated" the debt market. As early as 1968, there were over
6,700 bond issues listed on the New York and American Bond

Exchanges, with the highest volume being traded in non-investment-grade issues. Over the past twenty years, high-yield securities were sold by more than 200 different investment-banking firms, which underwrote over 1,500 issues. There were 200 market-makers trading these bonds in the secondary marketplace. Over 100 law firms representing underwriters or issuers issued opinions on the validity of these transactions. All of the large accounting firms audited these transactions. Major mutual funds, pension funds, financial institutions, foreign investors, and individuals invested in these markets. From 1980 to 1990 the number of high-yield mutual funds grew from 26 to 83. In short, the debt market was hardly a shell game, but a complex market that matured over the 1980s.

How did investors fare during this period? For the ten years from 1981 to 1991, the high-yield market averaged returns of 14.1 per cent, outperforming ten-year Treasury bills (10.4 per cent) and the Dow Jones Industrial Average (12.9 per cent). Unlike a Ponzi scheme, the high-yield market rebounded last year to be the best-performing securities once again. In 1991, new issues rose to $9.9 billion, from $1.4 billion in 1990. Non-investment-grade companies raised $11.5 billion in the equity markets. Mutual funds that had fled the market returned with $3.65 billion of new investments, more than offsetting their total outflow for 1990. In short, between the time the alleged "Ponzi scheme" collapsed and the present, the high-yield debt market resurged by $80 billion in value.

Into the Nineties
The fear and loathing aroused by debt in the 1980s is an anomaly in the long sweep of U.S. history. Despite Calvinistic abjurance of debt, the extension of credit, in a nation where economic growth was not held captive by inherited wealth or seigneurial rights, became the central means of access to productive assets, which, together with operating skills, talent, and hard work, have produced enormous wealth and income. With the cauterizing of new flows of capital, the economy's capacity to respond to change has atrophied. The companies and communities that created the most jobs during the past decade are now being redlined. Young companies eager for growth capital are strapped, and whole sections of the country are threat-

ened by the capital cut-off that began as a credit crunch and now threatens greater financial disruptions. The total dollar volumes of commercial and industrial loans dropped sharply in 1991, after edging down in 1990. Decreased lending has restricted expansion plans and polarized recovery for many economic sectors. A shorthand way of understanding this is that big business and big government (with sometimes blind and self-destructive cheerleading by big labor) sought to limit and regulate economic competition, not sustain it.

Our future depends on our ability to learn from the past, not distort it. The Eighties were a period of enormously creative financial innovation. Perhaps by demystifying debt in the Eighties, we can learn to apply our new financial and economic tools to build the future instead of compulsively destroying the gains of the past.

Race and Poverty

Edwin S. Rubenstein

Myth: Ronald Reagan's policies were particularly hard on blacks.

"After eight years of what many see as the Reagan Administration's benign neglect of the poor and studied indifference to civil rights, a lot of those who lived through this week in Overtown seemed to think the best thing about George Bush is that he is not Ronald Reagan."
—ABC's Richard Threlkeld, reporting on how
George Bush's inauguration was received
in Miami's black section of Overtown

"[The War on Poverty], along with a healthy economy, brought the poverty rate down from 19 per cent in 1964 to 11 per cent in 1973 . . . Compare that enviable record with the Reagan-Bush years. Even though the economy recovered for seven straight years, poor people did not. Poverty rates did not drop back to pre-recession levels."
—*New York Times* editorial, "War Against the Poor,"
May 6, 1992

In fact, the total poverty population shrank by 3.8 million between 1983 and 1989, and the poverty rate (the fraction of people living in poverty) fell from 15.2 per cent to 12.8 per cent. Poverty rates had risen throughout the Carter years and continued rising until Ronald Reagan's economic policies took hold.

Between 1978 and 1982 the number of poor blacks rose by more than two million; between 1982 and 1989 the number of poor blacks fell by 400,000.

According to David Ridenour (*Human Events*, October 12, 1991), from the end of 1982 to 1989 black unemployment dropped 9 percentage points (from 20.4 per cent to 11.4 per cent), Hispanic unemployment dropped 7.3 percentage points (from 15.3 per cent to 8.0 per cent), while white unemployment dropped by only 4.0 percentage points.

Table 2-11. Persons Living in Poverty

| | ———— (Millions) ———— | | | ———— Poverty Rate (%) ———— | | |
	White	Black	Hispanic	White	Black	Hispanic
1978	16.26	7.63	2.61	8.7	30.6	21.6
1980	19.70	8.58	3.49	10.2	32.5	25.7
1982	23.52	9.70	4.30	12.0	35.6	29.9
1989	20.79	9.30	5.43	10.0	30.7	26.2
1990	22.33	9.84	6.01	10.7	31.9	28.1

Source: Bureau of the Census, *Poverty in the U.S.: 1990*, August 1991, pp. 16–17.

A black entrepreneurial class flourished. According to the Census Bureau, the number of black-owned businesses increased from 308,000 in 1982 to 424,000 in 1987, a 38-per-cent rise. At the same time, the total number of firms in the U.S. rose by only 14 per cent. Receipts by black-owned firms more than doubled, from $9.6 billion to $19.8 billion.

In some areas of the country the black-white income gap has vanished entirely. Census Bureau figures show that black families in Queens, New York, had a median income of $34,500 in 1990, virtually identical to the $34,600 reported for the borough's whites. The median income for all New York State families was $32,965 that year.

Table 2-12. Black Families with Children

| | — Married-Couple Families — | | — Single-Parent Families — | |
	Number (Mils.)	Poverty Rate (%)	Number (Mils.)	Poverty Rate (%)
1980	2.154	15.5	2.311	54.1
1988	2.181	12.5	2.829	54.4
1990	2.104	14.3	2.965	53.5
Percentage Change, 1980–90				
	−2.3%	−1.2 pts.	+28.3%	−0.6 pts.

Source: Bureau of the Census, *Poverty in the United States: 1990*, August 1991. Table 4, p. 22 (calculations by author).

A recent *New York Times* article, "Blacks Reach a Milestone In Queens: Income Parity" (Sam Roberts, June 8, 1992), also reported that, from 1980 to 1990, the median income of black households grew 31 per cent above inflation, compared to 19 per cent growth for white households. The black-white income gap in Queens shrank from 9.5 per cent in 1980 to 0.2 per cent in 1990.

Unfortunately the very poorest of blacks—and whites too—missed out on the Eighties boom. Reaganomics is not the reason, however. Between 1980 and 1990 the number of black single-parent families grew by more than 650,000, while the number of intact black families fell.

By 1990 three out of every five black families were maintained by a single parent.

The poverty rate for black single-parent families was stuck above 50 per cent throughout the Eighties. The poverty rate for married-couple black families with children was only one-fourth as high, and declined during the decade.

E. Learned Misbehavior

Heads I Win, Tails You Lose

William Niskanen

Mr. Niskanen, who served on the Council of Economic Advisors from 1981 to 1985, is currently the chairman of the Cato Institute.

No, Virginia, Ronald Reagan did not cause the savings-and-loan crisis. The time bomb that became that crisis was designed in the 1930s, tested in the 1960s, and ignited in the 1970s. A July 1981 report to the Federal Home Loan Bank Board (the federal agency that regulated the S&Ls) concluded that the industry's net worth "was overstated by $152.3 billion, on a market-value versus book-value basis, at the end of 1980." Since the book value of the S&L industry at the end of 1980 was only $32 billion, this implies that its market value was *minus* $120 billion at that time—before Reagan took office, before the deregulation of deposit rates and the types of assets the S&Ls were allowed to own.

In most industries, of course, such losses would be borne by the investors in the affected firms. As a consequence of a series of unwise policy decisions that date back to the 1930s, however, most of the losses of the S&L industry ended up as liabilities of the Federal Government, i.e., the taxpayers.

After this time bomb exploded, some negligence at damage control by the Reagan Administration and overt obstruction by several members of Congress compounded the problem, but its general nature and magnitude were a consequence of policies that Reagan inherited. As of 1992, federal taxpayers will probably be liable for about $200 billion to close or reorganize the insolvent S&Ls, about the same (adjusted for inflation) as the negative net worth of the industry in 1980. More disturbingly, the basic policies that led to the S&L crisis (and a similar but smaller problem for the commercial banks) have not yet been changed.

How did this happen?

First, the structure of the savings-and-loan industry was designed

261

in Washington, rather than by evolutionary market processes. A 1932 act created the Federal Home Loan Bank System, with a structure much like that of the Federal Reserve System, to increase the funds available to reasonably solvent S&Ls to finance home mortgages. A 1933 act authorized the Federal Home Loan Bank Board to charter and regulate federal savings-and-loan associations; most of the loans by the member associations were initially restricted to mortgages secured by houses within fifty miles of the association's home office. These restrictions made the assets of S&Ls unusually vulnerable to conditions in the local real-estate market.

More important, the S&Ls faced unusual interest-rate risks. Most of their liabilities were savings accounts (and, later, demand deposits) with variable interest rates and subject to withdrawal on short notice. Most of their assets, however, were thirty-year mortgages at fixed rates. This made the solvency of S&Ls unusually vulnerable to an increase in short-term interest rates.

No financial intermediary with these types of restrictions could survive in a free market. For several decades, however, the S&Ls were sustained by three types of preferences. Solvent associations are allowed to borrow from the Federal Home Loan Banks and securitize their mortgages through the several government-sponsored mortgage associations, each of which has an implicit federal guarantee that reduces their borrowing costs.

S&Ls were exempt from federal income taxes until 1951 (although starting then, this tax preference was gradually reduced until it was nearly eliminated by the Tax Reform Act of 1986). And from 1966 to 1984, the S&Ls were allowed to pay a slightly higher interest rate, initially half a percentage point, than commercial banks on similar accounts. The combination of the post-World War II housing boom and these several preferences sustained a rapid growth of the S&L industry through the early 1970s, despite the unique asset and interest-rate risks to which these associations were subject.

Second, the unique vulnerabilities of the S&Ls would, even so, have been a problem only for their depositors and investors in the absence of another policy innovation of the 1930s. A 1934 act created the Federal Savings and Loan Insurance Corporation to insure the accounts at all federally chartered S&Ls and at those state chartered

S&Ls that elected this insurance. The terms were the same as for commercial banks. The premiums were set at a low flat rate, regardless of the risks to the insurance fund from individual associations. Accounts were first insured up to $5,000, a limit that was increased in steps to $100,000 by 1980. Moreover, the typical procedure for closing an insolvent bank or S&L effectively extended this insurance to accounts of any size.

The objective of deposit insurance was to prevent the types of runs to which even solvent banks were subject in the early 1930s, and it has been effective in this regard. The problems of deposit insurance, however, were also recognized by scholars, bankers, and key public officials at that time. Both the American Bankers Association and Franklin Roosevelt, who did not agree on many issues, opposed deposit insurance for three reasons: First, it means there is no incentive for depositors to monitor the solvency of the banks and S&Ls in which their funds are deposited. Second, the flat-rate premiums provide no incentive to the owners to maintain solvency; in effect, these premiums represent a subsidy from solvent institutions to weak ones. Most important, deposit insurance creates a moral hazard for the owners of weak or insolvent banks and S&Ls, in effect setting up a one-sided bet. If they make unusually risky loans that do not later default, all the returns accrue to the owners; if these loans fail, the losses are borne by the insurance fund and, ultimately, the taxpayers. Heads I win, tails you lose. One should be surprised only that the insured depositories did not attract more crooks and frauds.

One consequence of these problems is perverse runs from solvent banks to insolvent banks, until the solvent banks increase their deposit rates to match those set by the insolvent banks. The most dramatic consequence, of course, is that the taxpayers have now been left with the bill for the insolvent S&Ls.

Ticking Away

All right, smart aleck, you may be asking, if these problems were so clear, why didn't this time bomb explode until the 1980s? The primary reason was that inflation and interest rates were low and stable until the late 1960s. In fact, this time bomb was severely tested (without exploding) by increases in short-term interest rates in 1966,

1969–70, and 1973–74. The first policy response to the interest-rate squeeze of 1966 was to establish controls on the deposit rates of the S&Ls, only compounding the longer-term problem. A 1968 act permitted the S&Ls to issue longer-term liabilities but allowed only minor diversification of their assets. These episodes of rising short-term interest rates reduced the earnings of the S&Ls but were too brief to induce many insolvencies or a major policy response. In the meantime, the controls on deposit rates contributed to a loss of deposits to the new (unregulated and uninsured) money-market mutual funds created by securities firms in the 1970s.

The spark that finally ignited this time bomb was the rapid increase in inflation and interest rates from 1978 through 1981. In this period, the typical S&L found itself with a portfolio of mortgages yielding 8 per cent, at a time when the inflation rate was 10 per cent and the smart money was going into money-market funds at 14 per cent. Most S&Ls were effectively insolvent, even if their books showed some positive net worth.

For the most part, the policy responses to this episode were correct. The S&Ls were authorized to issue variable-rate mortgages in 1979. A 1980 act phased out the deposit-rate controls and broadened the range of assets that an S&L could own; the one major mistake in this act, a last-minute decision of the conference committee, was to increase the limit on insured deposits from $40,000 to $100,000. A 1982 law further broadened the asset powers and enforced the due-on-sale clauses in existing mortgages. This deregulation of deposit rates and asset powers was necessary to avoid a precipitous collapse of most of the S&L industry.

As it turned out, however, such measures only delayed the day of reckoning. The S&Ls then faced a series of asset shocks, the most important of which were due to the 1981–82 recession, the collapse of oil prices in 1986, and the general weakness in real estate markets following the Tax Reform Act of 1986. Some of the insolvencies were due to irresponsible loans of the types recently authorized; most were not. In fact, two of the newly authorized assets, credit cards and high-yield "junk" bonds, had the highest net yield in the S&L portfolios. Deregulation gave the S&Ls greater opportunity for both irresponsible and prudent behavior. The incentive for irresponsible behavior,

264

however, was (and remains) attributable to the combination of deposit insurance and inadequate private capitalization of the depository institutions.

As part of the general assault on the Reagan years, a *Washington Post* editorial (April 28, 1992) concluded that "Deregulation, combined with the egregious failure to enforce the remaining rules, led to the gigantic costs of cleaning up the failed S&Ls." Some people never learn! The failure of the S&Ls was primarily due to the combination of the excessive regulation and the increase in inflation prior to 1981. The cost of this failure to the taxpayers is entirely attributable to the flawed system of federal deposit insurance. The policy of general reluctance to close the failed S&Ls in the 1982 act was wise, based on a correct expectation that the interest-rate problem would soon be resolved. The later forbearance toward specific S&Ls, usually in Texas and California, was primarily due to strong pressure from leading members of Congress, such as House Speaker Jim Wright and the Keating Five. Management of the savings-and-loan crisis by the Reagan Administration was faltering but not egregious, given the overwhelming burdens on regulators working for an agency that reported to Congress and was unusually responsive to industry concerns.

The appropriate charge against the Reagan Administration and Congress was that they failed to change the major policies that led to the S&L crisis. *Unfortunately, these still have not been changed.* A 1989 act authorized funds to close many of the insolvent S&Ls and reassigned the regulators to the Treasury but did not change the deposit-insurance system. Capital standards were increased but the asset powers of the S&Ls were reduced. This act reflects a misperception that some of the effects of deregulation, such as brokered deposits and investment in "junk" bonds, were the primary causes of the S&L crisis. The premise of this act is that conscientious regulators can identify and close weak S&Ls before they become insolvent. Maybe so, but I doubt it. This patchwork of policies may be sufficient in the absence of another surge of inflation. In the meantime, however, the Bush Administration has persistently (and recently) pressured the Federal Reserve for a more expansive monetary policy.

Stay tuned for another episode in the continuing saga of your friendly neighborhood S&L.

Moving Up

Edwin S. Rubenstein

Myth: Reagan policies made it harder for the poor to advance.

"[R]ags to riches remains the economic exception, not the rule . . . If anything, economists say, the climb out of poverty has become harder in the last decade or two."
—Sylvia Nasar, "Rich and Poor Likely to Remain So,"
New York Times, May 18, 1992

"The President says that we should avoid class warfare. Well, as the income numbers show all too graphically, we had class warfare during the 1980s. And the wealthy won."
—Sen. Edward M. Kennedy,
Congressional Record, March 13, 1992

In fact, although the rich as a class have gotten richer relative to the poor, the mix of individuals that make up the "rich" and the "poor" is constantly changing. A banker's son getting a stipend from dad will appear "poor" in the statistics, as will a retired couple who own their own home, or a laid-off executive living off his savings until something turns up. Similarly, a middle-class businessman will find himself in the top 1 per cent the year he sells his business.

Many individuals who were in the bottom half of the American population in 1980 saw their incomes rise to the top 20 per cent by 1990, while others—real-estate speculators and oilmen, for example—plummeted from the top group.

Two recent studies have measured economic mobility in the Reagan years. A Treasury study, done at the request of the Joint Economic Committee of Congress, traced the income reported by 14,351 taxpayers between 1979 and 1988. This sample was restricted to individuals who filed tax returns each of those years, thereby understating mobility since people are always dropping out of or coming into the system.

Nevertheless, Treasury found that 85.8 per cent of taxpayers who were in the bottom quintile in 1979 had climbed to a higher quintile

Table 2-13. Incomes and Social Mobility				
1991 Dollars			
	Average Family Income of 1977 Quintile Members in		
1977 Quintile	**1977**	**1986**	**% Change**
Bottom 20%	$15,853	$27,998	77
Second 20%	31,349	43,041	37
Third 20%	43,297	51,796	20
Fourth 20%	57,486	63,314	10
Top 20%	92,531	97,140	5
All	48,101	56,658	18

Source: Urban Institute.

by 1988. Only 14.2 per cent remained stuck at the bottom; 14.7 per cent rose to the top quintile. *In other words, a person in the bottom quintile in 1979 was more likely to be found in the top quintile than in the bottom quintile in 1988.*

Those at the top have no place to go but down. Accordingly, more than half—52.7 per cent—of the wealthiest 1 per cent in 1979 were gone by 1988. (Again, mobility is understated since deaths are not included.)

Not surprisingly, young workers percolate up at a faster clip than the elderly, most of whom do not work full-time. Census Bureau data show that 29.6 per cent of young adults (18–24 years of age) who were in the lowest quintile in 1987 moved to higher quintiles the following year. By contrast, those who drop to a lower quintile are likely to be older retirees. As Representative Dick Armey put it, "As the poor get older they get richer, while as the rich get older, they retire."

These lifetime trends are ignored by the CBO and the media. Isabel V. Sawhill and Mark Condon of the Urban Institute, however, recently tracked the incomes of individuals over a nine-year period.

Miss Sawhill and Mr. Condon explain the pattern: "People who start at the bottom have nowhere to move but up, and are likely to do so as they become older, gain work seniority, and earn higher incomes. People who start at the top, some of whom may be there because of temporary sources of income like capital gains, have nowhere to go but down. This pattern, however, may be surprising to the general public, which has been led to believe that the poor were literally getting poorer over the past decade or two, and that the incomes of the rich were skyrocketing. This is simply not true."

The static model used by CBO and the media to "prove" that the poor got poorer never allows that the bottom 20 per cent filled up with younger, inexperienced workers during the Eighties—many of them immigrants happy to be here, many of them American citizens who couldn't find work during the Carter stagflation. Nor does it allow that the larger amount of income going to the richest 20 per cent reflects a higher floor for entering that group rather than an increase in income for the individuals who were in that group at the beginning of the period.

Inventing Homelessness

Carl F. Horowitz

Mr. Horowitz is the Washington Bureau
correspondent for Investors Business Daily.

"Mr. Reagan and Congress's housing cutbacks are directly responsible for the homeless problem," announced the late grand provocateur Mitch Snyder on the eve of the October 1989 Housing Now! march. Representative Charles Schumer (D., N.Y.) was also getting in his licks: "The Reagan Administration systematically decimated the nation's [low-income] housing supply." Homelessness, as much as AIDS, became during the Eighties an issue fully engaging Left-collectivism's passions for attaching guilt to the accumulation of wealth, rejecting empiricism, and projecting political explanations onto personal problems.

Homelessness was destined to become a national problem during the 1983–89 economic boom, precisely because it was a political, rather than an economic, phenomenon. By anointing derelicts as "homeless," overstating their presence, and attributing their status to the false consciousness of people in a rat race for success, activists found an effective strategy to encourage Americans to disavow the values that lead to prosperity (including good housing). Consider this comment by homeless activist Jeff Dietrich, in a guest editorial in the November 26, 1988, *Los Angeles Times.*

> We in the Catholic Worker Community believe that the problem of homelessness in America goes to the heart of our problems as a culture. And we believe that our country's culture is rotten because our system is rotten. . . . The driving force of our culture today seems to be the elimination of all those who do not have a degree in computer science, sell Tupperware, or teach aerobics.

Oh, that fiendish Tupperware!

With a few stray exceptions like Richard White, author of the recent *Rude Awakenings* (ICS Press), almost no one understands how homelessness became a super-issue, and why the major media still

269

present as "news" the fabrications of homeless activists. The case rests on two statistical falsehoods—one concerning the number of homeless people; the other, the availability of affordable rental housing.

Maestro of Homelessness
"The first thing a man will do for his ideals is lie," Joseph Schumpeter once wrote.

It is 1982, and Mitch Snyder is about to "go national." Snyder had been known since the mid Seventies in the Washington, D.C., area as something of a zany. He and fellow members of the Community for Creative Non-Violence (CCNV), originally an anti-war group, having discovered the issue of homelessness, instigated hunger strikes, squatting, vandalism, and other happenings for the local homeless.

In 1980, Mr. Snyder, along with a colleague, Mary Ellen Hombs, conducted an informal nationwide survey of homeless-shelter operators. In 1982 they summarized the results in a monograph, *Homelessness in America: A Forced March to Nowhere*. According to the authors, 1 per cent, or some 2.2 million, of all Americans lacked shelter. They added: "We are convinced the number of homeless people in the United States could reach 3 million or more during 1983." Mr. Snyder and Miss Hombs failed to explain how they arrived at such estimates. The General Accounting Office in 1988 reviewed 83 studies on homelessness, finding only 27 to be useful. *Homelessness in America* was not among them.

The major media, on the other hand, saw the CCNV survey as a springboard for a crusade against President Reagan. In short order, "3 million homeless" became enshrined in newspaper headlines and television feature stories. (Old habits are hard to break. On the March 26, 1991, *CBS Evening News*, Harold Dow reported: "In New York there are an estimated 70,000 homeless people, three million across America. A problem that got a lot worse during the boom times of the Eighties.")

The Department of Housing and Urban Development (HUD), for months on the hot spot, conducted a study of its own. Thorough and professional, *A Report to the Secretary on the Homeless and Emergency*

Shelters (1984) concluded that the number of homeless probably ranged from 250,000 to 350,000, and that emergency shelters, far from bursting at the seams, were only about two-thirds full.

The Left, understanding the political cost if HUD's analysis were widely accepted, reacted with swift outrage. Mitch Snyder coaxed Congress to inquire into the "undercount." Though Mr. Snyder admitted in testimony that his own estimate was meaningless (in 1989 Miss Hombs told me the same thing), House Joint Committee Chairman Henry Gonzalez (D., Tex.) was moved to compare HUD's estimate with denials of the Nazi Holocaust.

Recklessly inflating the number of homeless on a local basis is also good sport. This spring, former President Jimmy Carter observed that when he left office, the homeless in Atlanta numbered 1,200, but they now number 15,000. Carter did not cite his source of information.

Finally, the homeless can be redefined to include people "at risk" of losing their housing. In 1989, for example, David Schwartz and John Glascock, of the American Affordable Housing Institute at Rutgers University, authored a frequently cited study, *Combatting Homelessness*, which concluded that 4 million to 14 million American families are "living on the knife edge of homelessness." That's a lot like saying that millions of American married couples are "living on the knife edge of divorce."

Second String

The second element in the statistical charade was that there was a Reagan-inspired cut in federal rent subsidies by some 70 to 85 per cent, and that it forced people out of their dwellings. Richard Celeste, then Democratic governor of Ohio, speaking at the "Housing Now!" rally, denounced "the $24 billion that was denied to the poor and the powerless who depended on HUD for housing." Sociologist Richard Applebaum, of the University of California at Santa Barbara, referred to a "cut" in the federal housing budget from $32 billion to $6 billion and raised the possibility of housing riots at some time in the future.

Let the record show: The reduction in the HUD budget during fiscal years 1981–83 was from $34.2 billion to $16.6 billion (a little

271

more than 50 per cent). More important, it was a cut in *authorizations*, not outlays. As Annelise Anderson explains (p. 275), an authorization merely sets a spending limit, much as a Visa or a MasterCard account establishes a personal credit line. Money authorized reveals nothing about money spent. A federal agency conceivably can receive a zero-dollar authorization for a given year, and still raise its outlays by drawing upon unspent authorizations from prior years.

Table 2-14 reveals that HUD outlays went up during the Reagan years (fiscal 1981–89) by roughly one-third and are increasing, even more rapidly, under President Bush. Also going up substantially since the early 1980s has been the number of low-income households on the housing dole.

Table 2-14. The Amazing Expanding HUD Budget

Year	HUD Outlays (Millions)	Low-Income Households Receiving Housing Subsidies
1980	$12,735	3,107,070
1981	14,880	3,297,451
1982	15,232	3,507,896
1983	15,814	3,663,328
1984	16,663	3,859,676
1985	28,720 *	3,943,238
1986	14,139	4,076,783
1987	15,484	4,151,252
1988	18,938	4,227,330
1989	19,680	4,315,317
1990	20,167	4,386,365
1991	22,751	4,432,077 **
1992	24,159 **	4,577,616 **
1993	28,141 **	4,703,625 **

* The unusually high outlay figures for 1985 resulted from HUD's buying back of loans from public housing authorities; the loans eventually were forgiven.

** Estimate.

Sources: Executive Office of the President, Office of Management and Budget, *Budget of the United States Government: Fiscal Year 1993*, Supplement, Part Five, Historical Tables, February 1992, pp. 60–62; U.S. Department of Housing and Urban Development, *Expanding the Opportunities for Empowerment: New Choices for Residents*, FY 1993 Budget, January 29, 1992.

The anomaly of rising outlays and falling authorizations is attributable mainly to Congress's cancellation of programs committing HUD to subsidizing rents over several decades in new apartment projects, and its shift of funds toward the rent-certificate and voucher programs, which subsidize tenants of existing housing. Ironically, because of the backlog of construction projects approved during the Carter years, a great many federally subsidized apartments opened their doors under President Reagan anyway. Indeed, as William Tucker reported in *National Review* (September 25, 1987), almost three times as many apartments were completed under the public-housing program during 1981–84 as during 1977–80.

Federal subsidies aside, the total year-round housing stock grew from 89.6 million dwellings in 1981 to 102.8 million in 1989 (14.7 per cent), according to the U.S. Census Bureau's *American Housing Survey*. There was especially room at the inn for renters, presumably the population most at risk of becoming homeless. In 1981 the rental vacancy rate stood at 5.0 per cent; by 1989 the rate was 7.1 per cent, according to the Bureau's H-111 Series.

Homelessness Visible

So the two statistical linchpins of the Reagan-did-it hypothesis stand as frauds. The statistical phase of the homelessness debate, by any reasonable expectation, ought to be over, and Mr. Reagan ought to stand exonerated. Yet the Left will not yield. They know the political value of making the homeless visible to as many random observers as possible.

Homelessness, Eighties-style, has its genesis in 1972, when the U.S. Supreme Court handed down its decision in *Papachristou* v. *City of Jacksonville*, overturning the convictions of several persons on vagrancy charges in Jacksonville, Florida. Writing for the majority, Justice William O. Douglas rationalized: "Persons 'wandering or strolling' from place to place have been extolled by Walt Whitman and Vachel Lindsay."

This radical redefinition of rights gradually acquired a deadly political force. Local governments found it difficult to evict vagrants from parks, sidewalks, bus terminals, and other public amenities. Indeed, fearing the bad publicity that now greeted attempts to evict, they allowed the problem to get worse, despite growing complaints from commuters and residents.

New Age liberalism, fulfilling its own prophecy, in turn described the highly visible street people as the castaways of Reaganism gone mad, people whom Snyder & Hombs called "surplus souls in a system firmly rooted in competition and self-interest."

Whether in San Francisco's Civic Center Plaza or in New York City's Tompkins Square Park (both of which experienced rioting during eviction attempts), whether on sidewalks or in subway stations, derelicts had become political love objects, all the better to be seen, so as to shame passers-by whose apathy had supposedly allowed the situation to happen. (A. M. Rosenthal likened tolerating homelessness to being a silent witness to the Kitty Genovese murder.)

Here one comes to the heart of the matter. Homeless activists' boilerplate was made possible by the integration of collective guilt into our political culture. By assigning blame for homelessness to nearly all housed, employed Americans, and by shoving the homeless into their full view, political activists transformed the homeless into "victims" of the pursuit of self-interest (i.e., Reaganism). Until collective guilt as an operational doctrine is defeated, "Reagan did it" will continue to serve as an explanation for homelessness regardless of the evidence that, in or out of the White House, Mr. Reagan is blameless.

E. Learned Misbehavior

Homeless in America

Annelise Anderson

Mrs. Anderson is a Senior Research Fellow at the
Hoover Institution, Stanford University, and a
former Associate Director of the Office of
Management and Budget.

In the *Wall Street Journal* of May 19, 1989, reporter Andy Zipser claimed that "pretty much everyone agrees . . . that by any standard homelessness has multiplied enormously in a period of general affluence . . . and that if finger-pointing is called for, the fingers should point to Washington. . . . As need has escalated in recent years, total spending has plummeted."

Total spending did not plummet, as Carl Horowitz demonstrates in the preceding article. Like the other mythmakers, Mr. Zisper has taken budget-authority numbers and used them as spending—or budget-outlay—numbers.

If the Congress appropriates funds for an aircraft carrier, it doesn't fund just next year's expenditures—it bites the whole bullet. Actual spending may occur over five years or more. It funds the construction of subsidized housing the same way—up front. In 1982, there was $240 billion for housing in budget authority appropriated in earlier years that hadn't yet been spent.

The budget *authority* for subsidized housing did decrease in the Reagan years, from $27.9 billion in 1980 and $26.9 billion in 1981 to an average of $10 to $11 billion in the years 1982–88. Thus there were annual opportunities for claiming that the budget had been cut. In a masterpiece of confusion, *Time* magazine claimed (May 21, 1990) that "Since 1980 federal outlays for rent subsidies and home-building for the poor and elderly have dropped from $41 million to $10 million," thus mixing up not only authority and outlays, but millions and billions as well.

In spite of reductions in budget authority for housing subsidies, annual *outlays* kept on increasing; construction funded in earlier years was built; the number of households and people subsidized increased.

Expenditures for low-income assisted housing doubled between

1980 and 1984; it took until 1990 for 1980 GNP to double. Federal outlays for low-income housing thus increased as a percentage of the GNP. With the dollar increases came increases in the number of beneficiaries—from 10.6 million people in 1980 to 14 million in 1990, an increase of almost one-third while the population increased by only one-tenth. The number of households assisted also increased, from 3.1 million in 1980 to 4.4 million in 1990. Additional beneficiaries were served by the Farmers Home Administration.

In sum, federal spending increases for housing during the Reagan Administration rivaled those for national defense; the percentage of the population receiving benefits increased; a record percentage of the population was employed; and yet the problem of homelessness began to appear—supposedly because of the Reagan "budget cuts."

If budget cuts caused homelessness, the solution would be obvious and simple—increase the budget. Just the opposite is the problem: homelessness occurred as a social phenomenon at a time when increasing cash outlays were subsidizing housing for an increasingly great percentage of the population.

Some writers have sought explanations in rent control and overregulation as contributors to a decreased availability of low-cost rental housing, and indeed the consumer price index for rental housing increased somewhat faster than the overall CPI; on the other hand vacancy rates generally increased in the 1980s, and other costs—such as transportation and food—increased at a lower rate than the overall CPI. More significant may be the constitutional challenges to vagrancy and loitering laws; by the 1980s, it had simply become legal to live and sleep on the streets.

The Fading American Dream?

Edwin S. Rubenstein

Myth: Home ownership became increasingly beyond the reach of ordinary American families during the Reagan years.

"Middle-class families can't buy a house because they're too busy paying for people to have mansions in Chevy Chase, second houses in Malibu, and empty office buildings everywhere."

—C. Austin Fitts, former federal housing commissioner (1989-90), quoted in *The National Journal,* June 22, 1991

In fact, lower inflation and interest rates during the Reagan years greatly increased housing affordability. The Housing Affordability Index indicates the degree to which median-income households can afford a median-priced home. When the index equals 100.0, the median family income equals exactly the amount needed to qualify for purchase of a median-priced home, using conventional financing and making a 20-per-cent down payment.

Housing affordability plummeted during the Seventies. Soaring home prices and mortgage rates, along with stagnant real incomes, pushed the affordability index down to 120.6 in 1977 from 154.8 in

Table 2-15. Housing Affordability Index

	Median Home Price	Median Income	Mortgage Rate	Annual P&I Payment as % of Income	Affordability Index
1970	$ 23,000	$ 9,867	8.35%	17.0%	147.3
1971	24,800	10,285	7.67	16.5	151.9
1972	26,700	11,116	7.52	16.2	154.8
1977	42,900	16,010	9.02	20.7	120.6
1981	66,400	22,388	15.12	36.3	68.9
1988	89,300	32,191	9.31	22.0	122.0
1992 (Feb.)	103,800	36,788	8.43	20.1	138.3

Source: National Association of Realtors; all prices given in nominal dollars.

Table 2-16. Housing Prices and Sizes
1989 Dollars

| | — Median House Price — | | — Average New House — | |
	Existing	New	Sq. Ft.	$/Sq. Ft.
1970	$73,600	$ 74,800	1,385	$44.62
1980	93,700	97,100	1,595	47.06
1988	93,700	112,500	1,810	48.62
	Percentage Change			
1970–80	27.3%	29.8%	15.2%	5.5%
1980–88	0.0	15.9	13.5	3.3

Source: Congressional Research Service, as cited by Warren Brookes.

1972. By 1981 the index had dropped below 100.0, indicating that the median U.S. family could no longer afford the median-priced house.

The turnaround started in 1981. By 1988 the index was above 120.0, and today, by this measure, housing is more affordable to the typical family than at any time since 1976.

In addition, U.S. homebuyers are demanding, and getting, bigger and better houses than their parents ever dreamed of. A Congressional Research Service study showed that the average size of new homes rose 15.2 per cent between 1970 and 1980, and another 13.5 per cent between 1980 and 1988.

The CRS study shows that the 16-per-cent rise in new house prices between 1980 and 1988 was accompanied by a 13.5-per-cent rise in house size. As a result, housing prices rose a mere 3.3 per cent per square foot. Even this rise is largely accounted for by amenities such as air-conditioning and multiple bathrooms, which became far more prevalent over this period.

The CRS study goes on to point out that prices of *existing* homes were flat, after adjusting for inflation, during the Eighties. This, combined with higher median family income and lower interest rates, means that housing was markedly more affordable at the end of the decade than at the beginning.

Warren Brookes, in an article on the CRS study (January 17, 1990), quoted its author, analyst Richard Bourdon: "The rapid rise in home prices has made some think that the current generation of young people may have to settle for less housing than their parents. However, a significant explanation for rising house prices is that homes are getting bigger and better. Media reports often inappropriately refer to the high prices of these bigger and better homes in their stories about how hard it is to buy a first home."

F. Good Samaritans

Decade of Greed?

Richard B. McKenzie

*Mr. McKenzie is Walter B. Gerken Professor of
Enterprise and Society in the Graduate School of
Management at the University of California, Irvine.
This article is drawn from the book:*
What Went Right in the 1980s
(Pacific Research Institute, 1993).

Worrying that the 1990s would be the decade in which the bills of the 1980s would come due, a *Time* magazine reporter declared, "The past decade brought growth, avarice, and an anything-goes attitude," and then glibly summarized the 1980s with five words: "Get rich, borrow, spend, enjoy." A month later another *Time* reporter picked up on the same theme of a decade of decadence when reviewing five recently released books: "Doesn't anyone have a kind word for Wall Street's gilded '80s? The new decade is barely six weeks old and already stores are piled high with books that portray the past ten years as a sink of avarice and excess. The melodramatic titles depict the American free-enterprise system as overrun by barbarians and liars, ambition and greed."

Dubbed the "Decade of Greed," the 1980s were seen by many as one long consumption binge, fostered by the Reagan Administration and characterized by what political pundit Kevin Phillips called "conspicuous opulence." The evidence offered in support of this contention includes casual references to the jump in the sales of luxury automobiles, the number of MBAs (most of whom, presumably, set their sights on making money on Wall Street), the number of get-rich and self-help books, and the number of Wall Street brokers who went to prison.

John Kenneth Galbraith, of course, won't let the decade die. It lives on, he says. How? In the recession. In a recent article titled "The Economic Hangover from a Binge of Greed," the venerable professor says it's time to cut through the excuses: "The present recession is not an autonomous, self-correcting economic drama. It is the wholly predictable response to the speculative extravagances and insanities—and specific government policies—of the 1980s." The country's continuing problems could be blamed on a simple five-letter word: Greed.

That's the widely believed bad news. The good news is that the bad news never amounted to anything more than bad reporting.

More Blessed to Give

While many critics suggest Americans were more selfish and less charitable during the last decade, none have actually looked at the most direct means of assessing greed—the pattern of charitable giving. If they had, they would have quickly discovered that they had told only half the story, leaving out the most positive and striking parts. Measured by giving, the 1980s were not the "Decade of Greed" at all. On the contrary, charitable giving by individuals *and* corporations jumped dramatically. This finding holds for giving measured not just in absolute terms, but also in total real dollars contributed, real charitable contributions per capita, and charitable contributions relative to national income.

Indeed, giving in the 1980s was above the level that would have been predicted from the upward trend established in the 25 years prior to 1980. This conclusion holds even after adjusting for several economic and policy changes that might reasonably be expected to have boosted charitable contributions. In view of total, aggregate giving from 1955 to 1989, the 1980s in America were actually a decade of unusual generosity.

Total giving is composed of gifts from individuals (including bequests), corporations, and foundations. Figure 2-3 (p. 283) shows the pattern of giving from 1955 through 1989. In the 25-year period prior to the "Decade of Greed," total charitable giving, in real terms, more than doubled, increasing from $34.5 billion in 1955 to $77.5 billion in 1980—or at a compounded annual growth rate of 3.3 per cent. Between 1980 and 1989, total giving in real dollars expanded by 56 per cent to $121 billion, or by a compound growth rate of 5.1 per cent. *The annual rate of growth in total giving in the 1980s was nearly 55 per cent higher than in the previous 25 years.*

Because giving by living individuals accounts for more than 80 per cent of all giving, it is not surprising that this category also more than doubled, from $30.2 billion to $64.7 billion between 1955 and 1980 (a compounded growth rate of 3.1 per cent a year). Individual giving reached $102 billion in 1989, after expanding at a compounded rate of 5.2 per cent since 1980.

Moreover, the growth in private giving over the decade (58 per cent) approximated or exceeded the growth of expenditures on a variety of goods and services that might be considered extravagances—for example, new automobiles (60 per cent), jewelry and watches (41 per cent), alcoholic beverages (1 per cent), meals eaten outside the home (22 per cent), tobacco products (–12 per cent), and personal services such as health clubs and beauty salons (38 per cent). The increase in total giving by individuals even exceeded the increase in total consumer credit outstanding.

Corporate-giving levels are much more erratic, in large part because of fluctuations in the business cycle. Before-tax corporate profits represented nearly 15 per cent of national income in 1955 and only a little more than 7 per cent in 1989. After-tax corporate profits represented 8 per cent of national income in 1955, falling to half of that share in 1989. Nevertheless, corporate giving in real terms rose during the period from just under $1.9 billion in 1955 to nearly $5.3 billion in 1989, increasing in the 1980s at a compound rate of 4.1 per cent. *The growth rate in corporate giving was 52 per cent higher in the 1980s than in the earlier decades covered by this study.* In spite of a drop-off in corporate giving after 1986 (due in large part to changes in corporate tax laws), charitable contributions by corporations as a percentage of profits before and after taxes remained higher in the late 1980s than in the decades preceding.

When measured per capita, individual giving and corporate giving both followed the same pattern that we have already observed. Total per-capita giving in real dollars expanded relatively rapidly in the late 1950s and 1960s, rising from $208 per person in 1955 to $324 per person in 1970. Per-capita giving dropped as a result of the economic slump brought on by the OPEC oil-supply shocks in the first half of the 1970s, but remained within the range of $308 to $343 for the rest of the decade. Total per-capita giving then began rising

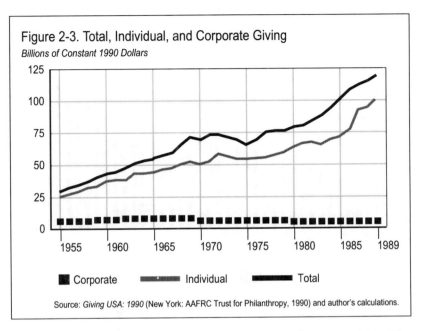

Figure 2-3. Total, Individual, and Corporate Giving
Billions of Constant 1990 Dollars

Corporate   Individual   Total

Source: *Giving USA: 1990* (New York: AAFRC Trust for Philanthropy, 1990) and author's calculations.

markedly in the 1980s, from $340 in 1980 to $486 in 1989. The annual compound growth rate over those years—4 per cent a year—is robust when compared with the 2 per cent average annual increase in the 25 years prior to 1980.

The same trends are observed in charitable giving as a percentage of national income. Charitable giving has never absorbed more than a very small fraction of national income in the United States, remaining below 3 per cent of national income between 1955 and 1989. However, total giving as a percentage of national income began a marked decline in the 1970s, and *made a marked turnaround in the late 1970s and continued generally upward throughout the 1980s.* Specifically, total giving as a percentage of national income rose irregularly from 2.3 per cent in 1955 to 2.5 per cent in 1970, only to fall to a low of 2.1 per cent in 1979. By 1986, total giving as a percentage of national income had surpassed its former high; it reached 2.7 per cent in 1989.

The unusual surge in giving in the 1980s could be explained in part by favorable changes in economic conditions during the dec-

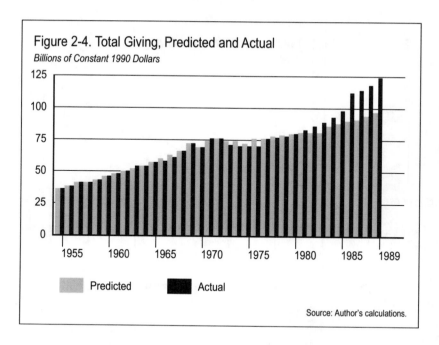

Figure 2-4. Total Giving, Predicted and Actual
Billions of Constant 1990 Dollars

Predicted   Actual

Source: Author's calculations.

ade. It might be said that Americans were giving more not because they were more charitable, but because they had higher incomes and varying tax rates. Some also point to a long-term upward trend in giving that could be attributable to a host of difficult-to-quantify factors, such as changes in religious convictions. Thus it might be argued that the growth in giving in the Eighties was merely an extension of economic changes and historical trends.

The Real Reason

But if that were the case, a statistical analysis of the economic determinants of total, individual, and corporate giving for the 1955–80 period should have predicted actual levels of giving in the 1980s. That was not the case.

Giving in real dollars is directly related (to a statistically significant degree) to real GNP per capita, to the tax rates, and to the population. The levels of total real-dollar giving by year were computed for the Eighties, using the regression formulas developed from 1955–80 data, and the predicted total giving is shown by the gray bars in Figure 2-4.

But the actual real level of total giving during the 1980s was higher in every year than would have been predicted from the statistical relationships established in the 1955–80 period. Indeed, actual total giving exceeded predicted total giving by an annual average of $14 billion, or by 16 per cent. Real individual giving exceeded predicted real individual giving by an annual average of $13 billion, or 18 per cent.

Perhaps in some measures not considered here, the 1980s were a "Decade of Greed." There were, no doubt, individual incidents of conspicuous consumption and selfish disregard for the welfare of others. As the editors of the *Wall Street Journal* noted, "The greedy are undoubtedly always with us." But they prophetically ask, "Were the 1980s really the Greed Decade?" In terms of charitable contributions, the answer is a resounding "No." American individuals and corporations in the 1980s outpaced by a wide margin their giving patterns established in earlier decades. This occurred at a time when real tax payments, part of which were intended to serve charitable goals, were on the rise, and at a time when, because tax rates fell, the after-tax cost of giving rose. No matter how the record of giving is measured, the 1980s were in fact a decade of renewed charity and generosity.

G. Sacred Garden

Barbarians Within?

Peter Samuel

*Mr. Samuel is a journalist specializing in
environmental and other regulatory affairs.*

In the fall of 1981 *Amicus,* the official journal of the Natural
Resources Defense Council, published a piece titled "Barbarians at
the Gate"; it said that the Reagan Administration and its allies were
"abusing the environment in so many ways that it is as if the barbarians were swarming through the gates of Rome, burning and loot-
ing." And what precisely was it that agitated the author of this piece,
one Bartle Bull, to predict the fall of American civilization at the
hands of Hunnish Reaganites?

The first offense was the installation as head of the U.S. Forest
Service of John Crowell, a man who had actually worked for a timber company once and believed in logging on some federal lands.
Ranching too. And oil and gas exploration. Even mining. Crowell
clearly deserved the "barbarian" label for the uncivilized thought
that it may be possible to combine some resource development with
conservation on federal lands. (Not to be confused with national
parks, federal lands constitute 30 per cent of the nation's total land
area and a majority of the land in many Western states.) The possible revival of policies of using government lands for human benefit
that were generally accepted prior to the environmental revolution
of the 1970s sent environmentalists into paroxysms of hysteria.

In fact during the Hunnish occupation of Washington, D.C., the
environment did pretty well, according to data assembled by the
Council for Environmental Quality. Reforestation shot up from
around 2 million acres annually in the 1970s to 3 million—perhaps
because of an improved economic climate. Land in wilderness pres-
ervation increased from 80 to 91 million acres over the Reagan
years. Wetland losses slowed from an average 290,000 acres annually
to 120,000. The Great Lakes continued to get cleaner. Lake Michigan, for example, went from a phosphorous loading of 6,600 tons in

1980 to 2,900 tons in 1988. Water quality in rivers and streams showed mixed trends. In terms of dissolved oxygen, fecal bacteria, and suspended nutrients such as phosphorous and potassium, there was general improvement, though in chlorides, sodium, magnesium, and nitrogen and in both alkalinity and acidity there was regress. Oil spills decreased from an average of 14 million gallons in the 1970s to under 9 million in the Reagan years. The air got cleaner according to most measures. Declines were: sulphur oxides 12 per cent, nitrogen oxides 4 per cent, volatile organic compounds (gasoline fumes, etc.) 14 per cent, suspended particulates (dust, etc.) 12 per cent, carbon monoxide 18 per cent, lead 89 per cent. Use of fertilizers and pesticides declined. Soil erosion was down. Numbers of ducks were down quite sharply, but geese increased. The number of endangered and threatened species increased sharply, though much of this is an artifact of the process of government listing.

Reasonable Standard?
But issues like the environment can be argued various ways. Those who want more environmental quality simply frame their discussion in terms of what remains to be done to meet a standard. Some standards are reasonable objectives (though even then, there is legitimate argument about how fast you should go). Some standards are arbitrary. Some keep being tightened so you never meet them. Others are plain ridiculous. A National Academy of Sciences panel on urban air quality recently pointed out that even the elimination of all human activity in some American cities would not allow the EPA's volatile-organic-compound standards to be met because emissions from surrounding trees exceed them! But standards, reasonable or not, provide a constant measure of deficiency used to beat up on any government. And environmentalists used them to the full against the Reagan Administration.

The environmentalists' most odious barbarian was Secretary of the Interior James Watt.

Not that Watt really deserved all the vilification. He never seriously threatened to roll back any of the environmental movement's achievements. He mostly annoyed them by refusing to show them the respect to which they had grown accustomed. And he did for a while threaten their main Washington redoubt by cutting the funding and staff of the EPA. At 10,400 in 1975, it had grown to 13,000 in the Carter Administration. Under Watt the EPA had a short period of decline in numbers to around 12,000 but it quickly recovered, and toward the end of the Reagan Administration and under President Bush has grown rapidly. It is now at 17,500.

Early on Watt initiated a Cabinet review of the Clean Air Act, hoping to reduce some of its inefficiencies—for example its extraordinary requirement that power plants install expensive sulphur-collecting scrubbers in their smokestacks even when they burn completely non-sulphurous coal. But according to William Niskanen, who represented the Council of Economic Advisors on the review group, the Reagan EPA administrator, Anne Gorsuch (later Burford), was captive to the EPA staff and killed all reform proposals by branding them "radical." Proposals to reform the Clean Water Act met similar opposition and were withdrawn.

The creation of Superfund—aimed at cleaning up toxic wastes—was rushed through the Congress in Jimmy Carter's lame-duck period and has turned out to be a fabulously expensive drain on taxpayers and shareholders. Its main effect seems to be to provide work for EPA inspectors and lawyers, with only a small proportion of funds going for reclaiming toxic materials and disposing of them.

Preoccupied with trying to contain budgetary outlays on Superfund, the Reagan Administration devoted all its intellectual energy to limiting the immediate costs to the federal budget, with sad consequences for industry.

Here was an opportunity to ask some serious questions. Much of the thinking about toxic cleanup is based on the romantic notion that nature is a pristine and benign setting contaminated by mankind. It follows that manmade toxics should be completely reprocessed into benign substances, regardless of the cost of doing this or of the actual risk they pose. Under Superfund, the absurd situation obtains where tens of millions are spent removing a toxic heavy metal from ground water because it is deemed the result of improper human dumping, while other ground water nearby, contaminated by *natural* deposits of the same metal, is completely untreated.

Instead of seizing the high ground and opening a debate about fundamentals, the Administration left proposals for reform of Superfund to the Environmental Protection Agency—akin to deputizing the fox to reduce the number of disappearing chickens. The EPA built a constantly growing program and everyone got promoted in the expanding bureaucratic empire needed to administer it.

None of the barbarian rulers of the Reagan era quite worked out how to cope with Washington scaremongering. Mostly they just got panicked into playing along. Take the case of Times Beach, Missouri, a tiny town where high levels of the trace chemical dioxin were measured and publicized in 1986. Some ten years before, to reduce dust nuisance, the dirt roads in Times Beach had been sprayed with a sealing oil containing the chemical.

Dioxin has never been known to do more than cause skin rash even when people have been soaked in high concentrations of the chemical, as in industrial accidents. But the anti-war crowd had successfully anathematized dioxin because of its presence in Agent Orange, used in Vietnam. Agent Orange air crews who mixed and loaded the chemical and spent hours daily in its spray mist showed no higher incidence of disease than their colleagues who had nothing to do with the chemical. Similarly, despite the hullabaloo about Times Beach's road spraying, there was no evidence of higher disease rates in the little town. No special health problems, and no public-health justification for doing anything at all—except perhaps to send in some non-ideological scientists from the American Council on Science and Health to tell residents the facts about dioxin.

Yet Anne Gorsuch played the green scare game to the hilt. People who had lived there all their lives without any sign of trouble were ordered out of their houses. Miss Gorsuch personally traveled to the benighted little town to announce that the EPA would spend $33 million to buy up all the homes and businesses and close the place down permanently. To placate the evil spirits of environmentalism, mankind (via American taxpayers) would pay its penance and be banished forevermore from the scene of this terrible crime against Mother Earth.

On the Plus Side

One thing the Reagan Administration did do was scare the bejesus out of the better-informed environmentalists by funding a solid scientific study of acid rain. Throughout the 1980s the greens had hustled up scares about acid rain. Typical of the sweeping claims was the statement in the spring 1986 issue of *Amicus* that "acid rain is destroying our soil, forests, and lakes—the basis of the earth's life-support system—and damage is occurring coast to coast." The Reagan Administration launched the National Acid Precipitation Assessment Project (NAPAP) to evaluate these claims. It involved five years of studies and over $500 million in research projects. It was scientifically unimpeachable, and concluded that the environmental zealots were talking through their hats. Lake and stream acidity was overwhelmingly the product of the relative acidity and alkalinity of local soils and rocks through which ground water passed, not precipitation, NAPAP discovered. This explained the presence of highly acid lakes in the pristine non-industrial environment of the South Pacific, and alkaline lakes in areas of "acid rain." The study found no evidence of damage to forests or crops from acid rain. Tree damage that had been attributed by many observers to acid rain was actually the result of pests, diseases, and climatic stress, the report said.

In short, it found that there was no scientific justification for forcing electric utilities to install expensive equipment to cut sulphur-dioxide emissions from their smokestacks, and that SO_2 was not the cause of forest dieback, lake acidity, or crop damage.

All of this was simply censored by environmental writers at the *Washington Post* and the *New York Times*. And the Reagan Administration, having gotten the NAPAP report, did nothing to break through the wall of silence surrounding it. It was left to incoming President George Bush to take the next step in obeisance to the greens by pushing a new Clean Air Act that incorporated $30-billion worth of anti-SO_2 measures. A number of economists have listed the wasteful Clean Air Act as one of a handful of events that ended the economic growth of the Reagan years and precipitated the economic malaise that has taken President Bush down from 80 per cent to 35 per cent public support in public-opinion polls.

Richard Stroup, who was director of the Interior Department's office of policy analysis for several years in the 1980s, says there were some limited accomplishments. He mentions:

—highlighting the skewed priorities of some existing programs and focusing some public attention on costs;

—introducing some limited markets in pollution rights;

—a speed-up of leasing coal-mining rights in federal land;

—the ending of federal subsidies to development of coastal barrier islands;

—a beginning in trades in water.

In an article in *Regulation* magazine Stroup wrote that the basic trouble ever since the founding of the Environmental Protection Agency under Richard Nixon has been that the government is "trying to provide environmental quality the way the Russians grow wheat—with central political control—and trying to preserve land and wildlife with straight socialism, namely ownership of the means of production."

Stroup says the Reagan Administration never challenged this own-it-or-control-it system, which is the heart of the problem. Under James Watt the environmentalists were teased. Under subsequent leadership the Administration tried to placate the environmentalists. It never did serious battle with them.

H. Their Disinformation Campaign

Fear of the Foreign

Evan G. Galbraith

Mr. Galbraith, who served as U.S. Ambassador to France from 1981 to 1985, is a Director of Morgan Stanley International.

In studying litigation at law school, one learns that pleading in the alternative is not only proper but often the only way the defendant is assured of a comprehensive defense. And never mind that the separate defensive arguments may appear contradictory. The old English case one read at Harvard involved a plaintiff claiming the defendant wrongfully held the plaintiff's vase. The defendant pleaded that he a) never took it; b) had given it back; and c) was the rightful owner.

It is thus that we must look at our trade deficit—in divergent ways: a) After necessary statistical adjustments, we do not for all practical purposes have a trade deficit; b) our trade deficit reflects a strength, not a weakness; and c) in the long term, it will probably disappear.

The biggest single factor in our trade deficit is oil, and if you take oil and Canada out of the calculations, our trade deficit disappears. It is advisable from a macroeconomic point of view that we make these adjustments because: a) Canada and the United States are one trading bloc—soon to be consummated—and one *de facto* monetary unit; b) oil is traded in dollars—no foreign-exchange transaction is triggered by the supplier's selling into the United States; c) and suppliers hold most of their reserves in dollars, i.e., the purchase money never leaves the United States. Other countries have to earn dollars to purchase oil. We do not. d) The fact that we purchase foreign oil is irrelevant to any judgment about whether or not our goods are competitive and whether we are relatively efficient—the making of such a judgment being one of the reasons why we keep trade statistics in the first place. e) Eventually, for environmental reasons, other sources of energy such as Canadian and Mexican natural gas will replace substantial amounts of imported oil, so in ignoring oil, we are not being unmindful of the future.

H. Their Disinformation Campaign

In most countries a chronic trade deficit reflects a problem, i.e., the non-competitiveness of a country's products: either their exported products don't measure up in quality or price in the world markets, or imported products are preferred by domestic consumers for the same reasons; or both. In these circumstances, the deficit country can run low on the foreign currency necessary to pay for essential imports—oil, minerals, and even food—and eventually the deficit country may have to restrict imports, either directly, or indirectly, by devaluing its currency. This will lower the country's standard of living.

Some countries overcome a trade deficit by the inward flow of foreign currency from so-called "invisibles"—e.g., tourism, insurance premiums, banking services. Indeed, one must look at the entire "current account" (of which trade in only one part) before reaching conclusions about deficits. If there is an overall current-account deficit, it must be matched mathematically by an equivalent positive amount in the "capital account," which records investment flows. A current-account deficit is covered in the capital account by the deficit country's borrowing abroad, receiving investment funds (equity or debt) from abroad, disposing of reserves of foreign currency, or diminishing capital outflows. If the capital-account surplus ceases, then the current-account deficit will also cease. Alternatively, if there is a surplus in the capital account, then there must be a deficit in the current account.

This brings us the proposition that a current-account deficit, or the trade component thereof, is not necessarily a sign of a nation's weakness. Indeed, during the hundred-year dominance of Britain from Waterloo (1815) to World War I (1914), Britain had a chronic trade deficit despite the captive market in the Empire for British exports. This was because money poured into the country on both the capital account (countries held sterling bonds; foreigners invested in the UK), and the current account (foreigners purchased British services, such as insurance from Lloyd's, banking from the City of London, engineering from the Midlands). This incoming money was used by the British to buy goods from everywhere, creating the highest standard of living in the world. Imports were good for Britain, not only because consumers benefited, but because the

293

foreign products often forced British products to be competitive. Only as Britain became more protectionist, toward the turn of the century, did she become less competitive.

During this hundred years, Britain also exported its excess capital around the world, which it could do thanks to the capital inflows and the stable, non-inflationary nature of its currency (there was almost no inflation during this hundred years; indeed, most items became cheaper as the Industrial Revolution progressed). This caused Britain to acquire substantial foreign assets, the earnings from which increased the current and capital accounts, allowing the luxury of a large trade deficit. All of this brings us to the Reagan trade deficit. America in the 1980s should be compared to Britain in its glory years, and not to a country that shows a trade deficit because its products are not competitive.

In the Reagan years, the trade deficit grew because the country became more prosperous, drawing in imports and raising living standards. Investment poured in (and more important, ceased flowing out) to take advantage of dropping interest rates (creating capital gains in the bond market, an increase in the value of the dollar, a rise in the stock market, and the availability of loans to acquire companies at reasonable prices). The export performance during the Reagan years was spectacular, more than doubling, with manufacturing and exports both increasing their percentages of U.S. GDP, but the large increase in household incomes sucked in imports even more rapidly, thus creating the trade deficit.

A High-Class Problem

The Reagan trade deficits were the result of the Reagan prosperity. That's what is called a high-class problem. But there are those who see it as a problem nonetheless—who cling to the notion that foreign-owned investment in the United States is a threat. These fears were sharpened by dislike of specific investors—oil-rich Arabs and efficient Japanese. The fact is that it takes two things for any country to grow: work and capital, which can include foreign capital. Growth not only creates new jobs, it creates better jobs, making dreams of upward mobility a reality. Just as British capital invested here contributed to pre-1914 U.S. growth, so does Arab, Japanese,

German, French, Taiwanese, Korean, et al. capital add to our present growth.

But what are we to make of the charge that we have become a debtor nation, Uncle Sam with a tin cup seeking handouts? First of all, the value of the assets we hold abroad—IBM, Coca-Cola, Exxon—must be recalculated to reflect their true value and not their historical cost or an arbitrary value established by the Commerce Department. The fact that Coca-Cola now makes more profit in Japan than it does in the United States is not adequately reflected in the evaluation of Coca-Cola Japan. Moreover, it is only in the last few years that interest and dividends paid abroad have exceeded, slightly, the earnings generated by our own foreign assets. Second, when the U.S. borrows abroad, it is in dollars, our own currency, not in a foreign currency as Brazil and Mexico have been forced to do; it makes no material difference if the holder of a U.S. Treasury bill is sitting in Nassau or in Miami. If foreigners stop holding our debt instruments, then they will lose us as a market for their goods. Third, the official figures mix debt and equity, and while both theoretically represent claims on the U.S., lending to the U.S. and investing in equity in the U.S. are different and have different consequences. Much of the $2.5 trillion of foreign holdings in the U.S. represents a rise in our stock and bond markets. We have been a good place for foreigners to invest. We could eliminate the $382-billion difference between our holdings abroad (officially, $2.1 trillion) and foreign holdings here by a brisk sell-off in our markets. The fact is that as long as we have the good sense to maintain a competitive, growing, non-inflationary economy, we will continue to attract foreign lenders and investors, all to the benefit of our economy.

The threat to our economy is not from abroad, it is from Washington, D.C. That is where protectionism, high taxes, crippling regulation, and excess spending come from.

And yet people still speak of the threat to American jobs from free trade with foreign countries. Jobs saved by protectionism always cost astronomical amounts: they cause domestic prices to rise, lessen the quality of domestic products, and lessen job creation to the point where, net, fewer jobs are available. A prosperous Mexico and Canada are in our best interests. They buy our products (creating jobs) and invest in our country and in theirs (creating jobs). What those who complain are really saying is that free trade is a threat to our unions—whose members often are our less productive workers. The raison d'être for unions is more for the union leaders than for the members. In any case, we should not subsidize the maintenance of the unions by protecting union jobs at the expense of other American jobs, at an enormous cost to the consumers, and to the detriment of our industries' competitiveness.

We came out of the Reagan years in competitive shape, with admittedly a mixed record in protectionism, but with a growing economy. The latter has been derailed by President Bush, but we still seem strong enough to recover despite the recent increases in taxes, regulation, and spending. Trade can bring added growth, and the Reagan years were growth oriented. While we may quarrel over certain aspects of President Reagan's policies—for example, an undervalued dollar and continued protectionism—he certainly recognized that it was in our best interests that our trading customers be strong. The trade deficit is a political weapon for the demagogues, and we should not allow ourselves to be stampeded into doing something dumb.

When the Losers Write the History

Martin Anderson

Mr. Anderson, a Senior Fellow at the Hoover Institution, was President Reagan's domestic and economic policy advisor, 1981–82. He is the author of Impostors in the Temple.

There is a great deal at stake in the writing of the history of the Reagan Presidency. For the past 25 years most of the men and women on the political Right—conservatives, neoconservatives, libertarians, and traditional Republicans—have focused their energies on creating new policies, forging political coalitions, electing Presidents, and fomenting peaceful worldwide revolution. They have been successful far beyond their wildest fantasies.

But while many of us have been basking in warm contentment and self-satisfaction, those who were beaten have been busily writing our history. Perhaps we should not be so surprised to read and hear with increasing frequency that the decade of the 1980s was a decade of greed and corruption, that the U.S. economy—after posting the greatest economic expansion in the history of the world—was a failure, that Communism fell because of the benevolence of Mikhail Gorbachev, and that America itself (now the most prosperous nation on earth, the most powerful military force on the globe, and the moral leader of the world) is a troubled nation, a terrible place to live—and all because of Mr. Reagan and his dreadful policies.

"Well . . ." as President Reagan might say, we have no one to blame but ourselves. We have largely let the Left write our recent history. A serious mistake. The future of this country will be powerfully affected by how well young men and women learn which policies were successful in promoting and securing liberty and prosperity and peace—and which policies were not. It is time to set the historical record straight.

The raw economic facts of the Reagan years are clear. From 1982 to 1990 the United States experienced 96 straight months of economic growth, the longest peacetime expansion in its history.

Almost 20 million brand-new jobs, most of them high-paying jobs, were created. Inflation fell dramatically to low levels and stayed there as the American dollar once again became sound. Interest rates also fell dramatically and stayed down. The stock market soared, nearly tripling in value. Government revenues—at the federal, state, and local levels—nearly doubled, making possible the largest increase in social-welfare spending in history. And, almost incidentally, we financed an enormous buildup in America's military power, checkmating the evil intentions of the old Soviet Empire, and ultimately causing the disintegration of Communism throughout the world.

But listen to what some of the most influential voices in the American media have been telling Americans in recent years.

"For ten years Ronald Reagan taught us there was a free lunch. Folks, he said, we're going to cut your taxes and we're going to spend like there's no tomorrow and you don't have to pay for it."
    —Sam Donaldson, on *This Week with David Brinkley*, ABC,
        October 7, 1990

"Reagan, as Commander-in-Chief, was the military's best friend. He gave the Pentagon almost everything it wanted. That spending, combined with a broad tax cut, contributed to a trillion-dollar deficit. . . . Social programs? They suffered under Reagan."
    —Tom Brokaw, NBC news special, *The Eighties*,
        December 27, 1990

"Bush was saddled with a lot of the supply-side voodooism of the Reagan era . . . Reagan was not the President of morning in America: he was the President of the free lunch."
    —Robert Healy, retired *Boston Globe* Washington Bureau
        Chief, October 11, 1990

"It is really Ronald Reagan's fault: His steady emasculation of federal domestic programs forced the states to increase

spending on essential services although they had no accompanying source of increased revenue."
   —Marianne Means, national columnist, April 29, 1991

". . . the evil excesses of the Reagan years."
   —Nancy Gibbs, associate editor, *Time* magazine,
      December 31, 1990

At first glance we could dismiss this as a natural consequence of a press corps dominated by left-liberals. I think the problem lies much deeper. After all, the men and women who write these falsehoods, the professional intellectuals of our land, are—by and large—honorable. The problem is that most of them seem to believe that what they say is true.

But why? I think the prime reason so many in the media persist in retelling the Reagan myths is that our academic intellectuals, those who profess to tell us the comprehensive truth free and clear of political prejudices, have lost their integrity. And when professors from Princeton and Harvard and MIT distort the Reagan economic record, it is not surprising that many in the media get it wrong.

Poisonous Fog

At the heart of this poisonous fog of misinformation is the attack on the very legitimacy of Reaganomics itself. The attack comes from two angles.

The first asserts that the economic ideas espoused by Ronald Reagan came from somewhat disreputable sources, implying that if the messengers are not expert the message must be wrong. Tales abound that Reagan listened to (besides himself) only a handful of non-economists—in particular Jude Wanniski and George Gilder. The truth of the matter is that, first, Wanniski and Gilder have said many sensible things about economics, and second, they were not Reagan's economic advisors.

To begin with, Reagan himself was a pretty good economist. He majored in economics in college and studied economic policy for many years, including his eight years as governor of California. But the driving force behind Reagan's economic policy was the large

299

group of economic experts he assembled in 1980. During the presidential campaign there were 461 distinguished policy experts who advised him on everything from welfare reform to nuclear- weapons policy. Of these, 74 were economic-policy advisors, organized into six different task forces, on: 1) the budget, 2) inflation, 3) international monetary policy, 4) regulatory reform, 5) spending control, and 6) tax policy. The most influential of these advisors were on the campaign's Economic Policy Coordinating Committee. Chaired by George P. Shultz, it included Arthur F. Burns, Milton Friedman, Alan Greenspan, Michael T. Halbouty, Jack Kemp, James T. Lynn, Paul McCracken, William E. Simon, Charls E. Walker, Murray L. Weidenbaum, Caspar Weinberger, and Walter B. Wriston.

It was this group of experts who who crossed every *t* and dotted every *i* of Ronald Reagan's economic policy. Reaganomics sprang from the heart of the traditional Republican establishment of policy economists, but you would never know it from reading the academic studies and most of the media coverage. As a consequence, much of the legitimacy of Reagan's economic policy has been wiped from the public record.

The second angle is to misrepresent (and perhaps in a few cases lie about) the substance of that policy. Two falsehoods are particularly egregious. The first is that Reagan claimed that one could substantially reduce tax rates, sharply increase government spending, and balance the federal budget simultaneously. The second, a corollary of the first, is that one could magically increase federal revenues instantaneously by reducing tax rates. The conclusion was rather simple: given the transparent nuttiness of such claims, the economic policy itself must be wrong.

As for the first falsehood, let us go back and look at the record. Yes, Reagan did in September 1980 call for substantially reducing tax rates, sharply increasing defense spending, and moving toward a balanced budget by 1983. And it was an eminently reasonable thing to do, for at the time virtually every economic forecaster in America (including in the Congressional Budget Office) was projecting *large, increasing federal surpluses* for the next five years. In September 1980 the consensus economic forecasts showed a federal budget deficit of $23 billion for 1981, a *surplus* of $2 billion in 1982, and surpluses of

$50 billion in 1983, $106 billion in 1984, and a whopping $182 billion in 1985.

I know all this sounds unbelievable in today's context of annual deficits in the neighborhood of $400 billion, but that's the way it was in the fall of 1980. The Democratic economists (and many of the Republican ones, for some unfathomable reason) have forgotten this historical fact. Given the huge, mounting surpluses forecast in 1980, there were essentially two choices: 1) spend more of the people's tax money to eliminate the surplus or 2) reduce tax rates and return that money to its rightful owners, the American people. In 1980 Ronald Reagan chose the latter course.

When Reagan was campaigning for the Presidency, the cumulative budget surplus over the next five years was projected at $317 billion. The savings he proposed by controlling the growth of federal spending added $195 billion, and the economic growth that was expected to result from tax-rate reduction added another $92 billion. The grand total was $604 billion.

> ". . . we are in the midst of the largest transfer of wealth in the nation's history . . . a transfer from the middle class to the rich and from the middle class to the poor.
>
> "Indeed, the growth of the middle class—one of the underpinnings of democracy in this country—has been reversed. By government action."
>
> —Bartlett and Steele
> *Philadelphia Inquirer*
> October 20, 1991

Reagan proposed to put fully 88 per cent of that surplus tax money back into the pockets of the American people by reducing tax rates. The remainder would probably have been used to pay off some of the federal debt. The Democrats saw it differently. They saw a windfall of $317 billion and were quietly licking their fiscal chops as they thought about spending it on domestic experiments.

Not a single extra penny was promised by Reagan in the fall of 1980 for increased defense spending. The Democrats, trying to put on a strong military face for the election, had already built increases into the future defense budget—from $134 billion in 1980 to a healthy $270 billion by 1985—that were more than sufficient.

But not everything turned out as planned. By early 1981 the economic indicators had begun to turn down, surprising the economic forecasters, all of whom had missed the kind of damage that recent Democratic economic policies had done. Then the economy went into the tank—a severe recession that could have turned into a bona-fide depression. The tax-rate reductions that Reagan pursued as President became not a luxury made possible by a surplus, but a necessity to fight off the deepening recession. The major cause of the rapidly growing deficits was the recession, not the tax cuts or increases in defense spending. At the time, there were few economists—not even the reliable left-liberal variety—who opposed the tax-rate reductions.

Finally, there is the myth that Reagan and his top advisors believed it was possible to increase tax revenues instantaneously by cutting tax rates. It is a damaging myth because it suggests that those in charge of economic policy in the early 1980s had a rather tenuous grip on reality.

> "To challenge the conservative hegemony, Democrats need to define the Reagan-Bush years—to create an imagery of Reagan-Bush America that supersedes the Carter years and impeaches the credibility of conservative governance for middle America. The battle to define the Reagan-Bush years is a critical political arena where Democrats have the opportunity to disrupt the Republicans' hold on the middle class . . ."
> —Stanley Greenberg
> Political consultant to
> Bill Clinton

In fact, in every economic speech and policy paper issued both during the 1980 campaign and during the entire eight years that Reagan was President, any proposed tax-rate reductions always showed immediate and substantial tax-revenue losses. On the other hand—and this is the point most people seemed to miss—total tax revenues were expected to continue to climb, but *not as much as they would have if the tax rates had not been cut.* The critical phrase here is "not as much as they would have." Some people seem to have become confused by statements to the effect that tax revenues would continue to rise even after the tax-rate reductions. Which, of course, is exactly what did happen. During the Reagan years, in spite of the large 1981 tax-rate reductions, federal tax revenues nearly doubled. The reason why Reagan was able to reduce tax rates and still see revenues rise was that the tax rates were way too high in the first place. And the fact that tax revenues doubled under Reagan suggests we did not cut tax rates nearly enough in the 1980s.

H. Disinformation

It should be noted here that the nasty current deficit problem is due entirely to the ingenuity of the federal bureaucracy, the avarice of Congress, and the recent ineptitude of OMB in controlling the growth of federal spending, spending which has managed to outrace the largest increase in federal revenue in U.S. history.

In the Heart of Academe

But the myth that the Reagan Administration thought it could raise more revenue immediately by cutting tax rates persists in the heart of the academic economic community, among intellectuals who pride themselves on separating fact from myth. Their false charge of Reagan's economic stupidity has been repeated in scholarly articles and at scholarly conventions. In my 1988 book, *Revolution*, I spelled out in some detail how men such as Martin Feldstein of Harvard, Walter S. Salant of the Brookings Institution, Herbert Stein of the American Enterprise Institute, Alan S. Blinder and William Branson of Princeton, and Robert Solow of MIT had all essentially made this damaging and false charge. When I asked Feldstein, Stein, Salant, and Blinder then if they had any evidence to back up their charges, they could not produce any. Four years have now passed, and still not one of them has deigned to correct the mistake.

After a while it makes you wonder. When scholars with distinguished reputations can make false statements to large audiences of their peers and not a murmur is heard, and when they can produce no evidence to support their false claims and yet they do nothing to correct the record, then one has to raise the possibility that something more may be afoot here than simple carelessness.

Finally, a Reaction

A case in point. In August of 1991 the *Wall Street Journal* ran an article consisting of the several pages from *Revolution* that dealt with some of these false statements. Although I had not heard a word from any of these scholars when the book was published in 1988, the article in the *Wall Street Journal* incited Professor Alan Blinder, the chairman of the economics department at Princeton, to respond with a furious letter-to-the-editor.

In his letter Blinder repeated the charges he first made in his

1987 book *Hard Heads, Soft Hearts.* He then deftly changed the subject by accusing me of a "rank violation of trust, manners, and the canons of scholarship" for printing what he had sent to me in response to my request for information, which I had specifically indicated would be used for my book. Although my patience was wearing a bit thin I responded with my own letter to the *Wall Street Journal,* again explaining that Professor Blinder had committed serious errors in his 1987 book and pointing out that in four years he still had not produced any evidence to support his charges.

That really set Blinder off. A few days later I received a rambling letter in which he accused me of being "short on content and long on malice," said I had called him "a liar," and said that I was a "liar." Furthermore, said Blinder, "every hearing person in America has heard Ronald Reagan claim that tax hikes lose revenue dozens of times," which is an

> "The Reagan legacy amounts to nothing less than the economic polarization of America. The rich got richer. The poor got poorer. And the hard-working middle class became more insecure than at any time since before World War II."
> —Bennett Harrison
> Professor of Economics
> Carnegie-Mellon University
> in the *Los Angeles Times*
> September 2, 1992

interesting comment if only because it has nothing to do with Blinder's original false statements. The letter concluded by accusing me of writing "content-free invectives," and saying my motive was "all too apparent" and "none too admirable."

Realizing that Princeton professors are mighty busy and may not have time to do the necessary research, I carefully put together a packet of materials for Professor Blinder that included 1) quotations of the passages from his 1987 book that contained the false statements, 2) Reagan's economic-policy speeches and fact sheets that spelled out the tax-revenue losses that were expected to result from the tax-rate reduction, and 3) the official 1982 budget documents from OMB that detailed the expected tax-revenue losses. I sent these materials to Professor Blinder with a letter that asked this question: "In the light of the evidence contained in the attached documents, don't you believe you should retract the false assertions you make in *Hard Heads, Soft Hearts?*"

A month later I got my answer. "I do not carry on correspondence with people who publish highly selected portions of my personal letters out of context," said Professor Blinder. Interesting. Not a word about the documents. Not the slightest attempt to defend his false statements. Not the slightest hint that he would retract his charges because of the documentary evidence provided to him. Just a new false charge that I was quoting him "out of context."

It is one thing to make an error or false statement unintentionally. It is quite another thing to let it stand uncorrected in the literature despite documentary evidence to the contrary. For to do so converts a simple false statement into a deliberate lie. Such actions from a person in a position of high trust seem inexplicable. But perhaps there is a simple explanation.

In 1983 Professor Blinder gave a long, personal interview that was published in a relatively obscure book called *Conversations with Economists*. In that interview he spoke passionately about his political views and bragged openly about how he intended to use economics as a political weapon. Here's what he said a few years before he wrote about President Reagan's economic policies:

> I guess I'm naturally a loudmouth. Part of it goes back to the attitude I had when I was 18 years old and first discovered economics. I saw social problems and thought the economics could contribute something to overcoming them. I feel more passionately involved recently because of the movement to the right, the election of Reagan, and the politics that Reagan has brought in. I have become more of an activist than I ever was before. . . . I am involved in an organization called the National Policy Exchange, which, while it doesn't want to be described as a Democratic think tank, really is. . . . I used to keep quiet, but if we keep quiet and the right-wingers keep yelling, what has happened will keep happening.

Professor Blinder is not the only member of today's academy who, while professing scholarly objectivity, writes about Reagan's policies with a bias and disregard for the truth that would make even a staff member of the Democratic National Committee blush.

PART THREE

THE RAW DATA TABLES

by Edwin S. Rubenstein

A. Clintonomics

Deconstructing Clintonomics

President Clinton claimed his first budget was "honest." Yet he is the first chief executive to use gross rather than net numbers for his budget presentation. The $500 billion deficit reduction figure ignores $109 billion in new spending and $60 billion in new tax cuts.

His claimed 1-to-1 balance between spending cuts and tax hikes was achieved by counting certain tax and fee increases as spending cuts, taking credit for spending cuts already in the pipeline, and claiming savings from unspecified managerial reforms and a hoped-for reduction in interest rates. Worse yet, some estimates suggest that the Clinton income-tax increase will raise only 30% of the revenues projected.

All this leads to about $6 in tax increases for every $1 in spending reduction, and a five-year deficit reduction of—at best—$284 billion.

Exposing the Clinton Economic Plan*

Billions of Dollars / Fiscal Year 1994–97

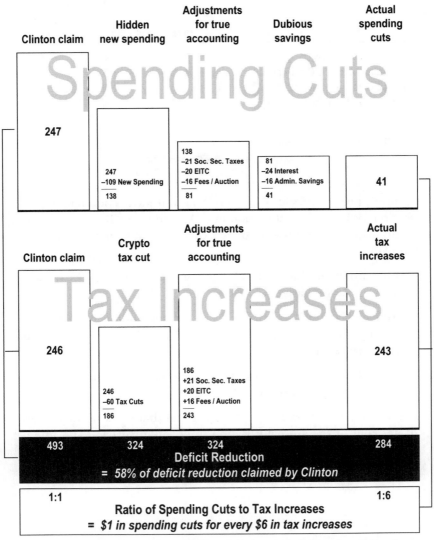

	Hidden new spending	Adjustments for true accounting	Dubious savings	Actual spending cuts

Spending Cuts

Clinton claim: 247

247
−109 New Spending
138

138
−21 Soc. Sec. Taxes
−20 EITC
−16 Fees / Auction
81

81
−24 Interest
−16 Admin. Savings
41

41

	Crypto tax cut	Adjustments for true accounting		Actual tax increases

Tax Increases

Clinton claim: 246

246
−60 Tax Cuts
186

186
+21 Soc. Sec. Taxes
+20 EITC
+16 Fees / Auction
243

243

| 493 | 324 | 324 | | 284 |

Deficit Reduction
= 58% of deficit reduction claimed by Clinton

| 1:1 | | | | 1:6 |

Ratio of Spending Cuts to Tax Increases
= $1 in spending cuts for every $6 in tax increases

* Before accounting for slower growth, tax-avoidance behavior, unbudgeted spending growth, or the coming health-care plan.

Source: American Enterprise Institute.

Economic Impact of the Clinton Plan

	1993	1994	1995	1996	1997	Average 1994–97
Tax burden without new taxes [1]	19.8	19.8	19.8	19.9	19.8	19.8
Projected tax burden w/Clinton plan [1]	19.9	20.1	20.2	20.5	20.9	20.5
Predicted increase in unemployment [2]	0.0	0.25	0.25	0.50	0.65	0.5
Predicted reduction in econ. growth [2]	0.0	−0.40	−0.50	−0.80	−1.10	−0.7

[1] Taxes as a percentage of GDP.

[2] As a consequence of higher taxes.

Source: House Republican Conference, "On the Wrong Track: The First 100 Days of the Clinton Administration" (April 1993).

Clinton's five-year, $300 billion tax hike will have a substantial contractionary impact on the enonomy. According to Republican staff economists at the Joint Economic Committee of Congress, the Clinton plan would:

- Increase unemployment by 0.6 percentage points by 1997. This is a loss of more than 650,000 jobs.

- Reduce economic growth by 1.1 percentage points by 1997. This is a loss of roughly 600,000 jobs and a reduction in output of about $60 billion.

- Raise the budget deficit by at least $100 billion above the Clinton Administration's projection for 1997.

The chart is based on an economic model that successfully tracked 70 per cent of the annual variation in economic growth and unemployment during the period 1960–1992.

Budget Projections Reflecting the Clinton Proposals
Billions of Dollars

	1992A	1993	1994	1995	1996	1997	1998
Receipts	$1,090.5	$1,145.7	$1,251.3	$1,327.7	$1,412.9	$1,476.1	$1,530.5
Outlays	1,380.9	1,467.6	1,515.3	1,574.4	1,624.6	1,690.1	1,781.0
Deficit	−290.4	−322.0	−264.1	−246.7	−211.7	−214.0	−250.4
Addendum							
On-Budget Deficit	−340.5	−366.5	−322.8	−311.5	−287.8	−296.6	−340.6
Off-Budget Surplus	50.1	44.5	58.7	64.8	76.1	82.6	90.1

—— As a per cent of GDP ——

	1992A	1993	1994	1995	1996	1997	1998
Receipts	18.6%	18.6%	19.2%	19.4%	19.6%	19.6%	19.4%
Outlays	23.5	23.8	23.3	23.0	22.6	22.4	22.6
Deficit	−4.9	−5.2	−4.1	−3.6	−2.9	−2.8	−3.2
Addendum							
On-Budget Deficit	−5.8	−5.9	−5.0	−4.5	−4.0	−3.9	−4.3
Off-Budget Surplus	0.9	0.7	0.9	0.9	1.1	1.1	1.1

Source: Office of Management and Budget.

The Clinton Deficits

Despite all the talk about the necessity of "sacrificing" for the future and the need to alleviate the burdens facing our children, deficit reduction under the Clinton plan is miniscule and short-lived. Clinton's plan envisions a $385 billion rise in tax receipts between 1993 and 1998. Despite this, the deficit is not expected to fall below $200 billion and actually starts rising after 1997. Spending, obviously, is unchecked.

A better measure of our operating deficit is the "on-budget" deficit, which excludes Social Security. The on-budget deficit is expected to reach $340.6 billion in 1998, virtually the same level as in 1992.

B. Health Care Spending

The Federal Health Budget
Billions of Dollars

	Medicare	Medicaid	Veterans Benefits	Other*	Total	Federal Health Spending as % of Total Federal Spending
	Federal Health Spending					
1965	—	$ 0.3	$ 1.3	$ 1.5	$ 3.1	2.6%
1970	$ 6.2	2.7	1.8	3.2	13.9	7.1
1975	12.9	6.8	3.7	6.1	29.5	8.9
1980	32.1	14.0	6.5	9.2	61.8	10.5
1985	65.8	22.7	9.5	10.9	108.9	11.5
1990	98.1	41.1	12.1	16.6	168.0	13.4
1992	119.0	67.8	14.1	21.8	222.7	16.1
1993E	134.1	80.3	14.9	24.9	254.2	17.5
1994E	152.3	91.9	15.7	26.2	286.1	19.0
1998E	239.3	145.9	18.0	31.0	434.2	23.6

Includes federal employee health benefits, other health benefits, and health-related research.

Source: Congressional Budget Office.

Health Care Is Crowding Out Other Spending

Health care is by far the fastest growing area of the federal budget. Medicare and Medicaid account for about 85% of all federal health spending. Spending on these two entitlements rose from a combined $46 billion in 1980 to $187 billion in 1992, an increase of 142% after inflation. By 1998 the CBO projects that Medicare and Medicaid will spend a combined $385 billion, an amount equal to more than one-fifth of that year's total federal spending.

Deficit reduction requires that entitlements be controlled, and this, in turn, requires that federal health spending be reined in. Indeed, even if we abolished Food Stamps, AFDC, farm price supports, child nutrition programs, and veterans' pensions—a scheme that no one is advocating—entitlements would constitute a larger share of the federal budget in 1998 than they do now unless Medicare and Medicaid costs are reduced.

Who Are the Uninsured?

Approximately 33 million people—13.5% of the U.S. population—did not have health insurance in 1989. Although most Americans equate the lack of health insurance with the inability to pay, statistics demonstrate otherwise:

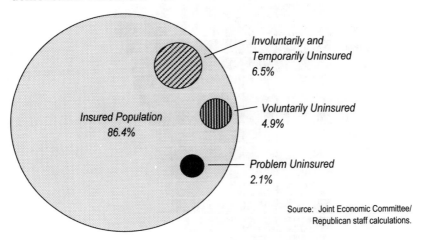

Involuntarily and Temporarily Uninsured 6.5%

Voluntarily Uninsured 4.9%

Insured Population 86.4%

Problem Uninsured 2.1%

Source: Joint Economic Committee/
Republican staff calculations.

—36% of the uninsured population is voluntarily uninsured. These are mainly young, healthy individuals who have chosen to risk paying health care expenses out of pocket rather than pay premiums up front.

—More than half (51%) of the uninsured population hold jobs. About 29% of all uninsured individuals are poor.

—Uninsurance is most frequent among young adults aged 18 to 25. Approximately 25% of this age cohort are uninsured.

—Uninsurance is usually a temporary condition. Federal surveys show that half of all uninsured spells end within four months while only 15% last longer than 24 months.

—Only 2.1% of the population (about 6 million Americans) are chronically and involuntarily uninsured.

—Having no insurance does not mean having no health care. The uninsured accounted for 11% of the nation's personal-health-care expenditures in 1988.

Per Capita Health Spending, 1989

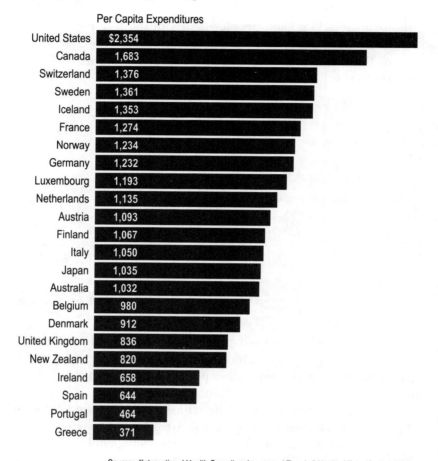

Per Capita Expenditures

Country	Per Capita Expenditures
United States	$2,354
Canada	1,683
Switzerland	1,376
Sweden	1,361
Iceland	1,353
France	1,274
Norway	1,234
Germany	1,232
Luxembourg	1,193
Netherlands	1,135
Austria	1,093
Finland	1,067
Italy	1,050
Japan	1,035
Australia	1,032
Belgium	980
Denmark	912
United Kingdom	836
New Zealand	820
Ireland	658
Spain	644
Portugal	464
Greece	371

Source: "International Health Spending: Issues and Trends," *Health Affairs* (Spring 1991).

On a per-capita basis we spend 40% more than our nearest competitor—Canada. See chart on page 315.

Per Capita Health Spending, 1989

Per Cent by Which U.S. Exceeds

United States	**0%**	
Canada	$$$$	**40%**
Switzerland	$$$$$$$	**71%**
Sweden	$$$$$$$	**73%**
Iceland	$$$$$$$	**74%**
France	$$$$$$$$	**85%**
Norway	$$$$$$$$$	**91%**
Germany	$$$$$$$$$	**91%**
Luxembourg	$$$$$$$$$$	**97%**
Netherlands	$$$$$$$$$$$	**107%**
Austria	$$$$$$$$$$$	**115%**
Finland	$$$$$$$$$$$$	**121%**
Italy	$$$$$$$$$$$$	**124%**
Japan	$$$$$$$$$$$$$	**127%**
Australia	$$$$$$$$$$$$$	**128%**
Belgium	$$$$$$$$$$$$$$$	**140%**
Denmark	$$$$$$$$$$$$$$$$	**158%**
United Kingdom	$$$$$$$$$$$$$$$$$$	**182%**
New Zealand	$$$$$$$$$$$$$$$$$$$	**187%**
Ireland	$$$$$$$$$$$$$$$$$$$$$$$$$$	**258%**
Spain	$$$$$$$$$$$$$$$$$$$$$$$$$$$	**266%**
Portugal	$$$	**407%**
Greece	$$$ . . .	**535%**

Source: "International Health Spending: Issues and Trends," *Health Affairs* (Spring 1991).

315

Total Health Expenditures as a Per Cent of Gross Domestic Product

Selected OECD Countries, 1970–1990

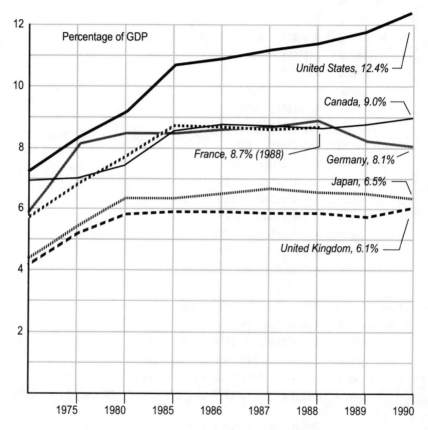

Source: George J. Schieber and Jean-Pierre Poullier,
"International Health Spending: Issues and Trends," *Health Affairs* (Spring 1991).

Total Health Care Spending
As a Per Cent of GDP

	1970	1980	1989	Increase, 1980–89
United States	7.4	9.3	11.8	2.5 % pts.
Sweden	7.2	9.5	8.8	(0.7)
Canada	7.1	7.4	8.7	1.3
France	5.8	7.6	8.7	1.1
Netherlands	6.0	8.2	8.3	0.1
Germany	5.9	8.5	8.2	(0.3)
Italy	5.2	6.8	7.6	0.8
Ireland	5.6	9.0	7.3	(1.7)
Spain	3.7	5.6	6.3	0.7
Japan	4.4	6.4	6.7	0.3
Australia	4.9	6.5	7.0	0.5
United Kingdom	4.5	5.8	5.8	—

Source: George J. Schieber and Jean-Pierre Poullier, "International Health Spending: Issues and Trends," *Health Affairs* (Spring 1991).

The Rapid Rise

The U.S. spends more of its income on health care than any other nation, and our lead is growing: between 1980 and 1989 the share of our GDP spent on health care rose by 2.5 percentage points—more than any other nation.

In 1990 the Department of Health and Human Services projected that the U.S. would spend nearly 15 cents of every dollar of GDP on health care in the year 2000. Only two years later, in 1992, actual spending reached 14% of GDP.

The Supply of Health Care

	Physicians per 100,000 Population	Medical Beds 100,000 Population	Days of Inpatient Care Per Capita	Average Length of Inpatient Stay
	(1987)	(1986)	(1986)	(1987)
Canada	215	1,628	2.0	13.2
France	250	1,070	3.3	12.5
Germany	281	1,104	3.5	17.1
Italy	111	799	1.6	11.0
Japan	157	1,485	3.9	52.9 *
United Kingdom	137	722	2.1	15.0
United States	234	533	1.3	9.3
OECD Average	215	857	2.7	16.1

* Includes nursing home patients in hospital settings.

Source: Organization for Economic Cooperation and Development; Health Care Financing Review.

As a nation: our ratio of physicians to people is only slightly more than the average found in the Organization for Economic Cooperation and Development (OECD) countries; we have significantly fewer hospital beds relative to population, and we go to the hospital less often and for shorter stays than the OECD average.

Our health-care problem is not the result of overuse. Nor is it that we spend enormous sums on health care: that is what you would expect in a rich country. What's wrong with health care is that its cost is growing much faster than the cost of other goods. Health care productivity—the amount of care delivered per dollar spent—has lagged behind the productivity of the economy as a whole.

Personal Health Care Expenditures

Billions of 1990 Dollars

	1970	1980	1990	% Increase 1970– 1980	1980– 1990
Hospital Care	$ 94.1	$162.5	$256.0	72.7%	57.5%
Physicians' Services	45.8	66.4	125.7	45.0	89.3
Drugs / Prescriptions	29.6	34.3	54.6	15.9	59.2
Nursing Home Care	16.5	31.7	53.1	92.1	67.5
Dentists' Services	15.8	22.8	34.0	44.3	49.1
Vision Products	6.7	7.3	12.1	9.0	65.8
Other	10.1	23.0	49.8	127.7	116.5
Total	$218.6	$348.0	$585.3	59.2%	68.2%

Source: Health Care Financing Administration (calculations by author).

Expenditures for physicians' services grew 89% (in 1990 dollars) during the 1980s, outpacing all other major categories of health-care spending.

Average Physician Income
1990 Dollars

	United States	Canada	West Germany	United Kingdom
1971	$131,751	$108,852	$95,490	NA
1983	130,125	79,017	88,948	$42,468
1986	137,390	91,828	88,411	45,428
1988	156,414	91,720	NA	47,148

Source: Congressional Budget Office.

The average income of U.S. physicians has risen, and is significantly greater than that of physicians in other nations. In 1986, U.S. physicians earned about 50% more than physicians in Canada, 55% more than West German physicians, and about three times as much as physicians in the United Kingdom.

Another approach to measuring physicians' income is to compare their earnings to that of the average worker. In 1986 the average U.S. physician earned 4.5-times as much as the average worker in the U.S. By contrast, Canadian physicians earned 3.7-times more than the average Canadian worker, West German physicians earned 4.3-times the average West German worker, and British physicians earned 2.4-times more than that country's average worker.

Half of the average U.S. doctor's income goes to pay for overhead (including malpractice insurance premiums) and expenses, according to the American Medical Association.

C. Public Sector Employment

Trends in Government Employment
Thousands of Dollars

	Public Sector Employment			Public Sector Employment as % of Total Employment
	Federal	**State & Local**	**Total**	**Employment**
1929	600	2,500	3,100	6.5%
1939	1,100	3,100	4,200	9.2
1949	2,047	4,156	6,203	10.8
1959	2,399	6,088	8,487	13.1
1970	2,881	10,147	13,028	16.6
1980	2,898	13,315	16,213	16.3
1988	3,112	14,476	17,588	15.3
1989	3,114	14,765	17,879	15.2
1990	3,105	15,263	18,369	15.6
1991	3,103	15,452	18,554	15.9

Source: U.S. Department of Commerce.

Between 1949 and 1991, federal employment rose about 50%, while real federal spending increased a whopping 450%. The rapid rise in federal spending reflected burgeoning transfer payments rather than money spent directly by federal agencies.

State and local government employment grew by 270% during the period from 1949 to 1991—more than five times as fast as federal employment. Public sector employment peaked at about 17% of total employment in the late Sixties, then fell slowly to 15.2% of the total in 1989 before rising in the recession.

Private Work and Public Dependence

	1950	1970	1980	1990
		Millions of Persons		
Private Sector Employees	39.20	50.40	74.17	91.48
Individuals Receiving Income from the Government:				
Government Employees	6.03	12.55	16.24	18.30
Government Beneficiaries:				
—Social Security recipients	3.48	23.56	30.94	35.57
—Civil Service retirees	0.16	0.70	1.30	1.59
—AFDC recipients	2.20	8.47	10.77	11.70
—Railroad retirement	0.26	0.65	0.69	0.61
—Unemployment insurance	0.84	2.05	2.83	2.60
—Black Lung	——	——	0.40	0.21
Total Beneficiaries	*6.94*	*35.43*	*46.93*	*52.28*
Total Persons Receiving Income from the Government	*12.97*	*47.98*	*62.77*	*70.37*
Total Income Recipients	*52.17*	*98.38*	*136.91*	*161.85*
		Percent of Total		
Private Sector Workers	75.1%	51.2%	54.2%	56.4%
Government Workers	11.6	12.8	11.9	11.3
Government Beneficiaries	13.3	36.0	34.3	32.3
Total Income Recipients	100.0	100.0	100.0	100.0

Source: Social Security Administration; Economic Report of the President (calculations by author).

Increasing Government Dependency

More than 70 million Americans depend on government as a major source of income, either as government workers (18.3 million) or as beneficiaries of transfer payments (52.3 million). This does not include millions of private-sector workers who are dependent on government contracts or grants.

Government employment more than tripled between 1950 and 1990. The number of transfer payment recipients rose more than 7-fold over the same period, accounting for the entire rise in dependency.

Not surprisingly, private-sector workers acccounted for a significantly smaller percentage of total income recipients in 1990 (56.4%) than in 1950 (75.1%).

D. Tax Policy

The Fairest of All: The Distribution of Income Taxes

Year	Top 1%	Top 5%	51–95 Percentiles	Lowest 50%
1981	17.89%	35.36%	57.22%	7.42%
1982	19.29	36.39	56.30	7.32
1983	20.73	37.71	55.18	7.11
1984	21.79	38.64	54.08	7.27
1985	22.30	39.28	53.61	7.10
1986	25.75	42.57	50.97	6.46
1987	24.81	43.26	50.67	6.07
1988	27.58	45.62	48.66	5.72
1989	25.30	44.04	50.25	5.71
1990	25.30	44.13	50.25	5.62

Source: Internal Revenue Service.

Income Tax Burden Shifted toward Wealthy
In 1981 the top 1% paid about 18% of all income taxes; by 1988 this group paid nearly 28% of all income taxes.

This wasn't just a case of "the rich getting richer." In fact, dividend and interest income, the best proxy for the wealthy, grew less rapidly than wages. Much of the gain reflects the shift of previously tax-sheltered income to more productive—and taxable—pursuits.

Wealthy Shoulder More of the Income Tax Burden

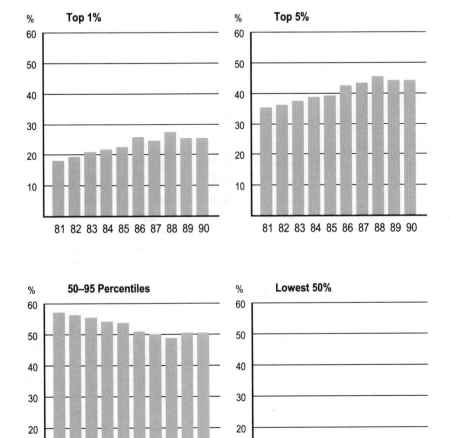

Source: Internal Revenue Service and Joint Economic Committee/Republican staff calculations.

Average Income Tax Payments, 1981–1990
1990 Dollars

Year	Richest 1%	Richest 5%	51–95 Percentiles	Lowest 50%
1981	$ 77,939	$30,802	$5,538	$647
1982	77,501	29,234	5,026	588
1983	78,195	28,453	4,625	537
1984	83,970	29,779	4,631	561
1985	87,615	30,874	4,682	558
1986	110,378	36,502	4,856	553
1987	99,234	34,605	4,504	485
1988	115,523	38,217	4,529	479
1989	102,961	35,841	4,545	465
1990	101,572	35,010	4,430	446
	───────	Per Cent Change	───────	
1981–86	41.6%	18.5%	−12.3%	−14.5%
1981–88	48.2	24.1	−18.2	−26.0

Source: Internal Revenue Service and
Joint Economic Committee/Republican staff calculations.

When Ronald Reagan cut the top income rate to 50% from 70%, the Congressional Budget Office predicted that average tax payments of wealthy taxpayers would fall, producing what Tip O'Neill called "a giveaway to the rich." IRS data show that the average tax paid by the top 1% of taxpayers rose 48.2% (in constant 1990 dollars) between 1981 and 1988. Meanwhile, the average paid by the bottom 50% fell by 26%.

The Economics of Envy

Were the Eighties a decade of Greed? Was Reaganomics a party for the rich paid for by the middle class? The networks think so. Sam Donaldson says: "The average pre-tax income of the richest 1 per cent has jumped 86 per cent in constant dollars since 1977, while the bottom four-fifths of Americans have seen their pre-tax income actually drop by almost 4 per cent . . . those in the top 1 per cent are paying 35 per cent less than they did in 1977." The Democrats agree: Democratic National Chairman Ron Brown has fashioned the entire "fairness issue" around these notions. And "leading Republican columnist" Kevin Phillips has added the ingredient of bipartisan support with his book *The Politics of Rich and Poor.* The 1990 budget deal responded to this new consensus by taxing luxury items and imposing the first increase in the top tax rate since World War II.

There's only one thing wrong with the new consensus. It's all wrong. To demonstrate exactly how it's wrong, let's look at a standard statement of the case, Barbara Ehrenreich's essay in *Time* (August 27, 1990), amusingly entitled "A Conservative Tax Proposal." Miss Ehrenreich gets to the point right away: "According to a study from the Congressional Budget Office, only the richest 10 per cent of Americans saw their taxes decline. The overwhelming majority . . . are now paying a higher share of their incomes in overall federal taxes than they did prior to the tax cuts of 1978 and 1981."

But the CBO table on which Miss Ehrenreich is relying is sleight of hand in two ways. First, it aggregates a whole series of taxes in order to reach the conclusion that the effective tax rate of the wealthiest 20 per cent is lower than it was in 1977—but that all other groups pay higher taxes now. It assumes, for example, that the entire rise in Social Security taxes was borne by employees (whereas employers pay half the tax) and that corporate income taxes are borne by both capital and labor (economists generally believe that they in fact fall on shareholders). The CBO also ignores non-cash government transfers such as Medicare, Medicaid, and Food Stamps, and employer-provided benefits such as health insurance. The second sleight of hand is to combine a period of high taxes with one of lower taxes, effectively concealing the income effects of tax cuts.

327

Effective Federal-Income-Tax Rates					
	1977	1980	1985	1990	Percentage Change, 1980–90
Poorest 20%	−0.6	−0.4	−0.1	−1.5	NA
Second 20%	3.5	4.5	4.0	3.5	−22.2
Third 20%	7.0	8.1	6.8	6.7	−17.3
Fourth 20%	9.6	11.0	9.2	9.0	−18.2
Richest 20%	16.0	17.1	14.4	15.6	−8.8

Source: Congressional Budget Office.

If we confine our attention to income tax, moreover, the CBO report clearly shows effective income-tax rates fell further for the poor and middle class than for the wealthy during the 1980–90 period and that these tax changes had far-reaching effects on the distribution of the tax burden and on incomes (see table above).

Watch the Numbers

What really happened to taxes in the last decade and a half? There was an increase in effective income-tax rates on everyone in the late 1970s, as the table shows, when inflation pushed taxpayers into higher nominal tax brackets. Indeed, this was a major reason for the tax reforms of the 1980s—a point Miss Ehrenreich curiously omits. Then in 1981 the top tax rate was cut from 70 per cent to 50 percent, and the rest of President Reagan's first tax cut was fully phased in by 1984. Inflation indexation followed in 1985. After that, the 1986 tax reform increased progressivity still further by removing 4.3 million taxpayers from the tax rolls and expanding the alternative minimum tax, which ensures that wealthier taxpayers cannot escape paying taxes altogether.

Between 1980 and 1985, therefore, effective federal-income-tax rates fell for all families except the poorest 20 per cent, who had found their tax rebates eroded by inflation in the Seventies, and now by real income growth after 1982. But the real change comes after the 1986 tax reform, which cut marginal tax rates on all taxpayers while expanding the tax base through limiting deductions. As a

328

result, the richest 20 percent of families found their effective tax rates rising from 14.4 per cent in 1985 to 15.6 per cent in 1990 at a time when other taxpayers saw their effective rates fall, and the poorest 20 percent saw their tax rebates rise from 0.1 to 1.5 percent of income.

So much for income taxes. Let us now accept, for the sake of argument, the CBO's calculations of the total tax rate including its tendentious treatment of Social Security and corporate-tax payments. Does the (alleged) decline in the top group's tax rate in fact signify a decline in progressivity? If the income of this group had remained static, or if it had increased at the same rate as that of the other groups, then a declining tax rate would indeed have meant this group paid a lower share of total taxes. That is plainly the conclusion which Miss Ehrenreich hopes to implant in the minds of her readers. Again, however, it's plain wrong. For, as the CBO study also shows, the *share* of federal taxes paid by the wealthiest taxpayers is higher now than it was during the Carter years, while the share paid by every other group is lower. In fact, the share of taxes paid by the wealthiest 20 per cent (see table below) increased during the Eighties for every tax studied—even Social Security taxes, long considered the most regressive feature of the federal tax system.

Percentage Shares of Total Tax Burden

	1977	1980	1985	1990	Percentage Change, 1985–90
Poorest 20%	2.0	1.6	1.9	1.6	−15.8
Second 20%	7.3	7.0	7.0	6.6	−5.7
Third 20%	13.5	13.4	13.1	12.6	−3.8
Fourth 20%	21.7	22.2	21.9	21.0	−4.1
Richest 20%	55.4	55.7	55.9	58.1	3.9
Richest 10%	38.7	38.7	39.0	41.8	7.2
Richest 5%	27.6	27.1	27.3	30.4	11.4

Source: Congressional Budget Office.

How do the liberal critics deal with this inconvenient fact? They simply deny that tax shares are a valid measure of progressivity. In their view the share of taxes paid by the rich goes up solely because the income of the rich has gone up still faster. But the incomes of all groups have risen since the Reagan tax cuts—and as the table on page 329 shows, the share of total taxes paid by everyone except the top 20 per cent has fallen.

Why Do the Rich Pay More?

Given that the liberal explanation is no explanation, the question then is: Exactly why are the rich paying a larger share? Lawrence Lindsey puts it this way in *The Growth Experiment*:

> The rich will pay more taxes at lower rates only if their *reported taxable* income goes up, which it did. This conclusion, however, is not very interesting in itself. The more important question is: why did the rich report more taxable income? If it happened because Reagan shifted the nation's economic playing field in favor of the rich (say by permanently increasing interest income as a share of national income, that is, by favoring capital over labor) then the critics have a point. But if the change occurred because the tax cuts simply encouraged the rich to expose more income to taxation or, even better, to work harder at producing more income, then the Reagan Administration can hardly be accused of unfairly boosting the rich.

Lindsey demonstrates, as conclusively as anything can ever be demonstrated in econometrics, that the financial rejiggerings of wealthy taxpayers ($200,000 and over) in response to the tax cuts were so pervasive that the government collected $11.5 billion more from them than it would have at the 70 per cent rate. His model establishes that *all* other income groups paid less under the new tax law than they would have under the old law, with the largest reduction—18 per cent—going to those earning less than $20,000.

Yet Miss Ehrenreich reaches a different conclusion: "According to the Washington-based Citizens for Tax Justice, the cumulative

Average Family Income 1988 Dollars	1977	1983	1988
Poorest 20%	$ 5,514	$ 5,061	$ 5,424
Second 20%	13,917	13,527	14,311
Third 20%	23,660	22,925	24,488
Fourth 20%	35,625	35,261	38,221
Richest 20%	63,101	65,101	72,759
All Families	28,364	28,375	31,041

Source: House Ways and Means Committee.

impact of the past 12 years of tax cuts for the richest 1 per cent will cost the Treasury $158 billion in 1990, not much less than the projected budget deficit."

This conclusion is based on a static line of reasoning: namely, that if 1977 tax rates were reimposed, wealthy taxpayers would continue to earn as much income—and *report as much income*—as they do now. Under such conditions we would indeed be collecting more from wealthy taxpayers. But the reasoning is fallacious—like arguing that taxpayers would continue to work if exposed to a 100-per-cent tax rate. The only respectable argument is over how much income taxpayers will conceal or forgo as tax rates rise. Lindsey's research shows that taxpayers—especially wealthy ones—are highly responsive to changes in tax rates, to the point that higher tax rates lead to a less progressive allocation of the tax burden. This simple point undermines all the arguments of Miss Ehrenreich and her allies; yet they have failed even to address it.

But overarching the tax issue is the question of distribution of income. Miss Ehrenreich again sinks into the conventional wisdom: "Real, after-tax income has been falling for most American families since the late Seventies. Only among the wealthiest 20 per cent have real incomes risen noticeably since 1977 . . ." What Miss Ehrenreich is doing here, of course, is lumping together two periods: 1977–81, in which statutory tax rates remained static (capital gains being the exception) while effective tax rates rose because of bracket creep;

and 1982–88, in which both statutory and effective tax rates were reduced across the board. Making allowances for time lags, the incomes of all groups except the wealthiest fell between 1977 and 1983, and subsequently rose between 1983 and 1988. Between 1983 and 1988 the average family income of the poorest 20 per cent of families increased 7.2 per cent, while that of the top group increased 11.8 per cent. The overall average increase was 9.4 per cent (see table p. 331).

Miss Ehrenreich might reply that the comparison is unfair since the period of high taxes was also one of high inflation and low growth, while the Reagan tax cuts were followed by low inflation and high growth.

Well, yes.

Top U.S. Income Tax Rate

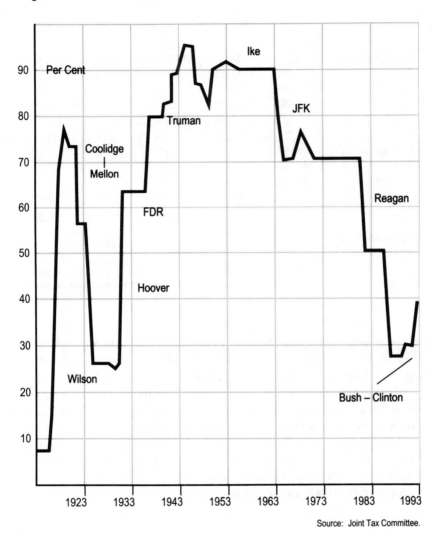

Source: Joint Tax Committee.

Will it be different now? Periods of rising income tax rates have traditionally been associated with war or depression. The Bush-Clinton years are the exception . . . so far.

The Mellon Tax Cut, 1921–1925

Net income class	Revenue ($ 1000s)		Change, 1921–25	Per Cent of Total	
	1921	1925		1921	1925
$0–5	$ 92,791	$ 13,909	–85%	12.9	1.9
5–10	68,871	19,150	–72%	9.6	2.6
10–15	51,807	22,419	–57%	7.2	3.1
15–20	41,183	25,090	–39%	5.7	3.4
20–50	146,808	147,353	0%	20.4	20.1
50–100	115,172	147,843	+28%	16.0	20.1
100–500	146,685	238,252	+64%	20.4	32.4
500–1,000	25,112	53,674	+114%	3.5	7.3
1,000 +	31,419	66,867	+113%	4.4	9.1
Total	$719,387	$734,555	+2%	100.0%	100.0%
Maximum marginal income tax rate	73%	25%			

Source: Internal Revenue Service, *Statistics of Income—1921–1925: Individual Income Tax Returns*; Tax Foundation.

At the urging of Treasury Secretary Andrew Mellon, income tax rates were slashed across the board in the early 1920s. The top rate fell to 25% from 73%, while the bottom rate went from 4% to 1.5%.

The result was a sharply progressive redistribution of tax burden. From 1921 to 1925 the amount of income taxes paid by individuals earning less than $20,000 dropped sharply; their share of total tax payments fell from more than 35% to less than 11%. Yet revenues paid by those with incomes above $20,000 increased enough that total income tax revenues rose somewhat. Taxes paid by those with incomes of $500,000 and above doubled.

The 1932 Tax Hike

Federal Income Tax Revenue by Income Class, 1931 and 1932
Millions of Constant 1931 Dollars

Income Class	Revenue Collected		Per Cent of Total	
	1931	1932	1931	1932
Less than $25,000	$51.6	$134.0	21.0%	36.5%
$25,000–$50,000	40.1	48.1	16.3	13.0
$50,000–$100,000	44.8	51.7	18.2	14.1
$100,000–$300,000	51.9	66.2	21.1	18.0
Over $300,000	57.8	67.4	23.5	18.4

Source: James Gwartney and Richard Stroup, "Tax Cuts: Who Shoulders the Burden?" Federal Reserve Bank of Atlanta, *Economic Review* (March 1982), p. 27.

Herbert Hoover's response to higher deficits after the 1929 crash was to raise taxes. (Sound familiar?) The Revenue Act of 1932 increased personal income tax rates across the board, with the top rate going from 25% to 63%. Corporate tax rates were boosted from 12% to 14.5%. Estate taxes were raised, a one-cent-per-gallon gasoline tax was imposed, and a 3% automobile tax, a telephone and telegraph tax, and many other excises were also imposed.

It was the sharpest increase in the federal tax burden in American history. Yet the $462 million deficit of 1931 jumped to $3.2 billion in 1932. Not only did PIT receipts decline sharply (falling to $427 million in 1932 from $834 million in 1931), but the higher rates actually caused the tax burden to be shifted to lower-income taxpayers.

The Kennedy Tax Cut

In January 1963, President Kennedy remarked in his economic report that "The main block to full employment is an unrealistically heavy burden of taxation. The time has come to remove it." The same month he proposed to cut all personal income tax rates across the board. On February 27, 1964, Congress passed the tax bill, lowering rates from the World War II-vintage 20%–91% range to 14%–70%.

The Treasury predicted a 19% fall in revenues based on a static model of the economy. As seen in the table on the preceding page, revenues remained approximately unchanged in real terms during the first two years of the tax cuts. In the income classes below $10,000, revenue declined, while in all higher brackets revenue progressively increased during the two-year rate reduction. The largest increase—85%—occurred in the $1,000,000+ income class.

By FY1966, income tax receipts climbed to $55.5 billion, or 17% above the amount collected the year prior to the tax cut, 1963. The 1966 budget underestimated FY1966 income tax receipts by $7.3 billion.

Unfortunately, the positive economic effects of the Kennedy tax cut were not long-lived. Starting in the late Sixties inflation pushed people into higher and higher tax brackets.

The Kennedy Tax Cut

Federal Income Tax Revenue by Income Class
Millions of Current Dollars

Adjusted Gross Income Class (thousands)	Revenue Collected			Change 1963–65
	1963	1964	1965	
$0–5	$ 5,911	$ 4,668	$ 4,337	−27%
$5–10	17,305	15,944	15,434	−11%
$10–15	9,430	9,972	10,712	+14%
$15–20	3,497	3,709	4,189	+20%
$20–50	6,681	6,882	7,440	+11%
$50–100	2,920	3,204	3,654	+25%
$100–500	1,890	2,220	2,752	+46%
$500–1,000	243	306	408	+68%
$1,000 +	327	427	603	+85%
Total	$48,204	$47,153	$49,530	+3%
Maximum marginal income tax rate	91%	77%	70%	

Source: Internal Revenue Service,
Statistics of Income—1963, 1964, 1965, Individual Income Tax Returns;
Tax Foundation.

The Reagan Tax Cut

In 1981 Ronald Reagan cut the top marginal income tax rate from 70%—where it had been since Kennedy's day—to 50%. The lowest rate was cut from 14% to 11%. The cuts stimulated investment income and economic growth and, as seen in the table on the preceding page, shifted the burden of income taxation to individuals earning $50,000 and over.

Economist Larry Lindsey, after studying the impact of the Economic Recovery Tax Act of 1981 (ERTA), concludes: "Personal income tax collections were lower under ERTA than they would have been had tax rates never been cut. . . . [H]owever, the reductions in very high tax brackets easily paid for themselves and produced a rather sizable increase besides" (Lawrence B. Lindsey, *The Growth Experiment*, Basic Books, 1990).

By 1985, according to Lindsey, the economy was between 2 and 3 per cent larger than it would have been without the tax cut.

The Reagan Tax Cut

$ Millions

Net Income Group (000s)	Revenue Collected					% Change
	1981	1982	1983	1984	1985	
$0–10	$ 7,975	$ 7,090	$ 6,148	$ 5,864	$ 5,475	−31.3%
10–20	39,511	34,567	31,463	31,283	30,352	−23.2
20–30	55,657	51,966	46,321	44,778	43,344	−22.1
30–50	86,592	84,995	82,629	87,280	91,835	6.1
50–75	36,299	35,892	38,353	47,355	56,385	55.3
75–100	14,715	14,595	15,393	18,759	21,683	47.4
100–200	21,506	21,869	22,014	25,763	30,218	40.5
200–500	12,750	14,032	15,613	18,775	22,423	75.9
500 +	8,988	12,592	16,122	21,648	27,005	200.5
Total	$283,993	$277,598	$274,056	$301,505	$328,720	15.7

Total Tax Burden (%)

Net Income Group (000s)	Percentage Distribution of Tax Burden				
	1981	1982	1983	1984	1985
$0–10	2.8 %	2.6 %	2.2 %	1.9 %	1.7 %
10–20	13.9	12.4	11.5	10.4	9.2
20–30	19.6	18.7	16.9	14.9	13.2
30–50	30.5	30.6	30.2	29.0	27.9
50–75	12.8	12.9	14.0	15.7	17.2
75–100	5.2	5.3	5.6	6.2	6.6
100–200	7.6	7.9	8.0	8.5	9.2
200–500	4.5	5.1	5.7	6.2	6.8
500 +	3.1	4.5	5.9	7.2	8.2
Total	100.0	100.0	100.0	100.0	100.0

Source: Internal Revenue Service.

Capital Gains Taxes: Rates vs. Revenues

Year	Taxes paid on capital gains income ($ mil.)	Maximum capital gains tax rate
1977	$ 8,232	49.1%
1978	9,104	48.3
1979	11,753	28.0
1980	12,459	28.0
1981	12,852	23.7
1982	12,900	20.0
1983	18,700	20.0
1984	21,453	20.0
1985	26,480	20.0
1986	52,914	20.0
1987	33, 714	28.0
1988	38,868	28.0
1989	35,258	28.0
1990	27,029	28.0

Source: U.S. Department of Treasury; Internal Revenue Service.

The case for cutting tax rates as a means of reviving the economy *and* reducing the deficit is overwhelming. Investors are particularly sensitive to capital gains rates. If rates are too high, they will avoid the tax simply by not selling the appreciated asset. When rates are cut, the accumulated gains are "unlocked," spurring large increases in realizations and tax revenues.

In 1978 the top capital gains tax rate was slashed from 49% to 28%. Revenues grew rapidly in subsequent years, an impressive feat in light of the sharp recession that occurred during this period. In 1982, rates were cut again—to 20%—and federal collections nearly quadrupled over the next four years. But when the levy was raised in 1987, receipts fell by more than one-third. They still have not regained their peak.

E. Federal Deficits

The Adjusted Budget Deficit

Billions of Current Dollars
Deficit as Per Cent of GDP in Parentheses

Year	Official Federal Deficit	Social Security	Official Deficit Adjusted for: Social Security and Federal Capital Expenditures	Social Security, Federal Capital Expenditures, State and Local Government Surplus, and Inflation
1953	$ −6,493 (−1.8)	$ −8,260 (−2.3)	$ 18,313 (5.0)	$ 21,481 (5.9)
1960	301 (0.1)	510 (0.1)	30,028 (5.9)	35,568 (7.0)
1970	−2,842 (−0.3)	−8,694 (−0.9)	45,497 (4.6)	73,838 (7.5)
1980	−73,835 (−2.8)	−72,715 (−2.7)	19,421 (0.7)	178,468 (6.7)
1990	−220,470 (−4.0)	−277,061 (−5.1)	−28,061 (−0.5)	141,072 (2.6)
1992	−399,733 (−6.8)	−449,125 (−7.7)	−201,524 (−3.4)	−53,490 (−0.9)

Source: Budget of the United States, FY 1993 (calculations by author).

Will the Real Deficit Please Stand Up?

Public opinion polls show almost everyone is against "the deficit." Yet few know what it means or how it is calculated. In fact, the official deficit measure violates basic bookkeeping rules followed by both private businesses and state governments.

For example, the official 1992 deficit includes a $49.4 billion "surplus" reported by Social Security. The trust fund will need this money to pay for future benefits, however. When we adjust for this by moving Social Security off budget, the deficit rises to $449.1 billion.

Similarly, the federal budget lumps capital and current expenses together when calculating the deficit. If companies followed this accounting methodology, not a single rapidly growing company in America would show a profit. When both Social Security and federal spending on physical capital and on R&D are removed, the 1992 deficit falls from $399.7 billion to $201.5 billion.

Two other factors should be reflected in a comprehensive deficit figure. Most obviously, the aggregate budget surpluses of state and local governments, which totaled $25.0 billion in 1992, should be deducted from the federal budget deficit.

Secondly, we should acknowledge that inflation is a tax that lowers the real amount of outstanding public debt. Calculations by A. B. Laffer, V. A. Canto & Associates, show that inflation reduced the level of real public debt by $123 billion in 1992.

After we have made all the adjustments, the 1992 federal deficit shrinks to $53.5 billion, or about one-seventh the official figure ($399.7 billion). In fact, the adjustments reveal budget *surpluses* for most of the last 40 years, including a $141.1 billion surplus in 1990.

Federal Tax Receipts (As Per Cent of GDP)

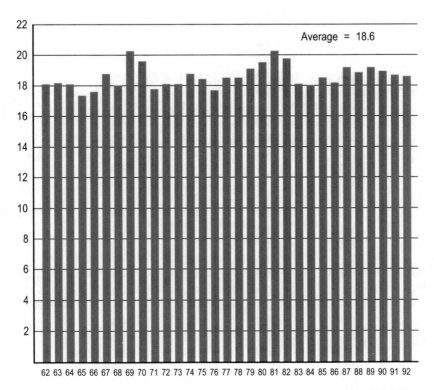

Average = 18.6

62 63 64 65 66 67 68 69 70 71 72 73 74 75 76 77 78 79 80 81 82 83 84 85 86 87 88 89 90 91 92

Source: Congressional Budget Office.

The per cent of GDP taken by federal taxes has remained remarkably stable for three decades, averaging 18.6%. On an annual basis, revenues have been as high as 20.2% of GDP (1969 and 1981) and as low as 17.4% (1965).

The stability occurred during a period when the top marginal tax rate ranged from a high of 92% to a low of 28%. This suggests that the deficit problem cannot be solved by tax hikes. Taxpayers find ways to avoid paying taxes when rates increase.

Federal Revenues, Outlays, and Deficits

Billions of Dollars

Year	Revenues	Outlays	Deficits
1962	$ 99.7	$ 106.8	$ −7.1
1963	106.6	111.3	−4.8
1964	112.6	118.5	−5.9
1965	116.8	118.2	−1.4
1966	130.8	134.5	−3.7
1967	148.8	157.5	−8.6
1968	153.0	178.1	−25.2
1969	**186.9**	**183.6**	**3.2**
1970	192.8	195.6	−2.8
1971	187.1	210.2	−23.0
1972	207.3	230.7	−23.4
1973	230.8	245.7	−14.9
1974	263.2	269.4	−6.1
1975	279.1	332.3	−53.2
1976	298.1	371.8	−73.7
1977	355.6	409.2	−53.7
1978	399.6	458.7	−59.2
1979	463.3	503.5	−40.2
1980	517.1	590.9	−73.8
1981	599.3	678.2	−79.0
1982	617.8	745.8	−128.0
1983	600.6	808.4	−207.8
1984	666.5	851.8	−185.4
1985	734.1	946.4	−212.3
1986	769.1	990.3	−221.2
1987	854.1	1,003.9	−149.8
1988	909.0	1,064.1	−155.2
1989	990.7	1,143.2	−152.5
1990	1,031.3	1,252.7	−221.4
1991	1,054.3	1,323.8	−269.5
1992	1,091.6	1,381.8	−290.2

Source: Congressional Budget Office.

The Lone Surplus

Since 1962 there has been only one budget surplus—$3.2 billion in 1969. The cumulative deficit over that period was more than $2.7 **trillion**.

Federal Revenues, Outlays, and Deficits

As a Per Cent of GDP

Year	Revenues	Outlays	Deficit
1962	18.0	19.3	−1.3
1963	18.2	19.0	−0.8
1964	18.0	18.9	−0.9
1965	17.4	17.6	−0.2
1966	17.7	18.2	−0.5
1967	18.8	19.9	−1.1
1968	18.0	21.0	−3.0
1969	20.2	19.8	0.4
1970	19.6	19.9	−0.3
1971	17.8	20.0	−2.2
1972	18.1	20.1	−2.0
1973	18.1	19.2	−1.2
1974	18.8	19.2	−0.4
1975	18.5	22.0	−3.5
1976	17.7	22.1	−4.4
1977	18.5	21.3	−2.8
1978	18.5	21.3	−2.7
1979	19.1	20.7	−1.7
1980	19.6	22.3	−2.8
1981	20.2	22.9	−2.7
1982	19.8	23.9	−4.1
1983	18.1	24.4	−6.3
1984	18.0	23.0	−5.0
1985	18.5	23.8	−5.3
1986	18.2	23.5	−5.2
1987	19.2	22.5	−3.4
1988	18.9	22.1	−3.2
1989	19.2	22.1	−3.0
1990	18.9	22.9	−4.0
1991	18.7	23.5	−4.8
1992	18.5	23.5	−4.9
1962–92 (avg.)	**18.6**	**21.3**	**−2.7**

Source: Congressional Budget Office.

Spending Is the Problem

Over the past three decades federal taxes have narrowly fluctuated about the average of 18.6% of GDP. Federal spending, however, has grown from 19% of GDP in the early 1960s to between 22% and 25% of GDP during the past 10 years. The deficit is clearly the result of too much spending rather than too little revenues.

Federal Tax Burden by Administration
As a Per Cent of GDP

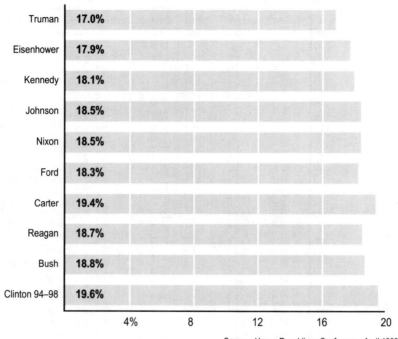

Truman	**17.0%**
Eisenhower	**17.9%**
Kennedy	**18.1%**
Johnson	**18.5%**
Nixon	**18.5%**
Ford	**18.3%**
Carter	**19.4%**
Reagan	**18.7%**
Bush	**18.8%**
Clinton 94–98	**19.6%**

4%   8   12   16   20

Source: House Republican Conference, April 1993.

The Tax Man Cometh

Ronald Reagan's 1981 tax cut (ERTA) reduced the tax burden to 18.1% of Gross Domestic Product in 1983 and 1984. But subsequent tax increases have eroded the beneficial effect of that tax cut. By the time Reagan left office, taxes were consuming more than 19% of GDP. Thanks to the 1990 Budget Agreement, the average tax burden under Bush was higher than under Reagan.

If President Clinton's program is adopted in full, the federal tax burden will exceed that of any other administration in history. Taxes as a share of GDP will rise to a level higher than under Jimmy Carter, who was swept from office in a nationwide tax revolt.

346

The Composition of Federal Revenues

Billions of Dollars

	Individual Income Taxes	Corporate Income Taxes	Social Insurance Taxes	Excise Taxes	Estate and Gift Taxes	Customs Duties	Miscellaneous Receipts	Total Revenues
1940	$ 0.9	$ 1.2	$ 1.8	$ 2.0	$ 0.4	$ 0.3	$ —	$ 6.5
1950	15.8	10.4	4.3	7.6	0.7	0.4	0.2	39.4
1960	40.7	21.5	14.7	11.7	1.6	1.1	1.2	92.5
1970	90.4	32.8	44.4	15.7	3.6	2.4	3.4	192.8
1971	86.2	26.8	47.3	16.6	3.7	2.6	3.9	187.1
1972	94.7	32.2	52.6	15.5	5.4	3.3	3.6	207.3
1973	103.2	36.2	63.1	16.3	4.9	3.2	3.9	230.8
1974	119.0	38.6	75.1	16.8	5.0	3.3	5.4	263.2
1975	122.4	40.6	84.5	16.6	4.6	3.7	6.7	279.1
1976	131.6	41.4	90.8	17.0	5.2	4.1	8.0	298.1
1977	157.6	54.9	106.5	17.5	7.3	5.2	6.5	355.6
1978	181.0	60.0	121.0	18.4	5.3	6.6	7.4	399.6
1979	217.8	65.7	138.9	18.7	5.4	7.4	9.3	463.3
1980	244.1	64.6	157.8	24.3	6.4	7.2	12.7	517.1
1981	285.9	61.1	182.7	40.8	6.8	8.1	13.8	599.3
1982	297.7	49.2	201.5	36.3	8.0	8.9	16.2	617.8
1983	288.9	37.0	209.0	35.3	6.1	8.7	15.6	600.6
1984	298.4	56.9	239.4	37.4	6.0	11.4	17.0	666.5
1985	334.5	61.3	265.2	36.0	6.4	12.1	18.5	734.1
1986	349.0	63.1	283.9	32.9	7.0	13.3	19.9	769.1
1987	392.6	83.9	303.3	32.5	7.5	15.1	19.3	854.1
1988	401.2	94.3	334.3	35.2	7.6	16.2	19.9	909.0
1989	445.7	103.3	359.4	34.4	8.7	16.3	22.8	990.7
1990	466.9	93.5	380.0	35.3	11.5	16.7	27.3	1,031.3
1991	467.8	98.1	396.0	42.4	11.1	15.9	22.8	1,054.3
1992	476.5	100.3	413.7	45.6	11.1	17.4	27.1	1,091.6

Source: Office of Management and Budget; Congressional Budget Office.

Revenues Outpace Inflation

Since 1980, aggregate federal tax revenues have grown 111%. Had revenues grown at the rate of inflation, the government would have collected $225 billion **fewer** dollars in 1992. Congress spent the additional money, and then some.

Percentage Composition of Federal Tax Revenues

	Individual Income Taxes	Corporate Income Taxes	Social Insurance Taxes	Excise Taxes	Estate and Gift Taxes	Customs Duties	Miscellaneous Receipts	Total
1940	13.8	18.3	27.3	30.2	6.1	4.6	——	100.0
1950	39.9	26.5	11.0	19.1	1.8	1.0	0.5	100.0
1960	44.0	23.2	15.9	12.6	1.7	1.2	1.3	100.0
1970	46.9	17.0	23.0	8.1	1.9	1.2	1.8	100.0
1980	47.2	12.5	30.5	4.7	1.2	1.4	2.5	100.0
1985	45.6	8.4	36.1	4.3	0.9	1.6	2.7	100.0
1990	45.3	9.1	36.9	3.4	1.1	1.6	2.6	100.0
1991	44.4	9.3	37.6	4.0	1.1	1.5	2.2	100.0
1992	43.6	9.2	37.9	4.2	1.0	1.6	2.5	100.0
1993 est.	44.5	9.2	38.0	4.1	1.1	1.6	1.5	100.0

Source: Office of Management and Budget; Congressional Budget Office.

Since 1970, *personal income taxes* have accounted for a stable 44% to 48% of all federal revenue. *Social insurance taxes* (mainly Social Security and Medicare payroll taxes and unemployment taxes) have contributed most to revenue growth. This source has risen from 11.0% of all revenues in 1950 to 38.0% expected in 1993. Corporate income taxes account for about two-thirds less of the total taxes than they did in 1950, reflecting a reduction in corporate profits relative to total income.

F. Federal Spending

The Composition of Federal Spending (1)
Billions of Dollars

Fiscal year	Social welfare	Net interest	National defense	Total other non-defense	Total federal outlays
1965	$ 36.6	$ 8.6	$ 50.6	$ 22.4	$ 118.2
1970	75.3	14.4	81.7	24.2	195.6
1971	91.9	14.8	78.9	24.6	210.2
1972	107.2	15.5	79.2	28.8	230.7
1973	119.5	17.3	76.7	32.2	245.7
1974	135.8	21.4	79.3	32.8	269.4
1975	173.2	23.2	86.5	49.3	332.3
1976	203.6	26.7	89.6	51.9	371.8
1977	221.9	29.9	97.2	60.2	409.2
1978	242.3	35.5	104.5	76.5	458.7
1979	267.6	42.6	116.3	76.9	503.5
1980	313.4	52.5	134.0	91.0	590.9
1981	362.0	68.8	157.5	89.9	678.2
1982	388.7	85.0	185.3	86.7	745.8
1983	426.0	89.8	209.9	82.6	808.4
1984	432.0	111.1	227.4	81.3	851.8
1985	471.8	129.5	252.7	92.3	946.4
1986	481.6	136.0	273.4	99.3	990.0
1987	502.2	138.7	282.0	81.1	1,003.9
1988	533.4	151.8	290.4	88.5	1,064.1
1989	568.7	169.3	303.6	101.7	1,143.2
1990	619.3	184.2	299.3	149.8	1,252.7
1991	689.7	194.5	273.3	166.3	1,323.8
1992	773.6	199.4	298.4	110.4	1,381.8
1993 est.	840.9	202.1	292.9	139.2	1,475.1
1994 est.	892.4	212.0	277.3	131.3	1,513.0
1995 est.	948.4	227.2	272.3	116.6	1,564.5
1996 est.	1,002.7	243.3	264.9	101.9	1,612.8
1997 est.	1,071.6	257.4	249.2	99.3	1,677.5
1998 est.	1,136.7	272.7	252.7	104.9	1,767.0

Source: Congressional Research Service,
based on data from Office of Management and Budget, January and February 1993.

The Composition of Federal Spending (2)
Billions of Constant 1992 Dollars

Fiscal year	Social welfare	Net interest	National defense	Total other non-defense	Total federal outlays
1965	$ 156.7	$ 36.8	$ 216.9	$ 96.2	$ 506.5
1970	263.8	50.4	286.0	84.8	685.0
1971	305.9	49.4	262.6	81.7	699.6
1972	339.2	49.0	250.5	91.2	729.8
1973	360.2	52.3	231.1	96.9	740.5
1974	380.2	60.1	222.2	91.8	754.3
1975	441.3	59.2	220.3	125.7	846.5
1976	481.5	63.2	212.0	122.6	879.4
1977	485.5	65.4	212.8	131.7	895.4
1978	493.0	72.1	212.6	155.6	933.4
1979	500.9	79.8	217.8	144.0	942.5
1980	538.1	90.2	230.1	156.3	1,014.7
1981	564.2	107.2	245.5	140.2	1,057.1
1982	563.8	123.4	268.8	125.8	1,081.7
1983	593.3	125.1	292.3	115.1	1,125.9
1984	576.4	148.2	303.4	108.4	1,136.4
1985	606.2	166.4	324.7	118.6	1,216.0
1986	600.9	169.8	341.1	123.9	1,235.8
1987	608.6	168.0	341.7	98.2	1,216.6
1988	623.8	177.6	339.6	103.5	1,244.5
1989	636.4	189.4	339.7	113.8	1,279.3
1990	664.7	197.7	321.3	160.8	1,344.5
1991	709.7	200.2	281.2	171.1	1,362.2
1992	773.6	199.4	298.4	110.4	1,381.8
1993 est.	821.2	197.4	286.0	135.9	1,440.5
1994 est.	851.1	202.2	264.5	125.2	1,442.9
1995 est.	884.1	211.8	253.8	108.7	1,458.5
1996 est.	913.7	221.7	241.4	92.9	1,469.7
1997 est.	955.5	229.5	222.2	88.5	1,495.8
1998 est.	991.7	237.9	220.5	91.5	1,541.6

The Republican Record 1980–92 Social welfare spending rose 44%. Defense spending rose 30%. Other non-defense spending fell 29%. And net interest rose 121%.

Federal spending grew by 173%, in real terms, between 1965 and 1992. By comparison, U.S. population grew 31% over that period, and real GDP rose by 99%.

The Composition of Federal Spending (3)

As a Per Cent of GDP

Fiscal year	Social welfare	Net interest	National defense	Total other non-defense	Total federal outlays	Gross domestic product ($ billions)
1960	5.2%	1.4%	9.5%	4.0%	18.3%	$ 504.6
1965	5.5	1.3	7.5	3.3	17.6	671.0
1970	7.6	1.5	8.3	2.5	19.9	985.4
1971	8.7	1.4	7.5	2.3	20.0	1,050.9
1972	9.3	1.3	6.9	2.5	20.1	1,147.8
1973	9.4	1.4	6.0	2.5	19.3	1,274.0
1974	9.7	1.5	5.7	2.3	19.2	1,403.6
1975	11.5	1.5	5.7	3.3	22.0	1,509.8
1976	12.1	1.6	5.3	3.1	22.1	1,684.2
1977	11.6	1.6	5.1	3.1	21.3	1,917.2
1978	11.2	1.6	4.8	3.5	21.3	2,155.0
1979	11.0	1.8	4.8	3.2	20.7	2,429.5
1980	11.9	2.0	5.1	3.4	22.3	2,644.1
1981	12.2	2.3	5.3	3.0	22.9	2,964.4
1982	12.4	2.7	5.9	2.8	23.9	3,122.2
1983	12.8	2.7	6.3	2.5	24.4	3,316.5
1984	11.7	3.0	6.2	2.2	23.1	3,695.0
1985	11.9	3.3	6.4	2.3	23.9	3,967.7
1986	11.4	3.2	6.5	2.4	23.5	4,219.0
1987	11.3	3.1	6.3	1.8	22.5	4,452.4
1988	11.1	3.2	6.0	1.8	22.1	4,808.4
1989	11.0	3.3	5.9	2.0	22.1	5,173.3
1990	11.3	3.4	5.5	2.7	22.9	5,467.1
1991	12.2	3.5	4.9	3.0	23.5	5,632.6
1992	13.2	3.4	5.1	1.9	23.5	5,868.6
1993 est.	13.6	3.3	4.7	2.3	23.9	6,173.0
1994 est.	13.7	3.3	4.3	2.0	23.2	6,508.0
1995 est.	13.8	3.3	4.0	1.7	22.8	6,855.0
1996 est.	13.9	3.4	3.7	1.4	22.4	7,202.0
1997 est.	14.2	3.4	3.3	1.3	22.2	7,543,0
1998 est.	14.4	3.5	3.2	1.3	22.4	7,873.0

After 12 years of Republican rule the U.S. today devotes a larger share of GDP to social welfare (13.6%) than ever before.

Defense spending is projected to fall to only 3.2% of GDP in 1998, the lowest since 1940.

The Composition of Federal Spending (4)
As a Per Cent of Total Federal Outlays

Fiscal year	Social welfare	Net interest	National defense	Total other non-defense	Total federal outlays	Total federal outlays ($ billions)
1965	30.9%	7.3%	42.8%	19.0%	100.0%	$ 118.2
1970	38.5	7.4	41.8	12.4	100.0	195.6
1971	43.7	7.1	37.5	11.7	100.0	210.2
1972	46.5	6.7	34.3	12.5	100.0	230.7
1973	48.6	7.1	31.2	13.1	100.0	245.7
1974	50.4	8.0	29.5	12.2	100.0	269.4
1975	52.1	7.0	26.0	14.8	100.0	332.3
1976	54.8	7.2	24.1	13.9	100.0	371.8
1977	54.2	7.3	23.8	14.7	100.0	409.2
1978	52.8	7.7	22.8	16.7	100.0	458.7
1979	53.1	8.5	23.1	15.3	100.0	503.5
1980	53.0	8.9	22.7	15.4	100.0	590.9
1981	53.4	10.1	23.2	13.3	100.0	678.2
1982	52.1	11.4	24.8	11.6	100.0	745.8
1983	52.7	11.1	26.0	10.2	100.0	808.4
1984	50.7	13.0	26.7	9.5	100.0	851.8
1985	49.9	13.7	26.7	9.8	100.0	946.4
1986	48.6	13.7	27.6	10.0	100.0	990.3
1987	50.0	13.8	28.1	8.1	100.0	1,003.9
1988	50.1	14.3	27.3	8.3	100.0	1,064.1
1989	49.7	14.8	26.6	8.9	100.0	1,143.2
1990	49.4	14.7	23.9	12.0	100.0	1,252.7
1991	52.1	14.7	20.6	12.6	100.0	1,323.8
1992	56.0	14.4	21.6	8.0	100.0	1,381.8
1993 est.	57.0	13.7	19.9	9.4	100.0	1,475.1
1994 est.	59.0	14.0	18.3	8.7	100.0	1,513.0
1995 est.	60.6	14.5	17.4	7.5	100.0	1,564.5
1996 est.	62.2	15.1	16.4	6.3	100.0	1,612.8
1997 est.	63.9	15.3	14.9	5.9	100.0	1,677.5
1998 est.	64.3	15.4	14.3	5.9	100.0	1,767.0

The tilt toward social spending has been under way since 1965. This will continue, as social welfare's share of the federal budget rises from 56% in 1992 to 64% in 1998. Net interest's share will rise from 14% to 15%.

Under President Clinton's plan, net interest will displace national defense as the second largest budget category in 1997.

Federal Outlays by Category
In Billions of Dollars / Fiscal Year 1965 to Fiscal Year 1998

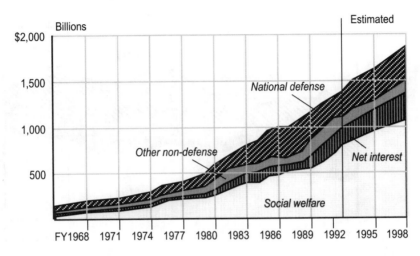

Source: Congressional Research Service,
based on data from Office of Management and Budget, January and February 1993.

Federal Outlays by Category

As Per Cent of GDP / Fiscal Year 1965 to Fiscal Year 1998

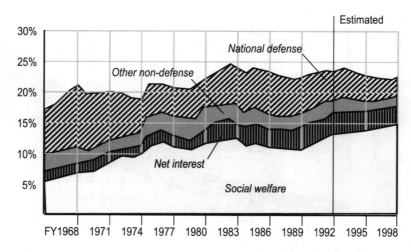

Source: Congressional Research Service,
based on data from Office of Management and Budget, January and February 1993.

Federal Outlays by Category

As Per Cent of Total Federal Outlays / Fiscal Year 1965 to Fiscal Year 1998

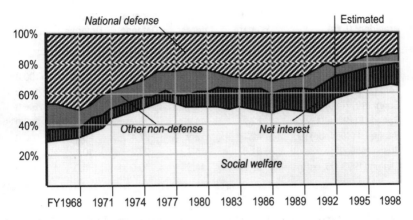

Source: Congressional Research Service,
based on data from Office of Management and Budget, January and February 1993.

The Composition of Federal Spending by Administration

As Per Cent of Total Spending

President (FYs)	Social Welfare	Net Interest	National Defense	Other Non-Defense	Total
	—— Spending as a per cent of total budget ——				
Nixon (1970–74)	45.5%	7.3%	34.9%	12.4%	100.0%
Ford (1975–76)	53.4	7.1	25.1	14.4	100.0
Carter (1977–80)	53.3	8.1	23.1	15.5	100.0
Reagan I (1981–84)	52.2	11.4	25.2	11.2	100.0
Reagan II (1985–88)	49.7	13.9	27.4	9.1	100.0
Bush (1989–92)	51.8	14.7	23.2	10.4	100.0
Clinton (1993–96, est.)	59.7	14.3	18.0	8.0	100.0

Source: Author's calculations based on Office of Management and Budget data, February 1993.

Social welfare and net interest will account for 74% of all federal spending during the Clinton Administration, up from 67% under Bush and 53% under Nixon

Defense and Other (a category that includes agriculture, energy, transportation, international affairs, space, technology, and environmental functions) have declined as a per cent of total spending.

Discretionary vs. Uncontrollable Spending

Billions of Dollars

		Mandatory Spending				
	Discretionary Spending	Entitlements and Other Mandatory Spending	Deposit Insurance	Net Interest	Offsetting Receipts	Total Outlays
1962	$ 74.9	$ 32.3	$ -0.4	$ 6.9	$ -6.8	$ 106.8
1963	78.3	33.6	-0.4	7.7	-7.9	111.3
1964	82.8	35.7	-0.4	8.2	-7.7	118.5
1965	81.8	36.1	-0.4	8.6	-7.9	118.2
1966	94.1	39.9	-0.5	9.4	-8.4	134.5
1967	110.4	47.4	-0.4	10.3	-10.2	157.5
1968	122.1	56.1	-0.5	11.1	-10.6	178.1
1969	121.4	61.2	-0.7	12.7	-11.0	183.6
1970	124.6	68.7	-0.5	14.4	-11.5	195.6
1971	127.1	82.7	-0.4	14.8	-14.1	210.2
1972	133.1	96.8	-0.6	15.5	-14.1	230.7
1973	135.0	112.2	-0.8	17.3	-18.0	245.7
1974	142.5	127.1	-0.6	21.4	-21.2	269.4
1975	162.5	164.4	0.5	23.2	-18.3	332.3
1976	175.6	189.7	-0.6	26.7	-19.6	371.8
1977	197.1	206.6	-2.8	29.9	-21.5	409.2
1978	218.7	228.4	-1.0	35.5	-22.8	458.7
1979	240.0	248.2	-1.7	42.6	-25.6	503.5
1980	276.5	291.5	-0.4	52.5	-29.2	590.9
1981	308.2	340.6	-1.4	68.8	-37.9	678.2
1982	326.2	372.7	-2.2	85.0	-36.0	745.8
1983	353.4	411.6	-1.2	89.8	-45.3	808.4
1984	379.6	406.3	-0.9	111.1	-44.2	851.8
1985	416.2	450.0	-2.2	129.5	-47.1	946.4
1986	439.0	459.7	1.5	136.0	-45.9	990.3
1987	444.9	470.2	3.1	138.7	-53.0	1,003.9
1988	465.1	494.2	10.0	151.8	-57.0	1,064.1
1989	489.7	526.2	22.0	169.3	-63.9	1,143.2
1990	501.7	567.4	58.1	184.2	-58.8	1,252.7
1991	534.8	634.2	66.3	194.5	-106.0	1,323.8
1992	537.4	711.2	2.6	199.4	-68.8	1,381.8

Source: Congressional Budget Office.

Discretionary spending consists of programs whose funding levels are set annually through appropriation bills. Nondiscretionary spending consists overwhelmingly of mandatory entitlement programs. Net interest is also nondiscretionary because its growth is wholly determined by government deficits and market interest rates.

Why Spending Is Out of Control:
The Rise of Non-Discretionary Spending
As a Per Cent of Total Spending

Fiscal Year	Total Outlays	Discretionary				Mandatory		
		Total	National Defense	Inter-National	Domestic	Total	Other Spending	Net Interest
1962	100.0%	70.1%	49.2%	5.2%	15.7%	29.9%	23.5%	6.4%
1963	100.0	70.4	48.3	4.7	17.4	29.6	22.7	7.0
1964	100.0	69.8	46.4	3.9	19.5	30.2	23.2	6.9
1965	100.0	69.2	43.2	4.0	22.1	30.8	23.5	7.3
1966	100.0	69.9	43.9	3.8	22.3	30.1	23.1	7.0
1967	100.0	70.1	45.7	3.4	21.0	29.9	23.4	6.5
1968	100.0	68.6	46.1	2.7	19.7	31.4	25.2	6.2
1969	100.0	66.1	45.0	2.2	18.9	33.9	27.0	6.9
1970	100.0	63.7	41.9	2.0	19.8	36.3	29.0	7.4
1971	100.0	60.5	37.6	1.8	21.1	39.5	32.5	7.1
1972	100.0	57.7	34.4	2.0	21.3	42.3	35.6	6.7
1973	100.0	54.9	31.4	2.0	21.6	45.1	38.0	7.1
1974	100.0	52.9	30.0	2.3	20.6	47.1	39.1	8.0
1975	100.0	48.9	26.4	2.5	20.1	51.1	44.1	7.0
1976	100.0	47.2	24.2	2.0	21.0	52.8	45.6	7.2
TQ *	100.0	50.0	23.2	3.5	23.3	50.0	42.7	7.2
1977	100.0	48.2	23.8	2.0	22.4	51.8	44.5	7.3
1978	100.0	47.7	22.8	1.9	23.0	52.3	44.6	7.7
1979	100.0	47.7	23.2	1.8	22.7	52.3	43.9	8.5
1980	100.0	46.8	22.8	2.2	21.8	53.2	44.3	8.9
1981	100.0	45.4	23.3	2.0	20.1	54.6	44.4	10.1
1982	100.0	43.7	24.9	1.7	17.1	56.3	44.9	11.4
1983	100.0	43.7	26.0	1.7	16.1	56.3	45.2	11.1
1984	100.0	44.6	26.8	1.9	15.9	55.4	42.4	13.0
1985	100.0	44.0	26.7	1.8	15.4	56.0	42.3	13.7
1986	100.0	44.3	27.7	1.8	14.9	55.7	41.9	13.7
1987	100.0	44.3	28.1	1.5	14.7	55.7	41.9	13.8
1988	100.0	43.7	27.3	1.5	14.9	56.3	42.0	14.3
1989	100.0	42.8	26.6	1.5	14.8	57.2	42.4	14.8
1990	100.0	40.1	24.0	1.5	14.6	59.9	45.2	14.7
1991	100.0	40.4	24.2	1.5	14.8	59.6	44.9	14.7
1992	100.0	38.7	21.8	1.4	15.5	61.3	46.9	14.4
1993 est.	100.0	**37.2**	19.7	1.5	16.0	62.8	49.1	13.7

* Transitional quarter, from FY ending 6/30 to FY ending 9/30.

Source: Congressional Budget Office.

To cut the deficit, all spending cuts have to be made in only 37% of federal outlays . . . unless entitlements and other mandatory spending are reined in.

Mandatory spending has grown from 29.9% of all federal outlays in 1962 to 62.8% in 1993. This represents more than a doubling of the share of the budget over which Congress and the Administration exercise no year-to-year control.

G. Comparative Spending of Governments

Government Spending: U.S., Europe, Japan
As Per Cent of GDP

	United States	Europe	Japan
1966	28.5%	34.6%	19.1%
1967	30.5	35.9	18.2
1968	30.7	36.9	19.2
1969	30.4	36.9	18.9
1970	31.6	36.6	19.4
1971	31.6	37.4	20.9
1972	31.3	38.1	22.1
1973	30.6	38.5	22.4
1974	32.2	40.4	24.5
1975	33.5	43.7	26.8
1976	32.6	43.5	27.2
1977	31.2	43.5	28.5
1978	30.0	44.4	30.0
1979	29.9	44.5	31.1
1980	31.8	45.4	32.0
1981	32.1	47.7	32.8
1982	33.9	48.7	33.0
1983	33.9	49.0	33.3
1984	32.6	49.0	32.3
1985	33.2	49.2	31.6
1986	33.7	48.6	32.0
1987	33.4	48.1	32.2
1988	32.5	47.3	31.6
1989	32.4	46.8	30.9
1990	33.3	47.8	31.7
1991	34.2	49.4	31.4
1992	35.4	50.7	32.2

Although there has been little change in the government spending/GDP ratio, real U.S. GDP has grown by 27% between 1982 and 1992.

Source: Organization for Economic Cooperation and Development.

The ratio of government spending to GDP is lower in the U.S. than in Europe, where public health insurance and unemployment insurance are larger expense items. The ratio has risen in all countries in the last 25 years—less here than elsewhere.

359

Government Spending vs. the Economy

	Government Spending as % of GDP 1992	GDP per capita 1991	Real GDP Average Annual % Change 1980–91	Inflation
United States	35.4%	$22,204	1.7%	4.2%
Japan	32.2	19,107	3.6	1.5
Germany	49.4	19,500	2.2	2.8
France	52.0	18,227	1.8	5.7
Italy	53.2	16,896	2.2	9.5
United Kingdom	44.1	15,720	2.6	5.8
Canada	49.7	19,178	2.0	4.3
Spain	45.2	12,719	2.8	8.9

Source: Organization for Economic Cooperation and Development; International Monetary Fund; The World Bank.

The Crucial Number

The U.S. and Japan have consistently had the smallest shares of government as a per cent of GDP among the major industrialized countries. And, perhaps not coincidentally, they also have, respectively, the largest output per capita and the fastest rate of economic growth. Inflation also seems to be lower in countries with smaller government sectors.

At the extremes are the collapsed communist economies, where government's share equaled 100%, and Hong Kong, where the government spends about 11% to 19% of a booming economy.

The universal rise in government as a share of GDP may explain two baffling phenomena: the twenty-year slowdown in productivity growth and the past three years of below-par economic growth.

Total Government Spending: Federal plus State/Local
As a Per Cent of GDP

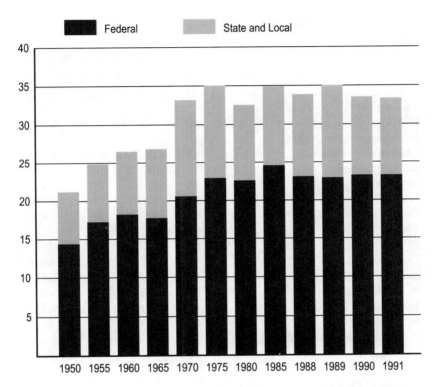

Source: Advisory Commission on Intergovernmental Relations.

Before Franklin Roosevelt's New Deal of the 1930s, government spending accounted for slightly less than 10% of GDP, with state and local government accounting for about three-quarters of the total. Since then the burden of national defense, interest on the national debt, and—most important—social programs such as Social Security and Medicare, has propelled the federal share to more than twice the state and local share.

In recent years government spending has stabilized at about 34% of GDP, with a rising federal share offset by a declining state and local share.

H. Social Program Spending

Social Program Spending
Billions of Dollars

	1970	1980	1992	Increase, 1980–1992 Amount	Per Cent
Social Security	$30.3	$118.5	$287.5	$169.0	142.6%
Medicare	6.2	32.1	119.0	86.9	270.0
Medicaid	2.7	14.0	67.8	53.8	384.3
Unemployment Compensation	3.1	16.9	37.0	20.1	118.9
Civil Service Retirement	2.7	14.7	33.5	18.8	127.9
Military Retirement	2.8	11.9	24.5	12.6	105.9
Food Stamps	0.6	9.1	21.8	12.7	139.6
Housing Assistance	0.5	5.4	18.9	13.5	250.0
Supplemental Security Inc.	—	5.7	17.9	12.2	214.0
Veterans' Benefits	7.9	19.8	31.5	11.7	59.1
AFDC	4.1	6.9	15.1	8.2	118.8
Farm Price Supports	4.6	7.4	12.5	5.1	68.9
Social Services	2.3	6.1	12.2	6.1	100.0
Student Assistance	0.5	5.1	10.5	5.4	140.3
Earned Income Tax Credit	—	1.3	7.8	6.5	500.0
Railroad Retirement	1.6	4.7	7.6	2.9	61.7
School Lunch and Child Nutrition Programs	0.4	3.5	6.1	2.6	74.3
Women, Infants, & Children (WIC)	—	0.7	2.6	1.9	271.4
Other	1.9	9.4	13.3	3.9	41.5
Total Social Programs	*$72.2*	*$293.2*	*$747.1*	*$453.9*	*154.8%*

Memo:

Total budget	$195.6	$590.9	$1,381.8	$791.0	133.9%
Non-defense budget	$113.9	$456.9	$1,083.4	$626.5	137.1%

Social Programs as a per cent of:

Total budget	36.9%	49.6%	54.1%		
Non-defense budget	63.4	64.2	69.0		

Source: Office of Management and Budget.

Escalating Entitlements

Social programs are taking over the federal budget and are responsible for most of the recent rise in the deficit. Between 1980 and 1992, social spending grew by 154.8%. (The inflation rate over the same period was only 68%.) Social programs accounted for 54% of all federal spending in 1992, up from a 37% share in 1970.

Entitlements—programs which are not directly controlled by Congress—account for more than 95% of all social spending. At one time the word was a euphemism for welfare. Today most entitlements go to middle-class individuals. Only one-quarter of entitlement payments are means-tested.

There are dozens of entitlement programs, ranging from Social Security and Food Stamps to obscure ones like money for witnesses in federal trials and subsidies to farmers who agree not to cultivate environmentally sensitive land. The largest three—Social Security, Medicare, and Medicaid—account for nearly two-thirds of all social spending.

Poverty Programs Miss Their Mark
1990

Means-tested Welfare Spending	$207.6 billion
The Poverty Gap	
Before means-tested spending	$ 79.6 billion
After means-tested spending	44.8
Net reduction	34.8
Number of Poor Persons	
Before means-tested spending	35.9 million
After means-tested spending	29.4
Net reduction	6.5

Source: U.S. Department of Health and Human Services (means-tested spending);
1992 Green Book (poverty gap, poverty population).

Total means-tested welfare spending by federal, state, and local levels of government equaled $207.6 billion in 1990. This was more than two and one half times larger than the amount needed to eliminate poverty—the poverty gap.

Unfortunately, the $207.6 billion anti-poverty expenditure reduced the poverty gap by a mere $34 billion. Clearly, most anti-poverty spending does not go to the poor. In fact, only 6.5 million poor persons, or 18% of the poverty population before receipt of means-tested benefits, were lifted out of poverty after receiving such benefits.

I. Poverty and the Family

Poverty and Family Values

	Number of Poor Persons (Millions)	Poverty Rate (%)	Poor persons living in: Female-Headed Families[1] (%)	All Other Families[1] (%)
1959	39.5	22.4%	26.3%	73.7%
1966	28.5	14.7	36.0	64.0
1975	25.9	12.3	47.4	52.6
1982	31.8	14.0	47.5	52.5
1985	33.1	14.0	49.5	50.5
1987	32.2	13.4	52.6	47.4
1988	31.7	13.0	52.9	47.1
1989	31.5	12.8	52.4	47.6
1990	33.6	13.5	53.4	46.6
1991	35.7	14.2	54.0	46.0

[1] *Includes unrelated or single individuals.*

Source: Bureau of the Census, "Poverty in the United States: 1991" (poverty data); *1990 Green Book*, p. 1286 (family composition data; 1991 data is from 1991 poverty statistics, p. xiv).

The largest declines in poverty occurred in the early 1960s, before the Great Society social-spending binge reduced work incentives. During the 1980s, economic growth again reduced the poverty rate—from 15.2% (1983) to 12.8% (1989).

Poverty has become increasingly behavioral rather than economic in nature, as seen in the persistent rise in the share of poor persons living in female-headed families. The real problem in poor communities is the breakdown in traditional values of family, marriage, meaningful labor, and individual responsibility.

Poverty, Work, and Marriage
1991

	Per cent of families living in poverty		
	All Races	White	Black
All Family Types	**11.6%**	**8.8%**	**30.8%**
No workers	31.5	22.9	74.6
One or more full-time workers	3.2	2.8	6.5
Married Couple Families	**6.0**	**5.5**	**11.2**
No workers	13.6	11.4	39.9
One or more full-time workers	2.5	2.4	3.3
Female-headed Families	**35.6**	**28.4**	**51.2**
No workers	76.0	67.4	89.4
One or more full-time workers	7.8	6.2	12.7

Source: Bureau of the Census, "Poverty in the United States: 1991," p. 113.

Working is the key to avoiding poverty. Only 3.2% of families with at least one year-round, full-time worker in 1991 were poor. By contrast, 31.5% of families in which no one worked were poor. Even among female-headed families, the presence of full-time workers cuts the chance of being poor by 90%.

Unfortunately, 42% of poor families in 1991—including 51% of female-headed families—had no workers whatever. Surprisingly, the lack of work effort cannot be explained by the lack of jobs. According to the Joint Economic Committee, only 7% of poor persons who did not work in 1990 gave "could not find work" as their reason for not working.

Number of Children in Never-Married and Single-Parent Families
Selected Years

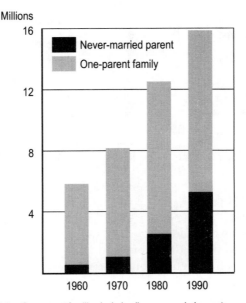

Note: One-parent families include all never-married parents.

Source: Bureau of the Census and U.S. Department of
Health and Human Services data.

Although the number of children under the age of 18 declined between 1970 and 1990, the proportion of children affected by family breakup grew dramatically. As a result, the number of children living with one parent grew 172%, from 5.8 to 15.9 million. Almost 25% of all children lived with one parent in 1990, compared with 9.1% in 1960.

The aggregate figures conceal enormous differences between blacks and whites. As seen in the accompanying chart, more than half (54.8%) of all black children lived with one parent in 1990, compared with 19.2% of all white children. The black/white gap is even wider when one looks at children living with a never-married parent: 28.3% of black children versus 3.7% of white children.

367

Living Conditions of Children
Under 18 Years Old

	1960	1970	1980	1990
	——————— Number in Millions ———————			
Total Number of Children	63.7	69.2	63.4	64.1
Living with:				
Two parents	55.9	58.9	48.6	46.5
One parent	5.8	8.2	12.5	15.9
Never married	0.2	0.6	1.8	4.9
Other relatives	2.0	2.0	2.3	1.8
	——————— Percentage Distribution ———————			
Total Number of Children	100.0%	100.0%	100.0%	100.0%
Living with:				
Two parents	87.7	85.2	76.7	72.5
One parent	9.1	11.9	19.7	24.7
Never married	0.4	0.8	2.9	7.6
Other relatives	3.2	2.9	3.7	2.8

By Race

	1960	1970	1980	1990
Per cent of children living with one parent:				
White children	7.1%	8.7%	15.1%	19.2%
Black children	21.9	31.8	45.8	54.8
Hispanic children	NA	NA	21.1	30.0
Per cent of children living with a never-married parent:				
White Children	0.1%	0.2%	1.1%	3.7%
Black children	2.1	4.5	13.2	28.3
Hispanic children	NA	NA	4.2	9.8

Source: Bureau of the Census, Current Population Reports, Series P-20.

Endangered Species: The Traditional American Family

	1970	1980	1988	1990
	Number in Millions			
All Families with Children	29.6	32.2	34.3	34.7
Two-parent families	25.8	25.2	25.0	24.9
One-parent families	3.8	6.9	9.3	9.8
Maintained by mother	3.4	6.2	8.1	8.4
Never married	0.2	1.1	2.7	2.8
Maintained by father	0.4	0.7	1.2	1.4
	Percentage Distribution			
All Families with Children	100.0%	100.0%	100.0%	100.0%
Two-parent families	87.1	78.5	72.7	71.9
One-parent families	12.9	21.5	27.3	28.1
Maintained by mother	11.5	19.4	23.7	24.2
Never married	0.8	3.3	9.0	8.0
Maintained by father	1.4	2.1	3.6	3.9

Source: House Ways and Means Committee, 1992 *Green Book*, p. 1078.

The number of two-parent families with children actually declined 3.5% from 1970 to 1990, falling from 25.8 million to 24.9 million. By contrast, the number of one-parent families skyrocketed from 3.8 million to 9.7 million, a 155.3% increase over the same period.

As a result of these trends, the composition of U.S. families has changed. Two-parent families accounted for 71.9% of all families with children in 1990, down from 87.1% in 1970. The declining incidence of two-parent families is especially severe among blacks, where such families accounted for only 39.4% of all families with children in 1990, down from 64.3% twenty years earlier.

Percentage of Births to Unmarried Mothers
By Race for Selected Years

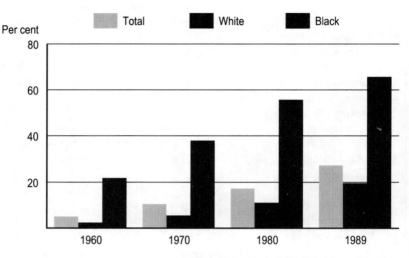

Source: National Center for Health Statistics, published data.

In 1989 there were approximately 1.1 million births to unmarried mothers, 64% more births than in 1980 (665,750). As seen in the chart, 66% of black children born in the United States in 1989 were born to unmarried mothers compared with 19% of white babies born that year.

Although white illegitimacy rates are lower, they are growing more rapidly than that of blacks.

Poor Families Headed by Females

Thousands of Families

Marital Status	1980	1988	% Change 1980–88
Previously married	1,500	1,482	−1.2%
Never married	548	912	66.4
Total	*2,048*	*2,394*	*16.4*

Source: General Accounting Office, "Poverty Trends, 1980–88,"
September 1992, p. 44 (calculations by author).

Illegitimacy Breeds Poverty

Never-married mothers accounted for the *entire* increase in female-headed families living in poverty between 1980 and 1988. The number of poor families headed by previously married females declined during this period.

Abortions: Estimated Number, Rate, and Ratio

	Number of Women Age 15 to 44 (thousands)	Number (thousands)	Abortions Per 1,000 Women	Per 1,000 Births
1972	44,588	586.8	13.2	184
1975	47,606	1,034.2	21.7	331
1977	49,814	1,316.7	26.4	400
1980	53,048	1,553.9	29.3	428
1985	56,754	1,588.6	28.0	422
1986	57,483	1,574.0	27.4	416
1987	57,964	1,559.1	27.1	405
1988	58,192	1,590.8	27.3	401

Source: U.S. Centers for Disease Control; The Alan Guttmacher Institute.

In 1988 there were nearly 1.6 million abortions in the United States.

The number of abortions per 1,000 live births rose from 184 in 1972 (the year before Roe v. Wade) to 331 in 1975. By the Eighties there were more than 400 abortions for every 1,000 births.

In 1988 there were 27.3 abortions for every 1,000 women of childbearing age (15 to 44). Among teenagers (not shown) the rate was 44.4 abortions for every 1,000 girls.

The former Soviet Union has the highest abortion rate (1990):

Per cent of pregnancies aborted (1990)		Number of abortions performed (1990)	
Soviet Union	54.9%	Soviet Union	5,000,000 (approx.)
United States	29.7%	United States	1,588,600
Denmark	27.0%	Japan	529,416
Japan	25.7%	Italy	230,080
Sweden	24.9%	E. Germany	185,037
Australia	20.4%	United Kingdom	160,160
United Kingdom	18.6%	Germany	86,296
Finland	18.0%	Canada	60,375
Canada	16.6%	Netherlands	17,796
Iceland	14.0%	Norway	14,805
New Zealand	13.6%	Finland	13,419
Belgium	12.2%	New Zealand	7,282
Netherlands	9.0%	Iceland	675

Source: United Nations.

Teenage Pregnancy and Birth Rates
Per 1,000 Women, Ages 15 to 19

Country	Pregnancies	Births
Netherlands	15.0	7.7
Sweden	33.2	11.7
Denmark	34.0	12.0
Finland	37.4	15.7
Canada	45.4	24.8
Norway	45.8	19.6
New Zealand	52.8	32.4
England and Wales	53.4	27.5
Czechoslovakia	79.3	53.7
Hungary	93.3	54.2
United States	109.9	51.7

Source: The Alan Guttmacher Institute, cited in *Adolescent Health,*
vol. 2, *Background and the Effectiveness of Selected Prevention and Treatment Services*
(Washington, D.C.: U.S. Office of Technology Assessment, November 1991), p. 329.

The teenage pregnancy and birth rates are significantly higher in the United States than in many other industrialized countries. Of the 11 countries listed in the table, the United States had the highest pregnancy rate of 109.9 pregnancies per 1,000 women ages 15 through 19, ahead of Hungary (93.3), England and Wales (52.8), and Sweden (33.2). The teenage birth rate in the United States was also high at 51.7, slightly below the rates of Hungary (54.2) and Czechoslovakia (53.7).

The Welfare Trap

A large underclass of chronically poor Americans persists despite increased economic opportunity. To understand why, compare the assistance received by an AFDC mother with two children living in New York City with the net income of a low-wage job:

Welfare		Minimum Wage Job	
Basic Grant	$2,856	Salary	$ 8,829
Home Energy Payments	636	Food Stamps	2,880
Shelter Allowance	3,432	Public Assistance	3,360
Food Stamps	2,784	Earned Income Credit	1,200
Total	9,708	*Income*	*$16,269*
		Day Care	$4,200
		Work-related Costs	2,500
		Social Security Taxes	678
		Expenses	*$7,378*
		Net Income	*$8,891*

Source: Public Policy Institute of New York State, "The Prisoners of Charity," May 1993 (charts).

The $9,708 received under welfare represents cash income only. It is supplemented by a fully paid health insurance policy (Medicaid), housing subsidies, school breakfast and lunch programs, special aid to pregnant women and young children, subsidized telephone rates, and numerous other in-kind benefits.

Even without the extras, the family of three has $817 *more* per year if the mother chooses welfare instead of a job paying the minimum wage of $4.25.

The choice of welfare over work is a rational response to the "incentives to fail" built into the current welfare system.

Federal Income Tax for Median Income Family by Family Size and Type, 1948–1989

Joint Returns

Year	Median Family Income	— No Children —		— 2 Children —		— 4 Children —	
		Tax	% of Income	Tax	% of Income	Tax	% of Income
1948	$ 3,187	$ 208	6.5%	$ 9	0.3%	$ 0	0.0%
1954	4,167	402	9.6	162	3.9	0	0.0
1960	5,620	625	11.1	385	6.9	145	2.6
1966	7,532	741	9.8	524	7.0	328	4.4
1972	11,116	1,201	10.8	916	8.2	631	5.7
1978	17,640	2,101	11.9	1,768	10.0	1,408	8.0
1980	21,023	2,643	12.6	2,176	10.4	1,756	8.4
1982	23,433	2,767	11.8	2,327	9.9	1,904	8.1
1984	26,433	2,844	10.8	2,421	9.2	2,061	7.8
1986	29,458	3,217	10.9	2,744	9.3	2,348	8.0
1987	30,853	2,876	9.3	2,306	7.5	1,736	5.6
1989	34,213	3,352	9.8	2,751	8.0	2,151	6.3

Source: Heritage Foundation.

Putting Parents Last

The tax burden for families with children has risen far faster than that of other groups. As seen above, while the average federal income tax rate for childless couples has not changed much since 1954, the rate for a typical married couple with two children has more than doubled. When Social Security and Medicare taxes are added in, this family now pays 24% of its income to the federal government.

The anti-family bias stems from a shrinking real personal exemption. In 1948 the exemption was $600—enough to shield 80% of a typical 4-person family's income from taxes. To shield the same fraction of income today the exemption (currently $2,300) would have to be raised to $8,200 per dependent child.

J. Distribution of Income

Real Average Family Income since 1973
Constant 1991 Dollars

Year	Lowest Fifth	Second Fifth	Middle Fifth	Fourth Fifth	Highest Fifth
1973	$10,746	$23,451	$34,457	$47,090	$ 80,794
1974	10,584	23,104	33,811	46,321	79,216
1975	10,205	22,226	33,119	45,351	77,481
1976	10,444	22,780	34,068	46,549	79,567
1977	10,282	22,865	34,483	47,588	81,584
1978	10,599	23,588	35,499	48,911	84,099
1979	10,765	23,750	35,870	49,395	85,589
1980	10,199	22,904	34,695	48,140	82,433
1981	9,782	22,126	33,958	47,682	81,741
1982	9,256	21,785	33,370	47,332	83,371
1983	9,236	21,823	33,648	47,964	84,381
1984	9,547	22,413	34,658	49,563	87,341
1985	9,675	22,711	35,132	50,356	90,627
1986	9,990	23,501	36,471	52,115	94,926
1987	10,157	23,872	37,069	53,053	96,956
1988	10,197	23,848	37,111	53,298	97,792
1989	10,359	24,184	37,571	54,055	101,780
1990	10,247	23,900	36,808	52,935	98,377
1991	9,734	23,105	35,851	51,997	95,530

Per cent change

Year	Lowest Fifth	Second Fifth	Middle Fifth	Fourth Fifth	Highest Fifth
1979–80	–5.3%	–3.6%	–3.3%	–2.5%	–3.7%
1979–89	–3.8	1.8	4.7	9.4	18.9
1981–89	5.9	9.3	10.6	13.4	24.5
1982–89	11.9	11.0	12.6	14.2	22.1
1990–91	–5.0	–3.3	–2.6	–1.8	–2.9

Source: Bureau of the Census and Joint Economic Committee/Republican staff calculations.

The Widening Income Gap

The gap between rich and poor has widened over the past twenty years. In 1991 the richest fifth of American families had an average income of $95,530, or 9.8-times larger than the average income of the poorest fifth ($9,734). In 1973 the average income of the rich was only 7.5-times larger than that of the poorest group.

A number of factors explain the widening income gap:

• The growth rate in the supply of college graduates decreased in the 1980s, forcing employers to pay a larger premium for well-educated workers.

• Marginal tax rates at the top of the income distribution fell from 70% in 1980 to 28% in 1987. This increased work incentives of upper-income taxpayers and reduced their incentives to defer income.

• The income figures reflect cash income only, thus ignoring the value of health and life insurance, employer Social Security contributions, accrued pension assets, vacation days, and other fringe benefits.

• Poor families are generally smaller and have fewer workers than rich families. The worker gap is especially important: the poorest fifth has only 19 full-time workers per every 100 households versus an average of 134 workers per every 100 households among the richest fifth.

A sizable share of the poorest fifth fall into poverty for a very short period of time. As a result, the distribution of spending is far more even than the distribution of income.

Poor No More: Economic Mobility, 1979–1988

1979 Quintile	Percent in Quintile in 1979	———— Per Cent in Each Quintile in 1988 ————				
		1st (poorest)	2nd	3rd	4th	5th (richest)
1st (poorest)	100%	14.2%	20.7%	25.0%	25.3%	14.7%
2nd fifth	100	10.9	29.0	29.6	19.5	11.1
3rd fifth	100	5.7	14.0	33.0	32.3	15.0
4th fifth	100	3.1	9.3	14.8	37.5	35.4
5th (richest)	100	1.1	4.4	9.4	20.3	64.7

Source: U.S. Treasury.

America on the Move

About 86% of those who were in the poorest quintile in 1979 had managed to raise their incomes by 1988 enough to have moved up to a higher quintile.

By 1988, 14.7% of these people had risen to the very richest quintile, while only 14.2% of them remained in the poorest quintile. In other words, a member of the bottom income bracket in 1979 had a better chance of moving to the top bracket by 1988 than remaining in the bottom bracket.

K. Infrastructure Spending

Federal Infrastructure Spending

	Total	Defense	Non-Defense
	Billions of Current Dollars		
1960	$ 19.1	$17.2	$ 1.9
1970	26.1	23.6	2.5
1980	40.5	32.5	8.1
1985	89.7	78.0	11.7
1990	102.8	87.7	15.1
1991	103.5	87.2	16.3
1992	103.3	82.1	21.2
1993 est.	100.0	77.1	22.9
	Billions of 1987 Dollars		
1960	$73.6	$66.4	$ 7.3
1970	76.7	69.4	7.3
1980	55.7	45.7	10.0
1985	89.1	77.0	12.2
1990	96.5	84.4	14.1
1991	97.0	81.9	15.2
1992	94.0	74.9	19.1
1993 est.	88.7	68.6	20.1

Source: Office of Management and Budget.

What Infrastructure Crisis?

President Clinton has called for a "Rebuild America Fund" to fund an additional $20 billion per year on public works projects. But the Federal Government already spent five times as much, or $103.3 billion, on physical projects and equipment in 1992.

Direct federal spending on civilian infrastructure came to $21.2 billion in 1992. This does not include $130 billion spent by state and local governments on highways, bridges, sewer systems, buildings, and other public works projects—much of it financed with federal grants.

Although the "crisis" is often blamed on 12 years of Republican neglect, federal civilian infrastructure spending rose by 91%, in real terms, between 1990 and 1992, including a 35% increase since 1990. The largest public works bill in U.S. history—a $151 billion highway bill—was passed with the Bush Administration's support in 1991.

The richest states have the highest levels of public investment. This just means that economic growth makes it easier to fund such projects, not that infrastructure "causes" growth.

President Clinton's $16 billion stimulus package included funding for a golf course, a gymnasium, a beach parking garage, and other politically inspired projects.

The Clinton plan would have created 219,000 jobs over the next year, but at a cost of $89,000 per job. That is almost three times the average cost of a private-sector job.

The economy created more than 200,000 jobs in both April and May 1993—without the aid of a stimulus package.

Depression-era projects such as WPA are often held up as examples of how infrastructure creates jobs. New research shows, however, that rapid growth in the money supply and World War II ended the Depression. Public works played a very limited role.

L. Federal Debt

Total Federal Debt, 1791–1991
Per Cent of GNP / Calendar Years

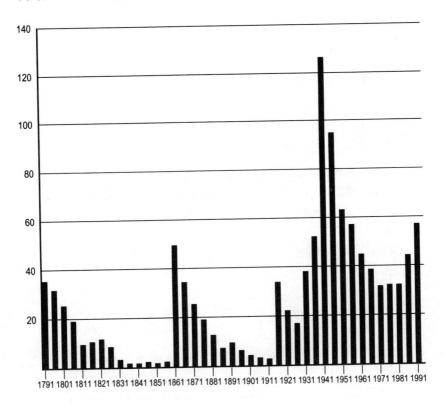

Note: 1980s debt levels are moderate by historical standards.

Source: Bureau of the Census; Bureau of Economic Analysis.

Gross Federal Debt, 1940–1991

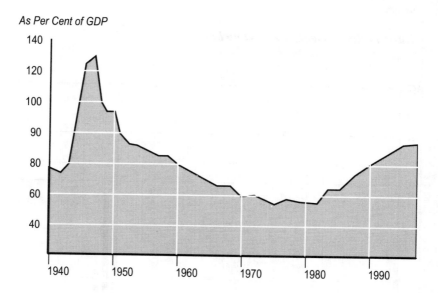

As Per Cent of GDP

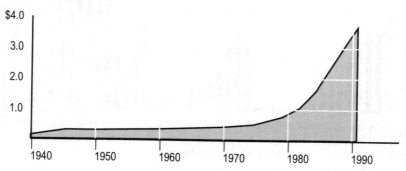

Trillions of Dollars

Source: Office of Management and Budget.

In dollar terms, the rapid growth of the national debt since 1980 dwarfs previous increases during World War II and later. The current ratio of debt to GDP, however, is still well below the levels reached in the late 1940s and 1950s. By this measure, the current debt burden is not unprecedented.

Federal Debt Trends

Billions of Dollars

	Debt Held by the Public			
	Current Dollars	**Current 1987 Dollars**	**As a Per Cent of GDP**	**Per Cent Held by Foreigners**
1950	$ 219.0	$1,094.0	82.4%	NA
1955	226.6	1,001.4	58.9	2.3%
1960	236.8	907.8	46.9	4.2
1965	260.8	922.1	38.9	4.7
1970	283.2	818.3	28.7	5.0
1975	394.7	829.6	26.1	16.7
1980	709.3	1,004.9	26.8	17.2
1981	784.8	1,009.2	26.5	16.7
1982	919.2	1,100.2	29.4	15.3
1983	1,131.0	1,229.8	34.1	14.2
1984	1,300.0	1,430.9	35.2	13.5
1985	1,499.4	1,589.7	37.8	14.9
1986	1,736.2	1,787.6	41.2	15.3
1987	1,888.1	1,888.1	42.4	14.8
1988	2,050.3	1,978.4	42.6	16.9
1989	2,189.3	2,021.5	42.3	18.0
1990	2,410.4	2,134.8	44.1	16.7
1991	2,687.9	2,282.4	47.7	16.3
1992	2,998.6	2,475.5	51.1	16.6
1993 est.	3,303.8	2,664.2	53.5	———

Source: Office of Management and Budget.

At the end of 1992 the government owed $2,998.6 billion to people who had loaned it money to pay for past deficits. The gross federal debt, including the amount held by Social Security and other trust funds, was $4.0 billion.

In 1946, after World War II, federal debt held by the public reached $242 billion, or 114% of the debt had grown to $709 billion, but had fallen to only 26.8% of GDP. The four-fold rise in debt, 1980 to 1992, resulted in a debt-to-GDP ratio of 51%, or less than half of its proportion just after the war.

Foreigners held 16.6% of all publicly held debt in 1992. The foreign share of federal debt, after rising rapidly during the oil shocks of the early 1970s, has remained fairly constant since 1975.

Federal Debt per Capita, 1990

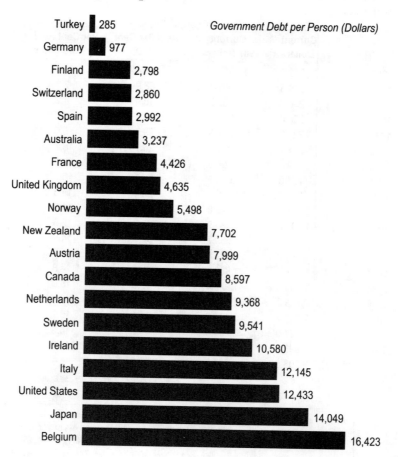

	Government Debt per Person (Dollars)
Turkey	285
Germany	977
Finland	2,798
Switzerland	2,860
Spain	2,992
Australia	3,237
France	4,426
United Kingdom	4,635
Norway	5,498
New Zealand	7,702
Austria	7,999
Canada	8,597
Netherlands	9,368
Sweden	9,541
Ireland	10,580
Italy	12,145
United States	12,433
Japan	14,049
Belgium	16,423

Source: Michael Wolff, *Where We Stand* (Bantam Books, 1991).

Total U.S. government debt, $3.2 billion at the end of 1990 (now estimated at more than $4.2 billion), came to $12,433 for every man, woman, and child. Only Japan and Belgium had higher per-capita debt burdens.

When total (state, local, and federal) government debt is measured as a per cent of GDP, however, the U.S. is below the average for the G-7 countries.

Foreign Ownership of Federal Debt, 1990

Billions of Dollars

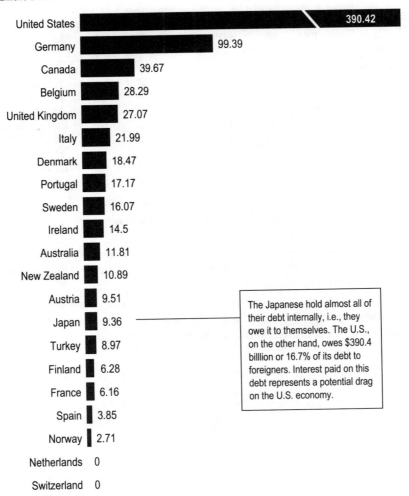

United States	390.42
Germany	99.39
Canada	39.67
Belgium	28.29
United Kingdom	27.07
Italy	21.99
Denmark	18.47
Portugal	17.17
Sweden	16.07
Ireland	14.5
Australia	11.81
New Zealand	10.89
Austria	9.51
Japan	9.36
Turkey	8.97
Finland	6.28
France	6.16
Spain	3.85
Norway	2.71
Netherlands	0
Switzerland	0

The Japanese hold almost all of their debt internally, i.e., they owe it to themselves. The U.S., on the other hand, owes $390.4 billlion or 16.7% of its debt to foreigners. Interest paid on this debt represents a potential drag on the U.S. economy.

Source: Michael Wolff, *Where We Stand* (Bantam Books, 1991).

Private Sector Debt

Selected Countries, 1975–90

Countries	Non-financial Companies				Households			
	1975	1980	1985	1990	1975	1980	1985	1990
	As % of GNP/GDP				As % of Disposable Income			
United States	36	36	41	49	67	75	80	97
Japan	94	86	101	135	45	59	70	96
Germany	66	68	73	74	62	76	88	84
France	63	57	60	69	52	56	54	69
Italy	NA	49	57	62	NA	NA	NA	NA
United Kingdom	46	41	49	82	47	49	77	107
Canada	89	98	97	99	77	85	72	90
Australia[1]	87	87	109	138[2]	NA	NA	NA	NA
Sweden	57	60	68	100	94	100	103	124

[1] *Total private sector, fiscal years.*   [2] *1988, as the series has been discontinued.*

Source: Bank for International Settlements (BIS), *Annual Report* (1992).

Contrary to conventional wisdom, U.S. corporations borrow less (relative to income) than companies in Japan, Germany, France, and other major countries.

Personal debt rose relative to income in many countries during the 1980s, reflecting not only the tax deduction for interest, but also optimism in the course of the recovery.

Contingent Federal Liabilities, 1992
Billions of Dollars

Gross Federal Debt	$ 4,002.7
Contingent Liabilities	
Government agency debt	1,162.9
Unfunded annuity programs	6,400.0
Private pension-fund insurance	850.0
Deposit insurance	2,800.0
Direct and guaranteed loans	744.0
Other insurance	1,080.0
Accounts payable	228.5
Total real and potential liabilities	$17,268.1

Source: 1994 Federal Budget;
National Taxpayers Union (unfunded annuity programs, accounts payable).

Hidden Bombs
The potential liabilities of the U.S. government now exceed $17 trillion, 4¼ times the conventional national-debt figure of $4 trillion.

The $17 trillion figure includes: unfunded liabilities of the Social Security and civil service pension systems, mortgage loans guaranteed by the government, deposit insurance for banks and S&Ls, flood insurance, student loans, commitments of the Pension Benefit Guarantee Corporation, and the debt of government-sponsored agencies such as the Federal National Mortgage Association (Fannie Mae) and Federal Home Loan Mortgage Corporation (Freddie Mac).

M. Federal Regulations

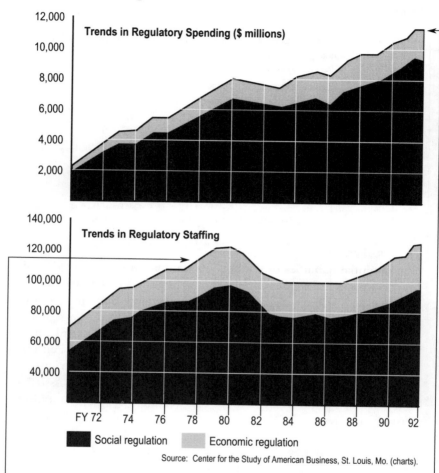

Source: Center for the Study of American Business, St. Louis, Mo. (charts).

The number of federal regulators grew to 122,000 in 1980 from fewer than 70,000 in 1970. Although the Reagan Administration succeeded in reducing this headcount for a time, the trend was reversed in 1988. In 1992 the government employed a record 125,000 regulators.

Tip of the Iceberg

The cost of complying with federal regulations has been estimated at between $400 to $600 billion annually, or a staggering $4,000 to $6,000 per household. The federal regulatory apparatus will spend $14 billion in 1993, or 5-times more than it did in 1970 (in constant dollars).

Federal Register *Pages per Decade, 1940s–1990s*

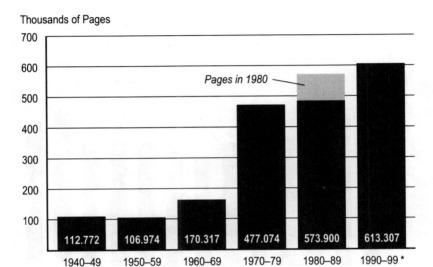

Thousands of Pages

Decade	Pages
1940–49	112.772
1950–59	106.974
1960–69	170.317
1970–79	477.074
1980–89	573.900
1990–99 *	613.307

Pages in 1980

Projection based on 3-year average.

Source: Laffer, Canto and Associates; Citizens For A Sound Economy Foundation (CSEF) calculations.

389

Federal Register *Pages per Year, 1980–1991*

Thousands of Pages

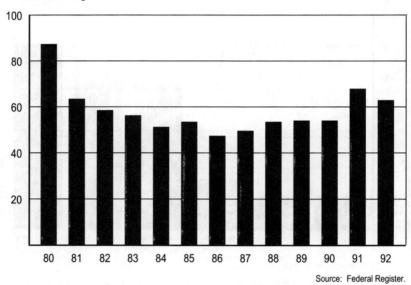

Source: Federal Register.

Number of Pages in the **Federal Register** *vs.* **S&P 500/GNP**

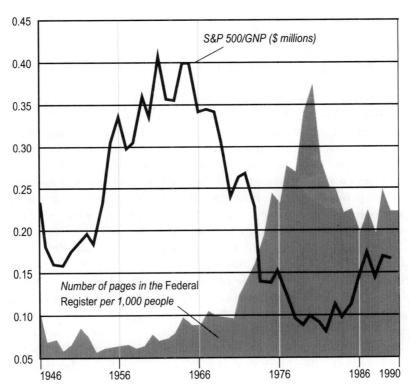

Source: Marvin Zonis & Associates; U.S. Bureau of Economic Analysis;
U.S. Bureau of the Census; Standard & Poor's Corporation.

Did Reagan-Era Deregulation Kill the S&Ls?

Contrary to popular understanding, the thrift industry was insolvent on a market-value basis throughout the 1970s. The industry as a whole was in the red by $110 billion by 1980, before any of the deregulatory reform initiatives were passed. Before 1980, savings and loans were required to invest the majority of their asset portfolios in 30-year, fixed-rate mortgages secured by real estate within a 50-mile radius of their home offices. Those loans were funded primarily by passbook savings accounts, generally payable on demand. Funding long-term, fixed-rate assets with short-term liabilities is a recipe for disaster if interest rates rise rapidly, as they did in the 1970s. It was the interest-rate risk—dictated by government regulation—that bankrupted the thrift industry initially. The government-mandated lack of geographic diversification helps explain the regional pattern of problems. Failures mounted most dramatically in regions with the most economic problems, such as Texas.

The steps toward deregulation taken in 1980 and 1982 were attempts to address the most immediate problem faced by the S&Ls—their overdependence on geographically concentrated fixed-rate mortgages—but policymakers failed to address the full range of problems. Congress and the White House left federal deposit insurance in place, and they allowed hundreds of insolvent institutions to remain open, their operations funded by a virtually unlimited claim against federal taxpayers. As Meigs and Goodman observed:

> Deregulation affected healthy and unhealthy institutions in different ways. It gave insolvent institutions more opportunities to throw Hail-Mary passes. However, these institutions were only being kept alive in the first place by federal deposit insurance. For healthy institutions, deregulation was a long-term necessity. Without it, many could not have survived the competition in the financial marketplace.
>
> —Catherine England
> Cato Institute Policy Analysis, March 12, 1991

S&L Failures and Maximum Deposit Covered by Federal Deposit Insurance

Date	Amount
1934	$ 2,500
1950	10,000
1966	15,000
1969	20,000
1974	40,000
1980	100,000

Source: Federal Deposit Insurance Corporation.

Adjusted for inflation, the original $2,500 guarantee would lead to deposit insurance of roughly $30,000 today.

Insuring the S&L Debacle

In 1980, deposit insurance was increased from $40,000 to $100,000 per account. This change brought in a new breed of depositor: many brokers from Wall Street, who pulled in $100,000 chunks of money from all over the country—for a fee. Because failing thrifts offered the highest rates, this helped keep alive the biggest money losers.

So an insurance program instituted to protect small depositors ended up financing the risky investments made by desperate S&L owners.

393

Number of Bank Failures, 1955–1990

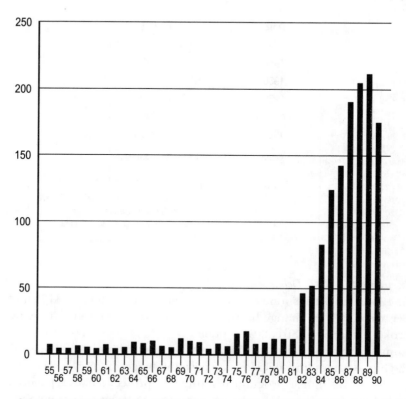

Source: Congressional Budget Office, *Reforming Federal Deposit Insurance* (Washington : CBO, September 1990), pp. 142–43; Federal Deposit Insurance Corporation (number of bank failures in 1990).

INDEX

Page references in bold italic refer to tables

Index